Foods of Association

FOODS OF ASSOCIATION

Biocultural Perspectives on Foods and Beverages that Mediate Sociability

Nina L. Etkin

The University of Arizona Press   Tucson

The University of Arizona Press
© 2009 The Arizona Board of Regents
All rights reserved

www.uapress.arizona.edu

Library of Congress Cataloging-in-Publication Data
Etkin, Nina L. (Nina Lilian), 1948–
Foods of association : biocultural perspectives on foods and beverages
that mediate sociability / Nina L. Etkin.
     p. cm.
Includes bibliographical references and index.
ISBN 978-0-8165-2777-9 (hard cover : alk. paper)
1. Food habits. 2. Drinking customs. 3. Nutritional anthropology.
4. Hausa (African people)—Food. 5. Hausa (African people)—Social
life and customs. I. Title.
GT2850.E876 2009
394.1′2—dc22

                                                      2009007538

Manufactured in the United States of America on acid-free, archival-
quality paper containing a minimum of 30% post-consumer waste and
processed chlorine free.

14   13   12   11   10   09   6   5   4   3   2   1

To my husband, Paul Ross,
for stimulating me intellectually,
being my best friend, and
encouraging me in so many ways

Contents

List of Figures   viii

List of Tables   ix

Acknowledgments   xi

1 Introduction   1

2 The Imperial Roots of European Foodways   50

3 Street Foods and Beverages   89

4 Foods and Beverages of Occasion, Circumstance,
   and Ceremony   127

5 Aspects of Health, Hype, and Identity in Bottled Water   171

6 Overview   206

Notes   209

References   213

Index   239

Figures

Hausa girls beside a dish of chile peppers   73
Author with Hausa women and children   112
Young Hausa men sharing cowpea fritters   116
Hausa boys removing seed coats from roasted groundnuts   118
Head of a Hausa household offers *goro* to guests at a *suna*   154
Hausa girls simulate the celebration of marriage   157
Hausa children wait in line for grinding mill   164
Hausa woman pounding millet with a mortar and pestle   165
Hausa water collectors at a well in Hurumi   195
Author and her associate interviewing a Hausa informant   197

All photographs are by Paul Ross, 1988.

Tables

1.1 Categories of USDA-authorized organic foods   30

1.2 Vitamin susceptibility to environmental conditions   30

1.3 A brief history of low-carbohydrate (CHO) diets   35

2.1 Caffeine and theobromine in beverages of association   78

2.2 Sites of action and relative strengths of methylxanthines   84

3.1 Polynesian botanical canoe foods   96

3.2 Hawaiian Plate Lunch nutrient values   100

3.3 Terms for semiwild fruit in Hurumi   119

Acknowledgments

I credit collaborations on Hausa research with Paul Ross and Malam Ibrahim Muazzamu and express gratitude to the people of Hurumi who taught me so much about Hausa medicine and animate my broader reflections on the meanings of food, medicine, and health. I applaud Jo Ann Steele, Laurie Ross Fielding, and Edward Steele for their encouragement. Thank you to a legion of stimulating University of Hawai'i anthropology graduate students and to Christine Szuter, Allyson Carter, and other energetically professional staff of the University of Arizona Press.

Introduction

THIS BOOK EXPLORES the biology and culture of foods and beverages that are consumed in communal settings, with special attention to the implications of these items for people's health. As defined for this book, foods and beverages of association are consumed by diverse social groups: these might be durable, such as the regular congregation of a church; impermanent, such as guests at a wedding; or some variation in between. In the case of public consumables such as street foods, eating and drinking overlap in time and space, although a social entity of consumption may exist only in the abstract or have limited longevity.

A substantial literature on food sociability that centers on the social context of food exists, but it largely neglects the foods and beverages that are consumed in social settings, which is the current volume's focus.[1] Food sociability foregrounds gastronomy, in which the central axis is the intersection of cultural and social features of food and eating. That literature does not consider physiology and food chemistry but instead focuses on how locus, praxis, and discourse—the context, social organization, and semantics—of eating are important means by which to understand diverse foodways. By employing a bio*cultural* perspective, I likewise acknowledge that foods are conduits of meaning and that they mediate social relations. However, my primary focus is on the biology of the foods themselves, how they impact individual and collective physiologies, and how the tangible aspects of foods contribute to their meaning. My analysis coheres around foods and beverages that fuel the body, induce physical satiety, provide nutrients, and have pharmacologic potential.

In a departure from much of the contemporary (largely popular) literature, this book does not promote certain foods or recommend dietary regimens. Instead, I advance an integrated perspective and draw on an extensive multidisciplinary literature to explore themes such as food chemistry, human evolution, history of cuisines, nutrition, and food and culture. I examine what exists, or once did, in real ethnographic contexts and consider the physiologic implications of those foodways. I also include my research on Hausa food and medicine.

The book is organized around a handful of circumstances in which foods and beverages of association are consumed. The criteria providing the framework for my research are that the foods and beverages should be ingested in the company, or at least proximity, of other people and that the communal consumption of these items contributes to their meaning. The key concern was to select foods and drinks for which there is sufficient scholarship on nutrients, pharmacodynamic constituents, physiologic actions, history, and ethnography.

The Structure of the Book

In this introductory chapter, I outline the theoretical foundations of my work and reflect on the physiologic and cultural circumstances of food sharing and other transfers in evolutionary perspective. I consider the evolution of food management strategies among noncaptive animals generally, nonhuman primates in near-natural environments, and archaeological and historical human populations. Following that, I discuss some dietary strategies in the contemporary and affluent West, where individuals form confederations around foodways that are designed to meet general and specific health goals: the Slow Food movement; vegetarian and low-carbohydrate diets; and foodways that accommodate the genetic conditions diabetes, gluten enteropathy, and lactose intolerance.

Chapter 2 offers a general treatment of European exploration and colonial activities to illustrate how certain foods and beverages were appropriated from other cultures and geographic regions and became items of association in European foodways. A more thorough biocultural analysis is applied to spices, which forge association as signatures of cuisines, and the social beverages coffee, cocoa, and tea. Chapter 3 is about street foods, that is, items that are consumed in public but not in conventional restaurants. A global overview serves as a backdrop for in-depth treatment of street foods in Hawai'i and northern Nigeria. In chapter 4, I explore foods and beverages consumed for all manner of ceremonies and occasions; they mark occasions that range from the mundane to the ritually sacred and have significant nutritional and pharmacologic potential. While celebratory customs and ritual elements are included to provide context, the primary focus is on the foods themselves. Chapter 5 traces the history and health potential of a very contemporary beverage of association: bottled water. I concentrate on the branded, individual-sized products that are vigorously promoted for a variety of health claims— which, I argue, have not been established or even substantially explored. The concluding chapter is an overview of themes that recur throughout the book and also suggests additional directions for research.

Theoretical Perspectives

My work is framed by a biocultural perspective that explores both the physiologic implications of consumption and the cultural construction and social circulation of food. This perspective is more comprehensive than are approaches in the biosciences, which commonly explore foods out of context, with the objective of identifying discrete constituents and specific activities. Biocultural analysis also expands many of the other anthropological inquiries on food, which center on issues of body, gender, identity, and commodification (e.g., Counihan 1999; Pence 2002; Bryant et al. 2003) but not on how those meaning-centered issues intersect food pharmacology and human physiology. I emphasize that people regard foods and beverages simultaneously as biodynamic substances and cultural objects: their pharmacologic profiles both transcend and contribute to their cultural signification. In other work, I conflate the biocultural perspective with the term *ethnopharmacology*, which is the intersection of medical ethnography and the biology of therapeutic action, a transdisciplinary exploration that spans the biological and social sciences (Greek etymology, from *ethno-*, "culture" or "people"; *pharm-*, "drug") (e.g., Etkin 2006a; Etkin and Elisabetsky 2005). I also invoke issues of globalization and political economy to illustrate how physiology and cuisine are influenced by asymmetrical access to food, knowledge, and other resources, disparities that bear directly and indirectly on nutrient sufficiency and other health issues.

My consideration of the physiologic implications of foods and beverages focuses primarily on botanicals. Logically, we understand that plants, which are not mobile and do not have the behavioral repertoires that animals employ, would have evolved attributes that support their survival. For example, plant reproduction is assisted by allelochemicals and structures that attract pollinators and seed dispersers or prevent competing species from sharing adjacent territories; toxins and other deterrents discourage herbivory and microorganismal infection. That many of these attributes benefit sympatric species of plants and animals, including humans, illustrates the coevolutionary relations among complex assemblages of flora and fauna. This means that an organism can be fully apprehended only through attention being paid to the context of its place in the world and the other life-forms that synchronically or diachronically share its environment.

Food Sharing

Scholars from many disciplines have contemplated intra- and cross-specific cooperative behaviors for millennia. Early philosophical reflections on humanity ranged among "questions of good and evil, of [people's] . . . tendency to be in a state of peace or war, and [their] . . . proclivity to cooperate or to cheat when the option presents itself" (Dugatkin 1997:4). Aristotle and the seventeenth-century philosopher John Locke portrayed people as naturally cooperative. Others held the opposite view, which was expanded by another English philosopher, Thomas Hobbes, in his classic work *Leviathan* (1651), in which he was absorbed by people's uncooperative tendencies and the laws necessary to counter these inclinations. Hobbes did not generalize his view to all taxa and remarked on cooperation among social insects (see the section on bees, below). In the nineteenth century, Charles Darwin struggled with how cooperation and altruism might compromise his theory of natural selection through survival of the most fit; he eventually resolved this apparent contradiction by drafting a theory of inclusive fitness, which was expanded and formalized a century later by the evolutionary biologist William Hamilton. In the late nineteenth century, Darwin's tenacious advocate Thomas Huxley emphasized lack of cooperation among many taxa, while Alfred Russel Wallace, who developed a theory of natural selection at the same time that Darwin did, took the position that cooperation in the animal kingdom is normative, not exceptional. In the 1930s, Warder Clyde Alee, cofounder of the Chicago school of animal social behavior, described what he perceived to be the ubiquity of cooperative behaviors, nuanced by dominance hierarchies, and was challenged by proponents who saw an uneven distribution of cooperative conduct among diverse taxa (Dugatkin 1997).

Unlike their earlier counterparts, Hamilton's 1960s publications on inclusive fitness were framed by a theoretical perspective and are regarded by some as a watershed that signals the modern era of cooperation and altruism studies, as well as the advent of modern sociobiology and behavioral ecology. A decade later, Edward O. Wilson reemphasized the central paradigm that cooperation should be more common among biological kin than among unrelated individuals. In *Sociobiology: The New Synthesis* (1975:4), he defined the field as "the systematic study of the biological basis of *all* social behavior" (emphasis added) and claimed that animal behaviors, including those of humans, are genetically inherited and subject to natural selection and other evolutionary processes. Like Hamilton's position, Wilson's theory was foundational and influential. It also was, and remains, controversial because of its rigidity and its implications for understanding social dynamics in human societies. For example, if demographics such as ethnicity and gender are defined genetically, can social policies adequately address inequities? During the same years, Robert Trivers offered his cornerstone argument that reciprocal altruism explains cooperation among nonkin. Lee Dugatkin and colleagues argue that at least three other categories of cooperative behavior signify: group selection, kin selection, and by-product mutualism (in harsh environments in which individuals more than groups are likely to be subject to predation) (Dugatkin 1997).

Social scientists who explore food transfer as a medium of nonverbal communication overlook that it also has substantial physiologic significance and in many instances and for many taxa has verbal components as well. Food sharing refers to the circumstances in which one individual allows another to consume all or part of a food that the holder could protect and withhold if he or she wished. It occurs among animals representing a spectrum of taxa, including insects, birds, cetaceans (whales, dolphins, porpoises), and other mammals. Much of that sharing is parent-offspring and other kin provisioning; nonkin sharing is less well understood, except among human groups. Jeffrey Stevens and Ian Gilby's (2004) review of nonkin sharing in species from arthropods to nonhuman primates offers a novel framework that explores two axes: the interval between when an item is shared and when the sharer accrues benefits; and the "currency units" in which the individual who shares receives benefits.

Although the terms *provisioning* and *sharing* are used interchangeably in some literature, they are not the same: provisioning embodies comprehensive rules that govern interactions within the social group; sharing refers to less formal, perhaps occasion-specific, circumstances. In the idiom of animal behavior, provisioning refers to one individual feeding another, including hierarchically vertical and horizontal kin feeding—parents to offspring and vice versa, siblings to siblings, cross-gender exchanges, and so on. This may take various forms: for example, *trophalaxis* refers to members of a colony feeding one another, and *mass provisioning* denotes the feeding of the different growth stages of a hive or colony by some subset of the whole population. In contrast, food sharing is one way to learn about foods. When social relations include interest in, and tolerance of, others' activities, individuals are likely to encounter, try, and eat the same foods. Reception of a novel food by naive group members of diverse taxa is more likely to occur in the proximity of other, more knowledgeable group members (Addessi and Visalberghi 2004).

Animals

Among social insects, honeybees (*Apis mellifera* L., Apiidae) offer an interesting example of the complexity of provisioning in the larger context of social relations that include caste, age, gender, and labor asymmetries. At the start of a season, each hive houses one queen, several dozen drones (males), thousands of foraging female workers, and about twice as many workers that maintain and defend the hive and convert nectar into honey for their hive mates. The honeybee colony has been described as a superorganism that houses individuals and groups of bees whose secretions and actions bring about physiologic and behavioral changes within the organism. The most potent individual is the colony's queen, who secretes a combination of chemicals that direct the workers in their tasks. These workers communicate about food sources in both phonetic ("buzzing") and kinetic ("dancing") modes that convey information about the smell and taste of the pollen and nectar that they forage for and carry back to the hive. Hive mates influence one another as specialized groups of workers, drones, and brood (eggs, larvae, pupae). Workers feed adults and the brood the honey-pollen mixture known as beebread. A more honey-dense version of this, called royal jelly, is fed to the worker egg that is designated to become the new queen. This complex and organized provisioning integrates primarily gene-based, but also learned, elements without whose orchestration the colony would not survive (Moritz and Southwick 1992; see below, mutualism and honeyguides; see also chapter 4).

While animals such as squirrels (*Sciurus carolinensis* Gmelin, Sciuridae) and some hawks (several genera, Accipitridae) do not come together for foraging or eating, many others are social foragers, a definition that does not extend to individuals who were attracted independently to a food source, whose propinquity is fortuitous, and who disperse as quickly as they appeared to come together. Social foraging occurs when the presence of conspecifics or heterospecifics attracts individuals to a feeding locale. This strategy typically is used when the success of foraging depends on the actions of associates in the same range of communication. The actions of associates can affect all phases of foraging, from the initiation of the search to food division and consumption. Social foraging can decrease predation risk as the number of vigilants increases so that food sources, especially those that are widely distributed, are seen by more group members more quickly. Vultures (several genera, Accipitridae) and seabirds (*Larus* spp., Laridae), for example, forage as groups over extended areas; when one or a small number identify a food source, the others quickly converge. Social foraging also can increase foraging skillfulness, because larger group size predicts better (more often, more specific) location of foods, and groups can take down larger prey than individual foragers can. Lions (*Panthera leo* L., Felidae) that forage alone take small prey, while groups can go after larger animals that can feed more individuals. In this example, labor is divided between stalkers and lions that wait to take down the fleeing prey (Beauchamp 2004; Smuts 2004).

Harris's hawks (*Parabuteo unicinctus* Temm., Accipitridae) hunt in cohesive groups, most commonly to surprise-pounce as several individuals converge on prey from different directions. They also flush and ambush after the prey has found cover, surrounding the location of the prey and sometimes penetrating the cover location. A third strategy involves sustained chase of prey with individual hawks rotating in the lead position. The rate of success increases with group size. Similarly, Aplomado falcons (*Falco* spp., Falconidae) that hunt in pairs are more successful than are solitary foragers (Dugatkin 1997).

Some animal species initiate food sharing by recruitment calling, attracting nearby foragers by drawing attention to the location of food, which the caller may or may not have already secured. This calling increases the likelihood that the larger group will capture prey; it can evolve through by-product mutualism, through reciprocity, or not at all. The food-signaling repertoires that evolved among gallinaceous birds are very extensive and diverse. On exploration of new food sources, male chickens (*Gallus gallus* L., Phasianidae) issue distinctive pulsatile calls whose number and frequency increase with the profitability (volume, organoleptic qualities) of the food. Males call more frequently when females are present, and females are more likely to join males that issue these distinctive calls. These observations illustrate the convergence of some, or parts of, courtship and feeding repertoires (Dugatkin 1997).

In mammalian and bird altricial species, or altrices, the newly born or hatched require parental care longer than the young of precocial species, whose young manage on their own sooner. When they are no longer provisioned by adults, altricial young generally disperse, but in some altrices, the young remain in proximity to parents even after achieving foraging independence. Adult pied babblers (*Turdoides bicolor* Jard., Sylviidae) issue recruitment calls to direct independent fledglings to foraging sites. Calling occurs more frequently when groups include independent fledglings and divisible food sources are abundant. The most common response to calls is from fledglings, which benefit substantially from parental care extended beyond the phase of direct provisioning (Radford and Ridley 2006). Similarly, anecdotal accounts suggest that cheetahs (*Acinonyx jubatus* Schreber, Felidae) use calls to direct their inexperienced offspring to prey, scavenging adult ravens (*Corvus* spp., Corvidae) are joined by juveniles through recruitment calls, and killer whale communications (*Orcinus orca* L., Delphinaceae) increase feeding efficiency by sharing pinniped (e.g., harbor seal, *Phoca vitulina* L., Phocidae) carcasses to maintain their buoyancy (through loss of prey weight and volume). Nonfood benefits of calling include reduced predation risk, as demonstrated by house sparrows (*Passer domesticus* L., Passeridae) that call more often in the presence of divisible food and reduce the number of calls as the size of the feeding group increases. Nonfood benefits also accrue from mate provisioning, support in dominance conflicts, status displays, and grooming (Stevens and Gilby 2004).

In populations of Harris's sparrow (*Zonotrichia querula* Nuttall, Emberizidae), dominant individuals permit subordinates to feed near them as long as the feeding benefit for dominants that is improved by food-location and other information from the subordinates is greater than the amount of food that subordinates eat. Better feeding efficiency also has been invoked to explain the use of communal roosts. These serve as information centers where individuals whose foraging was unsuccessful during one day can benefit the next day by roosting with, then following, successful foragers to locate food. Neighbor-following to food sites and perhaps the ability to identify and recognize foragers that have been more successful have been reported in communally roosting species such as weaver birds (*Quelea quelea* L., Ploceidae), herons (*Ardea* spp., Ardeidae), and heliconid butterflies (*Heliconius doris* L., Heliconidae). In some group-foraging species, both the individual search efforts and the resources found are combined. Sharing knowledge of food locations ensures that these places are more regularly encountered, offsetting the fact that food must be divided among the full group (Barnard 1983).

The definition of food sharing can be expanded to include interspecific behaviors. Behavioral biologists have been interested in group hunting because of the interrelations between cognitive function and cooperative action. Although few examples have been reported, cross-species hunting elicits the same interest and allows us to explore this kind of food sharing through a coevolutionary lens. Highly coordinated and communicative hunting has been reported for Red Sea moray eels (*Plectropomus pessuliferus* Fowler, Serranidae) and groupers (*Gymnothorax javanicus* Bleeker, Muraenidae). Ordinarily the eel is a nocturnal hunter that corners prey in reef crevices, while the diurnal fast-swimming grouper hunts in open waters. Bshary and colleagues (2006) report that eel-grouper associations are not random and that the frequency and duration of signaling depend on grouper satiety. Groupers initiate joint hunting with head shakes and dorsal fin displays that draw eels from their reef crevices and direct them to locations where prey fish conceal themselves —some having been chased there by the groupers. They also recruit eels after an unsuccessful single-species hunt. While pursuing an individual, eels displace other target fish; these escape to open waters, where they are caught by groupers. The coordination of two discrete hunting strategies yields more prey than does either species hunting alone. Bshary and colleagues suggest that this coordination emerged from associative learning, with each species linking increased prey yield to hunting in the vicinity of the other species. They note a similarity among coral reef commensal associations in which a "nuclear species" is followed by individuals of another fish species, although those associations are not coordinated and do not include signaling.

A more familiar cross-species example is people-dog coordinated hunting. Some researchers speculate that canine contributions to human hunting may have been one incentive for domestication of the wolf (*Canis lupus* L., Canidae). Thousands of years of selective breeding would have favored dog (*C. familiaris* L.) attributes such as superior olfactory sense, trainability, and companionability. Today, various fur-bearing mammals (e.g., raccoon [*Procyon lotor* L., Procyonidae]) are hunted with sighthounds (e.g., whippet) and scent hounds (e.g., coonhound). Many of the animals hunted by terriers (e.g., Jack Russell), such as prairie dogs (*Cynomus* spp., Sciuridae) and foxes (*Canis* spp.), have been deemed "pest species." Gun dogs are used to track small game and include retrievers (formerly categorized as "water spaniels"), poodles, cocker spaniels, and setters. Because contemporary hunting dogs are selected for different skill sets, we might logically assume that this has been the case throughout the history of people-dog associations.

On the basis of archaeological data, canine domestication is thought to have occurred 14,000–15,000 years ago, while recent molecular genetic studies of mitochondrial DNA suggest a date as long ago as 100,000 years. Another view, emphasizing the incomparability of archaeological and genetic data, hypothesizes that dogs diverged from wolves 100,000 years ago "naturally," without human agency, and had already evolved into dogs before being domesticated 14,000–15,000 BCE (Raisor 2004). Whatever the dates, evidence from many sectors underscores the longevity of dog-human relations, including hunting. Ruusila and Pesonen (2004) compared the hunting success of four variably sized Finnish hunting communities and found that the group of fewer than ten hunters bagged 56 percent more moose (*Alces alces* L., Cervidae) when hunting with dogs and were the most successful hunters. For groups of more than ten people, hunting success covaried with the number of dogs, but among larger groups, hunting success was independent of both group size and the presence of dogs.

Another human-other mutualism includes honeyguides, birds of the family Indicatoridae (*Indicator, Melichneutes,* and *Prodotiscus* are prominent species), whose vocalizations and movements guide people to beehives. Several honeyguide species issue rapid, abrupt calls and flutter back and forth across short distances and, if followed, repeat these actions until arrival at the hive.[2] They feed on insects, primarily bees and wasps. The Indicatoridae are unique among vertebrates in their ability to digest beeswax, but the smallness of their beaks precludes them from breaking into hives. The role of wax in the diets of honeyguides is not known, but the bacterium *Micrococcus cerolyticus* has been identified as the microorganism that promotes wax digestion in the honeyguide gut. When humans access the hive interior, honeyguides can feed on the comb, ingesting larvae, adults, and honey at the same time. The same kind of mutualism has been observed in baboons (*Papio* spp., Cercopithecidae) and the honey badger (*Mellivora capensis* Storr, Mustelidae). Because honeyguides tend to be solitary in feeding and other behaviors, their guiding actions are thought to be instinctive rather than learned from parents or age mates. Speculations about the coevolution of these behaviors suggest that humans learned from honey badgers, which is consistent with the observation that Zulu (observed in the 1950s) encourage honeyguides by imitating the badgers' grunts and knock on trees to simulate their breaking open hives. An alternative suggestion, although evidence for it is lacking, is that early humans observed that honeyguides were predictably good locators of hives and continued interactions resulted in the honeyguides' behavioral repertoire somehow becoming genetically hardwired. By whatever pattern the relationships among humans, honeyguides, and honey badgers developed, they are considered to be very long. Human-honeyguide relations also are "complete—there is no need for restraint . . . or training and retraining, as in the case of [people's] association with the birds of falconry or with the cormorant [and otter] involved in the fishing practices of China" (Hooper 1989:348).

The origins of fishing with cormorants (*Phalacrocorax* spp., Phalacrocoracidae) are not certain but might be traced to China or Japan as early as 212 BCE. It has been practiced (even on a commercial scale) on rivers, streams, and lakes. In traditional Chinese practice, a cormorant's wings were clipped to prevent the bird's escape, one end of a long string was attached to one foot and the other to a pole on shore, and a ring was placed around the neck to keep the bird from swallowing. When the cormorant caught a fish, the fisherman whistled to call the bird, took the fish, removed the band, and rewarded the bird with a small fish. Training was conducted for one month on shore and for the same duration on the fisherman's boat or raft. Eventually the string was removed, but the ring remained during fishing activities. Once widespread among both royalty, who used it for sport, and common people collecting food, cormorant fishing continues on a smaller scale today in China and Japan. The practice was adopted in France, Holland, and England in the late 1700s or early 1800s, perhaps introduced by the Dutch from Southeast Asia. Training birds for hunting in Europe was heavily influenced by falconry, which was largely reserved for sport and very different from Chinese customs (Simoons 1991).

In dispersed locations in contemporary North America and Europe, individual sports fishermen have trained otters to assist in fishing. In China, this ancient practice was systematized for commercial gain and employed teams of fishermen and otters. The freshwater otter (*Lutra* spp., Mustelidae) wore a harness that was clipped by a chain to a boat or pole on shore. The fishermen cast a large circular net, then pulled it to the surface; the otter, whose role was to chase fish from crevices or bottom mud, was previously placed in a small opening in the center of the net. When the net was pulled from the water and the fish unloaded, the otter received some as reward and reinforcement. Other descriptions position the otter outside the net, chasing fish into it as it descended. Fishing with otters has also been described in parts of Malaya and South and Southeast Asia (Simoons 1991).

Nonhuman Primates

Food sharing has been particularly well studied among nonhuman primates, including prosimians, New and Old World monkeys, and apes. Hunting has received a disproportionate amount of attention, overshadowing plant foods whose collection and sharing are less apparent but equally or more important for nutrition, growth and development, and sociability.

Small mammals are regularly hunted by only a few of the higher primates, including chimpanzees (*Pan troglodytes* L., Pongidae) and humans, both omnivores. Chimpanzees kill small mammals opportunistically upon encountering them while gathering plants. This behavior is notably different from that of social carnivores such as wolves and lions, obligate carnivores whose subsistence depends on daily decisions about where to locate prey and how to capture it. Red colobus monkeys (*Procolobus* spp., Cercopithecidae) are the primary prey of chimpanzees where the species are sympatric. Chimpanzee hunts are social; the groups comprise mixed demographics, although most of the kills are by males. Which prey is captured and the extent of female participation vary from one community to another as well as from one hunt to another. Communication among individuals to initiate a coordinated hunt has been reported for one group of chimpanzees, in Tai National Park, Ivory Coast. Cooperative hunting among chimpanzees has been suggested to include individuals assuming interdependent roles to drive, block, and ambush prey. In some communities, hunting frequency covaries with the availability of ripe fruit, suggesting that chimpanzees hunt more often when energy costs are met by other foods.

The patterns by which meat is shared are strategic and varied.[3] Chimpanzee sharing may privilege kin, sexually receptive females, political and agonistic allies, or hunt participants. Gilby (2007) argues that there is no evidence for the commonly cited idea that male chimpanzees trade meat for sexual relations. His observations in Tanzania and Uganda found that the probability of a hunt does not increase in the presence of sexually receptive females; sharing meat with these females does not increase mating success; and, when sharing, males do not privilege these females. But Hockings and colleagues (2007) report that male chimpanzees in Guinea who do not share wild plant foods or meat do share stolen crops—most commonly, papaya (*Carica papaya* L., Caricaceae), banana (*Musa* spp., Musaceae), and pineapple (*Ananas comosus* Merr., Bromeliaceae)—with sexually receptive females. In this case (and, presumably, other cases, too), anthropogenic landscapes present new challenges that select for adjusted feeding strategies; crop raiding provides males with favored foods that can be exchanged for other currencies. In short, sharing varies regionally, episodically, and with community demographics and dynamics; dominance orders are heavily improvised and context dependent (Boesch and Boesch 1989; Boehm 1999; Stanford 2001; Watts and Mitani 2004; Silk 2005).

Opportunistic hunting, primarily of nonmammalian species, also has been described for capuchin monkeys (*Cebus* spp., Cebidae). These omnivores have not been reported to hunt cooperatively as a social unit, but collaborations have been documented. A collaboration-cooperation continuum suggests increasingly systematic strategies and likely has implications for whether and how prey is shared. Most capuchin meat sharing occurs as provisioning of infants and juveniles. Adults are more likely to cofeed; when they do share, the strategies employed have the same goals as those of chimpanzees. Other food sharing that occurs among all nonhuman primates includes group feeding when large volumes of an item are encountered, for example, eating social insects or their products (e.g., honey, propolis, termite earth) from their nests. Similarly, an individual tree might be occupied by a group of primates to take advantage of the insects found on various plant parts. Individuals might alert one another when large stores of plant foods are encountered, during masting, for example, when many species flower and then fruit synchronously. In these circumstances, foods are shared, if only minimally as provisioning of the young by adults (de Waal 2000; Mitani and Watts 2001; Rose 2001; Stanford 2001; Reed and Bidner 2004; Rose 2004; Gilby 2006).

The same features of strategic sharing that I describe above for hunting by nonhuman primates also characterize gathering and intragroup distribution of botanical resources. Resonating coevolutionary themes, the phylogenetic diversification of angiosperms (flowering plants) is suggested to have been an important backdrop for adaptive radiations in the order Primates. By the late Paleocene (ca. 55 million years ago), some angiosperms had evolved large fruits with stored nutrients as coadaptations to small-animal-dispersed propagation. The increase in the variety of food resources—flowers, pollen, buds, nectar, fruit, seeds, gum, leaves, and bark—happened over the same period that a suite of adaptive radiations occurred in the order Primates. Some of the fundamental adaptations that evolved among early primates (e.g., nails, grasping, and visual acuity) are suggested to have included their more effective exploitation of plant parts: notably, reproductive organs (McGrew 2001; Di Bitetti 2005; Strier 2006).

Early Human Foragers and Horticulturalists

Our more than 30-million-year evolutionary history as anthropoid primates influenced our digestive physiology and nutrient requirements long before the earliest humans appeared. The types of foods from which we can derive nutrients are limited by such human features as body and brain size, dental and gut morphologies, and digestive kinetics: our relatively small gut holds only a limited amount of food, and transit time is slow. These inherited traits have been argued to require a high-quality diet to support a socially and physically active lifestyle through cultural (technological) and social strategies to obtain and prepare foods prior to consumption. The similarities of gut morphology and digestive kinetics shared by humans and the great apes suggest that human digestive physiology and nutrient requirements did not change appreciably during the early foraging stage of human evolution (Milton 2002). Many of the lay public are interested in our early foodways (and other behaviors) because they hope to learn what humans ate "naturally," while anthropologists understand that the circumstances are more complicated, having been shaped not only by genetics and the physical environment but also by culture, including aesthetics.

Debate among anthropologists about the origins of human sharing economies led many to the conclusion that diverse ecological and social processes helped to shape a variety of foraging patterns that are applied individually and also combined into complex, integrated strategies. Until the advent of agriculture about ten thousand years ago, human groups consisted of hunter-gatherers who exploited wild plants and animals. The incorporation of fire into hunting strategies and the production of hunting weapons and tools for plant collection and processing allowed early humans to take advantage of a greater number and diversity of plant and animal species. Foods were drawn from all trophic levels and included relatively simple algae and lichens, ferns, herbaceous and woody plants, invertebrates, aquatic and terrestrial animals, and end-point carnivores.

Foraging both depended on and fostered cooperative social interactions and contoured an assemblage of interrelated behaviors. Whereas scholars in the past advanced the script that men hunted and women gathered, in all likelihood gender and other divisions of labor in early human groups varied among populations, as is observed among contemporary groups who modify strategies, often in a short time frame, as environmental, social, and other circumstances shift. Researchers concur that foraging occurred remotely from a home base, a central place that provided, among other things, a safe environment in which to consume, preserve, and store food. Control of fire would have extended sociability and safety into the night. Cooking hearths might have been a site for group activities, including food preparation and sharing. Imagining that those early central sites were conducive for establishing nuclear families and other social alliances is not difficult. Under those conditions, food sharing would have included the provisioning of both adults and children and could have been a core from which still other associations would emerge. Cooking dramatically altered the biological character and quality of human diets by neutralizing plant toxins, softening meats and fibers, increasing palatability and the bioavailability of soluble nutrients, and assisting preservation (Kaplan et al. 2000; Stanford 2001; Ungar and Teaford 2002).

Human hunting and scavenging of animals (and consuming them) has conventionally been advanced as a primary influence on the evolution of early humans. However, the amount and regularity of animal products consumed continues to be disputed, and researchers of early humans currently lean toward less emphasis on animal foods, even though meat—especially that of hunted animals—continues to have an emblematic importance out of proportion with its role in past and present human diets (see chapter 4). A bias toward animal foods has been fueled by the fact that for much of hominid history, faunal remains predominate in the archaeological record. A review of the most recent literature suggests that in early foraging populations, this largely cooperative means of subsistence included in-the-moment decisions about whether to pursue animals as an opportunistic diversion from plant collecting or other activities. This is consistent with the characterization of early foraging lifestyles that included high residential mobility, encounter hunting, and immediate or near-kill-site consumption. Later, with advances in knowledge and technology, foraging was logistical, reflecting lower residential mobility, hunting by design of larger numbers of animals, and the consumption and storage of meat in places that were remote from the kill site. The increase in size of early hominid populations has been correlated to growth of the neocortex, which enabled cognitive development and progressively more complex sociality, within which comprehensive hunting and gathering strategies and sharing conventions developed. Rather than a unidirectional pattern of development, we should envision that command of more and better food (including animal products) contributed to brain development, which improved subsistence technologies. As group size increased, so did the likelihood that foraging and food distribution were nuanced by social hierarchies and other asymmetries (Kaplan et al. 2000; Ungar and Teaford 2002).

Much as hunting has captured the attention of scholars and the public, most intragroup food transfers in early human populations would have involved plants. Through systematic study of contemporary foragers, we comprehend the still substantial contribution of gathered plant products, which constitute an estimated 93 percent of human foods. Statistics drawn from global production data suggest that a small number of species provide most of the energy that people obtain from plants: in the family Poaceae, rice (*Oryza sativa* L.), maize (*Zea mays* L.), wheat (*Triticum* spp.), barley (*Hordeum* spp.), sorghum (*Sorghum* spp.), millet (*Pennisetum* spp.), and sugarcane (*Saccharum officinarum* L.); in other families, soybean (*Glycine max* Merr., Fabaceae), yam (*Dioscorea* spp., Dioscoreaceae), sweet potato (*Ipomoea batatas* Lam., Convolvulaceae), and potato (*Solanum tuberosum* L., Solanaceae). The economic significance of these major crops eclipses the diversity of plants consumed; of more than 300,000 vascular plants, an estimated 7,000 species today are cultivated and foraged by people around the globe, and roughly 3,000 wild, semiwild, and domesticated species are regularly exploited as food. The production of substantial dietary diversity by industrial agriculture is only an illusion (see the section on Slow Food below). Research based on per capita food supply data from 146 countries concluded that just over 100 species are eaten by 90 percent of the world's people but that thousands of other species are consumed by the other 10 percent and that the diversity of plant food resources is underestimated (Fresco 2007). That many of these plants are also used medicinally allows us to speculate that their physiologic impact extends beyond standard nutrient values (protein, carbohydrates, fat, calories, vitamins, minerals) (Etkin 1994a).

Among contemporary hunting and foraging groups, the !Kung of the Kalahari might be the most familiar, thanks to the film-documentation of their lifeways by John Marshall and scholarly and popular ethnographic accounts produced by other family members. Megan Biesele recounts that in the 1960s and 1970s, Lorna Marshall portrayed "a people whose culture is closely and visibly connected to the activities of subsistence. . . . Among these are many variations upon the theme of cooperation and harmonious social relations, enormously detailed knowledge of the environment . . . and strongly institutionalized patterns of sharing" (1993:9). She added, "Kinship ties . . . link individuals . . . and sharing patterns . . . draw together members of different groups in reciprocal obligations. . . . Meat-sharing has both social categorising functions and religious ramifications" (1993:42) and "The exchange of arrows among kin minimises the hunter's act and emphasizes the sharing process" (1993:91).

This is one depiction of sharing among a contemporary foraging and hunting community and cannot be generalized, especially not in the context of concerns expressed more recently that !Kung harmony and cooperation have been exaggerated. In any event, the conventional wisdom of a Paleolithic egalitarian ethos extended to present-day foragers has given way to a better understanding of the lifeways of these heterogeneous peoples. Visions of "automatic, unambivalent, totally altruistic sharing" have been replaced by complex models such as "vigilant" and strategized sharing (Boehm 1999:214). Contemporary foragers employ various strategies for the collection and distribution of plants and animals; these strategies include sharing, which, as in complex societies, occurs within and between households. The diversity of strategies reflects the confluence of ecological circumstances, historical processes, and social factors such as provisioning, supporting kin, elevating status, forging alliances, and otherwise using food transfer as biological and social capital (Boehm 1999; Stanford 2001; Gurven et al. 2004; Marlowe 2004; Kaplan and Gurven 2005; Prinz 2006). Recent observations among the Hadza of Tanzania, foragers in Siberia, and Nicaraguan and Ecuadorian horticulturalists reveal that patterns of food transfer are context specific and flexible and reflect both continuity and the changing circumstances of resource availability, household and community configurations, and political and social economies (Kishigami 2004; Koster 2007; Patton 2007; Wood 2007; Ziker 2007).

Among the permutations of sharing is "demand sharing," or "mutual taking." It is generally prevalent among foraging populations—for example, among the !Kung, Alaskan Inuit, northwestern Canadian Dogrib, and Malaysian Batek. It is widespread in Australia and has also been observed among some Melanesian horticulturalists and Bantu pastoralists. Demand sharing is a complex set of behaviors that are not based solely on need and in which food and other material items serve as currency. These behaviors include both verbal and nonverbal components (Peterson 1993; Saethre 2005).

Miller and colleagues characterize food transfers between opposite-gender young (human) adults along two axes: behaviors during the transfer, in which A feeds or shares food or drink with B; and the circumstances of the item transferred, in which B's food or beverage has or has not been touched or sampled by A. They designate the latter "consubstantiation," to denote "shared substance," a concept that overlaps principles of contagion that govern exchanges of all kinds cross-culturally (Miller et al. 1998:423). For example, food transfers among the Hua of the Eastern Highlands of New Guinea express social alliances and connect organic and inorganic forms through customs that bear on relatedness. Absolute rules are about contagion and define the relation between a consumer and a type of food: A should not eat X. For example, young men should not eat ash-cooked food unless the ashes are removed, because the quality "dry" will be transferred to their skin, whereas oily skin is preferred, as it reflects vitality. As another example, pregnant women should not eat dog, cat (*Felis catus* L., Felidae), or opossum (Didelphidae), because the inability of these animals to articulate will be transferred to the infant. Relative rules specify relationships between a consumer, a food, and its source and express the concept of *nu*, "vital essence," the centerpiece of the Hua theory of nurture. With the exception of wild species, all foods hold the nu of their producer. Thus, Hua people should not eat food prepared by strangers, that is, people with whom one does not share nu through common birth or residence; and male initiates should not eat *kito*, "leafy vegetables," because women wear these as ornaments (Meigs 1988). Similarly, among the Kaluli of the Southern Highlands, food is a social idiom that expresses connectedness through reciprocal exchanges of garden produce and food sharing. Someone eating should not be startled, and talking while eating is rude, as is imbuing a food with revulsion—

mentioning worms while someone eats fish, which eat worms, or the color of red pandanus (*Pandanus conoideus* Lam., Pandanaceae), which resembles blood. Before they are married, boys can consume virtually all meats, but after marriage they eat only smoked meat, as do their wives. This literally separates boys from men and signals a stronger connection between marriage partners (Schieffelin 1976).

Miller and colleagues (1998:323) state that transfers with "no sharing, sharing, sharing with substantiation, and feeding" represent increasing degrees of intimacy. This oversimplifies; one could argue that these four (and more) behaviors are better viewed as a continuum. Further, as examples in this chapter illustrate, food transfers reflect more than social intimacy. Notably, Miller and colleagues do not include other social dimensions, such as political asymmetries and motivations, and do not address outcomes that bear on nutriture and physiology.

Agriculture

Human subsistence was transformed by the advent of food production during the Neolithic, between twelve thousand and nine thousand years ago. Through domestication, people gained control over wild plants and animals by managing their reproduction. Which species were selected and for which characteristics varied in space, time, and cultural context. Plants were selected for such attributes as fruit size and perishability, organoleptic qualities, pharmacologic potential, and resistance to insects and pathogens. Similarly, animals were judged according to perceived food value or suitability for traction and medicine and as sources of milk, hide, eggs, and feathers. The domestication of these and other species also was driven by religious and other meaning-centered goals. The combination of practical and ideational factors that influence the selection of domesticates is reflected in the great diversity of cuisines and pharmacopoeias among contemporary populations.

Today, as in the past, different subsistence patterns occur along a foraging-farming continuum, the number and character of steps along the succession varies, and they grade into one another in ways that are neither unidirectional nor deterministic. Similarly, boundaries are blurred between wild and domesticated species. There is no consensus on how, or whether, to position plants along a wild-domesticated continuum and to characterize intervening categories. For example, cultivated plants are sowed, that is, defined by people's activities, and domesticated species technically embody genetic modifications that occur as a result of human agency. But cultivated plants may not be domesticated, and wild plants can be cultivated. In most of the world, truly wild species (i.e., not influenced by human actions) do not exist. The term *semiwild* applies to plants that are not specifically cultivated or actively tended but are nonetheless affected by human agency. It conflates *semidomesticated* with *wild* and implies no assumptions about whether genetic changes have occurred (Etkin 1994a, 1994b, 2006a:ch. 1). Hausa (in Nigeria), who have long practiced intensive agriculture, offer an example of mixed subsistence strategies. They foster semiwild species (each of which may be genetically different from its domesticated analogues) without actually cultivating them, by weeding around individuals that appear adventitiously on farms, by providing shade and occasionally water, and by protecting them from grazing herbivores (Etkin 2006b).

Overall, the management of domesticated plants and animals yielded larger, and to some extent more reliable, food stores than were available to early foragers. This fostered substantial population growth, a reshaping of the family and other social entities, the further division and specialization of labor, and a redirection of labor to nonsubsistence activities such as technology, trade, and the arts. However, what people gained through agricultural production was offset over the long term by the diminishing spectrum of food species. Arguably, this flattened our food aesthetic through reduction of the number and variety of species. More significantly, these circumstances led to an increasingly narrow range of foods that embodied fewer nutrients and pharmacologically active constituents.

Whereas sharing and other food exchanges are in some circumstances optional for foragers, the circulation of food is integral for populations in which not everyone produces food. This is most apparent in the modern era and in the developed world, where food production is technology-driven agribusiness, the commercial food industry grows exponentially, and more and more of the world's people are linked through globalization and economic and sociopolitical interdependencies, including complex systems of marketing with highly structured trade regulations.

A special case of resource transfer is alloparenting, which is more common among monotocous (producing one offspring at a time) than among polytocous mammals. Nonoffspring nursing is common among nonhuman primates even though lactation is physiologically expensive, suggesting that this kind of food transfer has social as well as nutritional functions (Dugatkin 1997). Similar practices occur among human populations and are characterized by class, gender, and other demographic asymmetries. The general term *wet nurse* applies to a woman who breast-feeds an infant other than her own. Most commonly, the wet nurse has recently given birth, but the term applies as well to women who induce lactation through neural reflexes in response to suckling. In European history, privileged classes used wet nurses to hasten another pregnancy (which is suppressed during lactation) with the expectation of producing more heirs or gender-appropriate heirs, while the wet nurse used the practice to generate income. In Europe and the United States today, wet-nursing is being revived, particularly among a privileged group who can afford the service and for whom the commodification and outsourcing of breast milk serves a number of functions that range among cosmetic, health, and lifestyle issues. Concern has been expressed about the impact of this practice on mother-infant bonding, although benefits of immuno-heterogeneity have been described when infants receive breast milk from more than one woman.

Diets of Association in Contemporary Western Populations

Contemporary affluent populations have access to a great assortment of commercially produced items whose natural origins are ambiguous. Commercial foods are suffused with salt, sugar, milled grains, and fats. The interrelations among these dietary excesses and obesity, cancers, and cardiovascular diseases have been recognized by health professionals for decades. Sedentary lifestyles and insufficient intake of vegetable and fruit fiber contribute to these problems as well. In the West today, there is growing concern about food and health among the public, fueled by increased media attention to the content and physiologic consequences of "bad diets."

Popular refrains about food and identity include "We are what we eat," "We are where we eat," and (although not for all palates) "We are who we eat." These statements can be further refined to "We are what we *say* we eat," which multiplies the layers by which identity is forged or shed and suggests different implications for pharmacologic potential and physiologic health. The long evolutionary trajectory that I trace in the first part of this chapter evidences the increasing complexity and versatility of human foodways. Early human populations had, and many people in the developing world today have, little of the flexibility enjoyed by the more privileged in contemporary societies, in which individuals who have the resources, interest, and presumed knowledge configure foodways to meet specific health goals. Here I discuss foods and diets of association that are characterized by inclusions and exclusions, constitute a nucleus of community and identity, and have significant potential to prevent and manage illness.

For the past fifteen years, many of the groups that cohere around particular foods or foodways have served as umbrella resource and social entities, which have proliferated with the growth of the Internet. These are interactive communities that maintain Web sites, publish electronic and paper journals, and otherwise disseminate information about health implications, sources of desired foods, substitutes, and efforts to influence the food industry. Although Web-centered interactions stretch my definition of association, there is a growing body of literature that examines the cultural construction and social negotiation of online communities and the diverse products of those communications. These computer-mediated social spaces are indeed sites of shared ideology and community; they are social networks that can be analyzed in terms of nodes (individual actors) and ties (relationships between and among actors). Since the mid-1900s, social network analysis has been systematically applied by social scientists to communities on all scales, and most recently to Internet sites. Further, some of those electronic interactions eventuate in what are more conventionally regarded to be social associations, such as announcements that convene membership groups, identify in-person educational opportunities, or connect individuals in geographic propinquity for in-person interactions and other face-to-face or same-place meetings (Wilson and Peterson 2002; Islam 2006; Knorr 2006).

Background: "Natural Diets" Evolve into Nutrients-as-Specific-Therapy

During the late nineteenth and early twentieth centuries, bioscience was so focused on clinical microbiology and related disciplines that nutrition science did not advance until much later. In retrospect, the characterization of essential nutrients seems to have been slowed by the work of Louis Pasteur and colleagues, who directed attention to the presence of something that causes illness, microorganisms, rather than to deficiencies of health-sustaining nutrients. Although the basics of metabolism and digestion had been sketched out in the early 1800s, the term *vitamin* did not come into use until 1911, most of the vitamins and essential amino acids were characterized only over the next few decades, and the U.S. National Research Council did not publish its first table of dietary standards until 1943. The dogmatic advocacy of infectious theories delayed the exposition of vitamins, even those for which the link between disease and diet had already been established (for example, scurvy and diets that featured few or no foods that contain vitamin C).

That nutrients might play a role in human health was compelling for the general U.S. public, who reinstilled "natural foods" into diet and health lore during the early 1900s. The number of what have been labeled retrospectively "food cults" expanded proportionate to whichever advocate or idea was most convincing, only to be superseded by some food regimen that seemed to be more healthful or at least different. Many of the allegedly natural diets were truncated, not supported by credible evidence from nutrition and other sciences, and framed as dogma that featured, for example, grapefruit (*Citrus* spp., Rutaceae), "organic foods," brown rice, or carrots (*Daucus carota* L., Apiaceae). Whereas earlier promotions of purportedly healthful foods had consisted of exaggerated claims and testimonials, by 1930 advertising had been polished into communications that were more discriminating and persuasive. Advances in nutrition and related disciplines were incorporated into advertising to infuse commercial products with the imprimatur of science (Young 1978).

Although the general public did not apprehend nutrition except at a low level of resolution, they were persuaded by product promotions that emphasized individual naturally occurring nutrients—for example,

"Grapefruit Juice: Excellent Source of Vitamin C" and eventually by products that had been enhanced with heterogenous nutrients, such as vitamin D–fortified breakfast cereals and dairy products. In addition to singlet foods and nutrients, more-comprehensive foodways were fashioned around themes that appealed to diverse and shifting adherents.

Slow Food

The Slow Food movement is a cultural posture that positions one's lifeways in contrast to the tempos and rhythms of modernity. A 1986 protest against the opening of a McDonald's restaurant in Rome's historical Piazza di Spagna is commonly identified as the origin of this movement, although such an ethos emerged with the Industrial Revolution (or earlier) and has simply been perceived by some to have accelerated. Efforts to slow daily activity patterns are evident in individual subscribers' daily routines and extend to wide-reaching social actions. The Slow Foods movement is propounded primarily by small autonomous groups that strive to (re-)create slow versions of cities, recreation, and communications by increasing "awareness, attention, and engagement" (Parkins and Craig 2006:105). What began as opposition to fast food has evolved and today has the more comprehensive goal of advancing dietary and biocultural diversity.

Food is a central site of the Slow Food movement. Advocates of slow food (SF) both reject fast food proper—and other nutritionally and culturally homogenized commercial foods—and promote traditional, regional, artisanal, and organic fresh foods and beverages. One goal is to advance the production and consumption of local specialties such as vegetable and fruit cultivars, cheeses, traditional beers and wines, and breads. The SF Ark of Taste project has fostered such foods as Sun Crest peaches from California, which taste "sublime" but travel poorly. On the strength of promotion through SF networks, the peach was featured in *Time* magazine, following which its small producer was flooded with inquiries and the volume of sales increased rapidly (Fastcompany 2007).

SF proponents are critical of fusion foods, citing the "decontextualization of culinary traditions [which] . . . is symptomatic of . . . the need for . . . innovation . . . which, paradoxically, erases differences." They regard fusion foods (see chapter 4) as "inauthentic, disconnected from relations with place, people and territory—which can only be . . . made meaningful by slowness" (Parkins and Craig 2006:105). Critics underscore the privileged nature of access to slow food. Carlo Petrini, one of the founders of the Slow Food movement, was a contributing author for the epicurean magazine *La Gola*, a word that means both "throat" and "desire for food" and is often translated as "gluttony." That he and other founders of the SF ideology were members of a Milanese leftist intellectual circle[4] fuels the critique that SF proponents are elitist, that the foregrounding of boutique foods is simply another iteration of the "power of consumerist capitalism to commodify everything, even [one's] opposition to commodification" (Wilk 2006a:22). The Slow Food movement's University of Gastronomic Sciences adds an academic piece that appeals, and is accessible, only to those who can afford it. The critique continues that featuring artisanal foods encourages dependence on niche markets, government regulation, and gastro-tourism (Guthman 2003). For example, the SF Progetto Presidia fosters the continued production in Cinque Terre, Italy, of the rare white wine Sciacchetrà, for which the Slow Food movement purchased land and gave it, rent-free, to one of the three remaining Sciacchetrà vineyards (Fastcompany 2007). The name "Presidia" is derived from the Latin *praesidia*, "military post," a metaphor that underscores the passion that marks this and other SF projects and advocacies.

A primary goal of this culinary aesthetic is to consume in the company of others, where pleasure and authenticity converge. By this definition, one might argue that the Slow Food movement is quintessentially about foods of association, but essentialism is not something I want to embrace intellectually. The Slow Food movement is distinguished as a foodway not by signaling low-fat or lactose-free goals (see below) but by improving health through shared production, distribution, preparation, and consumption of foods and beverages. In these sites, the foods are items of association and sociability that are embedded in broader socioeconomic and ecological settings (Miele and Murdoch 2002; Petrini 2003; Parkins and Craig 2006).

The community coalitions that make up SF networks are *convivia*, from the Latin *convivium*, "feast" (more comprehensively, a living together, from *con* + *vivo*), which shares a root with *convivial*, meaning fond of companionship, drinking, and feasting. Reference to SF convivia overlaps the literature on food sociability mentioned earlier. Analyzing the Slow Food movement from a biocultural perspective directs attention also to the biology of foods and beverages and how they affect us physiologically.

Heirloom and Heritage Foods and Beverages

In the past, farmers worldwide have produced thousands of breeds and varieties of animals and plants (see the section on early human foragers, above). Today, industrial food producers work with relatively few specialized species and varieties; thousands of noncommercial breeds and varieties representing substantial genetic diversity have disappeared. Some sustainable farmers conserve biocultural diversity by producing heirloom and heritage products, which have been embraced by gardeners, gourmets, and food hobbyists, including SF advocates (see chapter 3, section on street foods in Hawai'i). Although the terms *heirloom* and *heritage* are used interchangeably and mean more or less the same thing, some distinguish heirloom *plants* from heritage *animals*—which, by my interpretation, privileges meat (see above) by connecting it to our ancestors, while *heirloom* connotes items that have been important over a shorter time frame. These terms are applied to varieties of plants and animals that were produced by earlier generations of farmers and are genetically different from commercial, mass-produced foods. Growing heirloom plants sustains diversity and contributes to diet items that are unique in taste, appearance, and texture. Whereas heritage animals were bred to encourage characteristics adapted to local ecologies (climate, disease, altitude, and pasture and other free range), breeds favored by industrial agriculture were selected for the volume of meat, milk, and eggs produced over compressed time frames in confined installations (Fresco 2007).

Researchers of Africa's food heritage point out that the continent has more native grains than any other landmass. However, this began to change with the advent of exposure to other cultures: centuries ago, dhows (traditional Arabic sailing vessels) along the Mediterranean coast traded rice from Asia; in the sixteenth century, Portuguese colonists in Mozambique and Angola imported maize from the New World (see chapter 2); over the past several decades, wheat has been imported from temperate regions. Embracing the exotic and projecting what people associate with modernity, Africa has "slowly tilted away from its own cereal wealth" (National Research Council 1996:1). Indigenous populations lacked the support of authorities—principally agricultural researchers, missionaries, and colonial administrators—who had little interest in or knowledge of local ecologies, cuisines, and other customs. Local grains literally and metaphorically lost ground to "up-to-the-minute" aliens whose convenience was exaggerated by the introduction of automated grinding mills and other ease-of-processing technologies. Indigenous grains were "driven into internal exile," as they acquired the fictional stigma of having low yield and less flavor and being more difficult to produce and process. Some of Africa's "lost crops" have begun to take center stage, however, on the basis of recent research: West African red rice (*Oryza glaberrima* Steudel), cultivated in the Niger delta for 3,500 years; finger millet (*Eleusine coracana* Gaertner), cultivated in Ethiopia since 3000 BCE; *fonio* (*Digitaria exilis* Stapf and *D. iburua* Stapf), arguably Africa's oldest grain; and *teff* (*Eragrostis* spp.). All of these grains have nutritional values that are as high as or higher than some of their substitutes—notably, and variably, for calcium, thiamin, iron, phosphorus, manganese, and fiber (Mabberley 1993; National Research Council 1996).

Among heirloom crops, the purple carrot offers an interesting example that is gaining momentum in North America and Europe. Wild ancestors of the carrot probably evolved about five thousand years ago and are native to Afghanistan, which remains the center of diversity of *Daucus carota*; there, it is still used by hill farmers to make a traditional fermented beverage. Egyptian temple drawings from 2000 BCE depict a purple root that researchers speculate is a carrot; papyruses (made from *Cyperus papyrus* L., Cyperaceae) record the medicinal properties of carrot seed and leaves. People of the Roman era knew purple carrots, whose color is attributed to anthocyanins, and white cultivars, whose lack of pigment is attributed to a single gene. In the 1300s, purple, white, and yellow carrots were imported to southern Europe, where they were used as medicine and food. By the 1700s, the Dutch had introduced orange roots, pigmented by á-carotene and by even more ß-carotene than their yellow relatives. This emblematic food honored the Dutch national color, a metaphor for the political entity Huis van Oranje, "House of Orange."

The still-orange center of the purple root contributes to the stunning appearance of sliced carrots (World Carrot Museum 2008). These heritage or heirloom crops are not, or not primarily, promoted by food enthusiasts; instead, they are advocated by researchers who recognize better nutritional potential and wish to advance biocultural diversity.

Slow Food and Health

The physiologic implications of slow foods, including heirloom and heritage varieties, include the nutritional benefits of organically produced and fresh foods and beverages. Organic foods contain fewer or no pesticides, hormones, antibiotics, chemical fertilizers, and preservatives. The U.S. Department of Agriculture (USDA) certifies four categories of organic foods (outlined in table 1.1) according to standards established in 2002. Meat, dairy products, fruits, and vegetables are grown either organically or not and are thus 100 percent organic, if at all. The other three categories reference food blends and processed foods. Since the early 1990s, the conventional food industry has been stocking a small percentage of organic products, with astonishing sales increases of about 20 percent each year. This success can be explained by the large profit margin from what is still a small proportion of marketed foods (estimates range from 1 to 10 percent). The great abundance of food in the United States translates into slow growth of conventional food sales, about 1 to 2 percent annually (Nestle 2006). Organic foods carry the cachet of certification for consumers who seek agency in their health but are overwhelmed by the diversity of food varieties, brands, and health claims. Consequently, they are prepared to pay high prices for what they perceive to be assurances and better food. However, many of the organic foods that are sold in big-box grocery stores do not conform to the SF philosophy, because they are not locally grown; SF proponents count on local producers for what they perceive to be healthy foods.

The nutritional benefits of fresh local foods include the decreased likelihood of nutrient loss. For example, the stability of both fat- and water-soluble vitamins is compromised by heat, oxygen, ultraviolet radiation, and pH shifts that can occur during transport and storage (table 1.2). Reduced spoilage among locally sourced fresh foods might contribute to cost containment and thus further encourage supporting local producers.

TABLE 1.1. Categories of USDA-authorized organic foods

Organic ingredients content	Certified Organic seal on label[a]	Label statement
73% or less	no	organic ingredients only on information panel
74–94%	no	"Made with Organic Ingredients"[b]
95–99%	yes	"Organic"
100%	yes	"100% Organic"

Source: Nestle 2006.

[a] Labeling requirements are also established for livestock feed that has been organically produced, for containers in which organic products are shipped and stored, and for denoting bulk organic products in market information that is displayed or disseminated at the point of retail sale.

[b] Up to three organic ingredients can be listed.

TABLE 1.2. Vitamin susceptibility to environmental conditions

Vitamin	Destabilizers				
	Heat	Oxygen	Light	Acids	Alkalies
Fat-soluble					
A	no	yes	yes	yes	—[a]
D	no	no	no	—[a]	—[a]
E	no	yes	yes	no	yes
K	no	yes	yes	yes	yes
Water-soluble					
C	yes	yes	yes	no	no
Thiamin	yes	yes	yes	—[a]	yes
Riboflavin	no	no	yes	no	yes
Niacin	no	no	no	no	no
B_6	no	—[a]	yes	no	yes
Folic acid	yes	yes	yes	yes	no
B_{12}	no	yes	yes	yes	yes

Source: Lutz and Przytulski 2006.

[a] Inconsistent information.

Beyond these considerations, featuring wild or semiwild SF species suggests the contribution of significant amounts of macro- and micronutrients (Grivetti and Ogle 2000). These species also provide substantial pharmacologic potential: the manipulation of wild species during their domestication, notably their organoleptic characteristics, has in many cases bred out physiologically active phytoconstituents. For example, the anthocyanins in purple carrots and other novelty vegetables are antioxidants that have cancer-suppressive and cardiovascular-protective effects and are antimicrobial (Etkin 1994a; Johns 2000; Nicolle et al. 2003).

The SF philosophy also extends to the physical environment: "ecogastronomy" contextualizes people's foodways broadly and draws a parallel with species conservation by promoting what SF proponents label "endangered foods." A central theme links people who enjoy food and traditional foodways with environmentalists who seek to preserve local, small-scale production. The Slow Food movement offers these compelling statistics: since 1900, the loss of food-product diversity is 93 percent and 75 percent for the United States and Europe, respectively; 33 percent of livestock varieties are extinct or approach extinction (Fondazione Slow Food 2007).

Vegetarian Diets

The diverse foodways that are included under the rubric "vegetarianism" all cohere around the idea that consumption of plant foods is more healthful and ethical than eating meat and animal products. Vegans are the most strict and exclude all animal products from their diet, attire, cosmetics, and other use categories. Vegans also reject so-called hidden products, whose animal origins are more remote, such as gelatin (from connective tissues) and beeswax, propolis, and honey (see chapter 4). Animal-derived additives also are avoided: texture modifiers, including whey (milk plasma) and bone phosphate; emulsifiers, such as caseinate (milk protein); lactose (milk sugar) (see below) as a sweetener and flavor vehicle; dyes, including cochineal (scale insect, *Dactylopius coccus* Costa, Dactylopiidae); purportedly nondairy products such as whipped toppings and powdered coffee creamer to which whey, lactose, and milk solids are added for structural stability and bulk; and glazing agents such as shellac (lac insect, *Lacifer lacca* Kerr., Dactylopiidae). Vegans also reject cosmetics and other products that have been tested on animals, although the antipathy may not extend to animal-tested human medicines and to the many prescription and over-the-counter drugs that are manufactured with lactose (VRG 2004).

In the classic macrobiotic diet, whole (not milled) grains constitute 50 to 60 percent of the diet, and vegetables 30 percent; small amounts of fish may be included. Frugivore diets are defined by fruit, including tomato (*Lycopersicon esculentum* Miller, Solanaceae), cucumber (*Cucumis sativus* L., Cucurbitaceae), and others that, because they are not sweet, are commonly regarded to be vegetables. Other vegetarians avoid only certain animal foods: ovo-lacto vegetarians reject all animal flesh, including fish and seafood, but eat dairy products and eggs; lacto vegetarians consume dairy products but not eggs; ovo vegetarians consume eggs but not dairy products. Over the past fifteen years or so in the United States, the term *flexitarian* was popularized to refer to people who are flexible about how strict their vegetarian diets are. In other words, the flexitarian eats meat with unspecified frequency and in particular contexts, perhaps in restaurants or at friends' homes. Incentives for following vegetarian diets are varied and overlap. They include the injunctions of Buddhism, Islam, and other religions that reject consumption of all or some animals and animal products. Other motivations are ethical, such as advocacy concerns for animals and environmental integrity, including sustained biodiversity, and aversion to the manner in which animals are treated in the meat, dairy, clothing, and cosmetics industries (Perlo 2003; VRG 2004; Elmadfa 2005).

Vegetarian Diets as Foodways of Association

Although vegetarian diets tend to be defined by what they exclude, they also are statements of inclusion. Rather than a rejection of our omnivore roots (see above), they are foodways of association that forge identity through statements about people's relationships to one another, other animals, and the environment and statements about health and ethics. People tend to establish vegetarian regimens not in isolation but rather as a processual formalization of food rules whose organizational scaffold promotes community and may take on elements of social movements. Like all foodways, these grow as much out of social experiences as of individual ones (Maurer 2002). In this way, the term *flexitarian* is an in-the-moment statement (rather than a cryptic one) about fluid boundaries, pragmatic and social decisions, empathy for animals, and nutritional and other health concerns.

The Health of Vegetarians

The health benefits and risks of any diet are defined by which foods and beverages are consumed or excluded, in what volume, and with what frequency. Plant-dominant diets offer the advantages of lower levels of saturated fat and cholesterol; higher levels of fiber, potassium, magnesium, folate, the antioxidant vitamins E and C, and pharmacologically active phytoconstituents; fewer constituents that contribute to calcium loss; and less exposure to antibiotics, hormones, and other chemicals commonly administered to farmed animals. Compared to their meat-eating counterparts, vegetarians (variably defined) tend to have lower incidence of obesity, coronary artery disease, hypertension, cancer, and diabetes; greater longevity; and markedly lower all-cause mortality rates (Appleby et al. 1999; Burr 2000; Rajaram and Sabaté 2000; Elmadfa 2005; Rust and Elmadfa 2005). Conversely, the more restricted vegetarian diets pose health risks such as deficiencies of iron, vitamin D, calcium, and vitamin B_{12} in infants and children, the elderly, and pregnant women; impaired iodine uptake; and dental erosions (not including caries). These problems are exaggerated over the long term in individuals who eat primarily raw fruits and vegetables (Lightowler and Davies 1998; Ganss et al. 1999; Louwman et al. 2000; Koebnick et al. 2005).

Many vegetarians compensate for the nutritional limitations of their foodways by eating across a broader span of plant foods and taking vitamin and other supplements. One of the most versatile and nutritious elements of vegetarian diets is fermented soybean curd (e.g., tofu, tempeh), which is emblematic of low-meat or meatless foodways. Like other fermented foods and beverages, tofu adds vitamins and amino acids, improves nutrient availability and palatability, is antimicrobial, reduces toxicity, and preserves foods (Etkin 2006a:ch. 4). Soy isoflavones have been linked to the prevention of chronic disorders such as cancer, heart disease, and osteoporosis (Friedman and Brandon 2001; Messina et al. 2002). Lately, concern has been expressed about the risk of nonfermented soy products —for example, in some hormone-dependent cancers (Weiger et al. 2002).

Low-Carbohydrate Weight-Loss Diets

Low-Carbohydrate Diets as Foodways

At present, the Atkins Nutritional Approach (popularly known as the "Atkins Diet") is emblematic of a host of low-carbohydrate (CHO) diets, several of which are summarized in table 1.3. The recorded history of these diets suggests a web of intersecting processes or circumstances: people in all societies and times strive to manage body weight; even with efforts to conduct controlled trials, it is not clear whether weight loss and other advantages can be attributed to a particular food regimen; and the relative merits of different weight loss diets are difficult to assess. Still, these diets have been very popular and continue to be so in this era of epidemic obesity. Atkins's enterprises alone sold 45 million books since the 1960s (Astrup et al. 2004); by brand extension, his and others' diet names have been applied to other commercial lines such as supplements, foods, and cookbooks. Most of the creators of the more popular diets are physicians, members of a profession that carries substantial authority in health matters. Other low-CHO promoters are celebrities who claim knowledge of nutrition or are sufficiently charismatic to persuade potential subscribers to adopt their regimens. These observations contribute to the associative features of following particular dietary regimens. Whether or not adherents understand the composition and metabolism of carbohydrates, they establish membership in a group for whom identity includes making statements about health and having agency in improving or maintaining it.

Low-CHO Diets and Health

One thing that the historical outline in table 1.3 does not reflect is a unified or timeless perspective on physiology and biological processes. The rationale of most contemporary low-CHO diets centers on the metabolism of insulin, glucose, and cholesterol and other markers of

TABLE 1.3. A brief history of low-carbohydrate (CHO) diets

Diet name/date[a]	Author or creator	Refinements[b]
Harvey-Banting 1862	William Harvey, MD	High protein, high fat; no calorie restriction; begin phase two at near-target weight
Inuit Style 1929	Blake Donaldson, MD	Strict meat diet
Stone Age 1958	Richard Mackarness	Emulate our ancestors prior to the advent of agriculture; high fat and protein
Atkins 1972	Robert Atkins, MD	Unprocessed, nutrient-rich foods such as meats and fish; dietary supplements; sequence of phases
Fat Flush Plan 1988	Anne Gittleman	Whole natural foods; no salt; flaxseed oil and essential fatty acid supplements, no other oils; no dairy products
Protein Power 1995	Michael Eades, MD; Mary Eades, MD	Eat as our "cave-man ancestors" did; protein and fat from all meats and fish; limited dairy; avoid high-sugar fruit
Schwarzbein Principle 1999	Diana Schwarzbein, MD	Red meat, eggs, butter, cream; low CHO vegetables; unrefined carbohydrates in moderation[b]
Neanderthin 1999	Ray Audette	Eat as our ancestors did; reject technologically produced foods, including beans and grains; minimal fruit
South Beach 2003	Arthur Agatston, MD	High fiber and protein, low animal fat

Note: This compilation is shortened and modified from a popular website that promotes low CHO diets (Low Carb 2006).

[a] The date corresponds to the year of design or popularization of the diet; it may precede the date of publication of a diet book.

[b] Primarily to manage diabetes.

coronary heart disease. Gittleman's flush metaphor is appealing to subscribers whose knowledge base does not support critical judgment of such purported weight-gain factors as "water-logged tissues," "liver toxicity," and "the fear of eating fat." Thus, the common lay-friendly theme is *low carbs*. This is an injunction to eat fewer of what are commonly understood in the West to be carbohydrate-rich foods: bread, pasta, sweets, cereal, and root vegetables. The corollary instruction to eat more protein evidences a misplaced nostalgia for a hunter's diet that the public would like to believe centers on high protein and few polysaccharides (outlined above).

A sea of anecdotal accounts and limited surveys of individuals' and clinicians' experiences with low-CHO diets suggest, at least for the short term, successful weight loss without hunger. This is appealing to subscribers who otherwise might discontinue the regimen during the first and most restrictive phase(s). Two studies that compared low-fat and low-CHO diets reported no significant difference in weight loss after twelve months, although individuals following low-CHO diets lost significantly more weight during the first six months. Concern is raised, however, whether early success has any impact on modifying and maintaining dietary changes over the course of a lifetime. Further, low-CHO diets have been associated with fatigue, bowel irregularities, headache, increased protein burden on the kidneys, ketosis,[5] and modified pH, which can eventuate in bone demineralization and diminished integrity. Cancer risk may increase as a consequence of eliminating whole grains, vegetables, fruits, and legumes. The issue of high fat consumption is troublesome in view of its link with cardiovascular and other morbidities. Low-CHO diets have inadequate levels of fiber and vitamins A and C. A systematic review of low-CHO dietary intervention studies that were published between 1966 and 2003 reported that weight loss is associated more strongly with limited calorie consumption and duration of diet than with CHO restriction. The long-term effects of these variably restrictive diets are not known (Foster et al. 2003; Lichtenstein 2006; Lutz and Przytulski 2006; Steffen and Nettleton 2006).

Diets Adapted to Physiologies

During the past twenty-five years or so, complementary and alternative medicines (CAM) have captured a large and growing market share among "unconventional" health products and practices. The category "CAM" is defined by exclusion—anything that is not consistent with the preventive and therapeutic paradigms of medical doctors (MDs), doctors of osteopathy (DOs), and allied health professionals such as nurses, physical therapists, and psychologists. In other frameworks, the category also is inclusive, embracing virtually everything that claims to influence health, spanning an infinitely broad spectrum of perspectives that range from megavitamins to horticultural therapy (see chapter 5, section on therapeutic landscapes) to spirit mediums. Some of these customs can be traced back thousands of years to Chinese, Arabic, and other ancient traditions, which themselves no doubt represent customs that evolved from knowledge of the earliest humans.

Today's category CAM does not have the structure or paradigmatic integrity of an indigenous system of knowledge and practice but is instead configured by a variety of competing and converging understandings of illness, prevention, and therapeutics. Since the 1950s in the affluent West, the epidemiologic landscape has shifted: antibiotics and immunization have significantly reduced the impact of infections; cardiovascular and other chronic disorders account for a greater proportion of morbidity and mortality but are not curable and commonly are difficult to manage. A hierarchy still defines clinical encounters, but the absence of dramatic cures and a shifting ethos that flattens social stratifications have empowered patients who want to participate in their own health care. Simultaneously, bioscience has become more interested in the healthful qualities of foods, which reinforces the public's confidence in a more comprehensive ("holistic") and nonpharmaceutical management of health and disease. But the imprimatur of science is illusory. Most of the current bioscientific research on foods consists of reductionistic explorations of purified and other phytochemical constituents and their specific actions. Research findings are issued as factoids, disembodied statements that summarize reductionistic and acontextual studies whose findings may contradict one another (see chapter 4, section on wine and the French paradox). As scientists continue to debate incongruent findings, laypersons can become confused by information that is not connected to eating whole foods in the combinations and sequences that are the syntax of real meals. Even when medicine-like activities are confirmed by studies of (usually healthy) animals, that is not evidence of efficacy for sick humans. The health benefits of most CAM are potential rather than established.

Perhaps most prominent in the popularization of CAM is the commercialization of health and the globalization of products. CAM is one of the most rapidly growing sectors of U.S. health-product industries, a process accelerated by a series of legislations that constituted a "supplements" category that is not subject to rigorous, or even consistent, regulation by the Food and Drug Administration (FDA). Even when the constituents and activities of CAM have been well characterized, products vary widely in the bioavailability and activity of those constituents. For example, many pharmacologic effects have been rigorously and reproducibly established for garlic (*Allium sativum* L., Liliaceae)—antithrombic, antimicrobial, cholesterol-lowering, and more—but a study of garlic extracts sourced from different manufacturers, and even batches from the same producer, revealed significant variations in the amounts of allicin, citral, and other constituents.

In a very general and amorphous way, the aggregation CAM might be said to serve as a platform for association. The use of CAM does, after all, reflect a social phenomenon that includes taking agency in one's health care. But there are too many CAM products and claims to proceed in that direction. A more productive approach is to note that among the dizzying array of CAM products are fix-it or prevent-it foods and supplements for specific physiologic conditions that have been identified and characterized by conventional medicine. The foods of association that I discuss here reflect identities that cohere around metabolic circumstances that can be managed, fully or in part, by diet: diabetes, gluten enteropathy, and lactose intolerance. All three conditions confer identity through shared information about etiology and diet and lifestyle management. The example of lactose intolerance, however, is distinguished from the other conditions by the extent to which a food group (dairy) is manipulated by powerful commercial and government influences.

Diabetes

The term *diabetes* is a gloss for several chronic carbohydrate metabolism disorders. Diabetes mellitus (DM) is defined by a relative or absolute deficiency of insulin, a pancreas-secreted hormone that promotes utilization of glucose. Worldwide, DM is a major cause of morbidity and mortality that affects at least 171 million people. Of people diagnosed with DM, 95 percent have type 2, also called "non-insulin-dependent" and "adult-onset," in which some insulin production persists. The others have type 1 DM, "juvenile-onset," which responds to exogenous insulin. Other classifications include secondary diabetes, linked to pancreatic and other disorders and to drug reactions; and gestational diabetes. DM is an independent risk factor for cardiovascular disorders and often is associated with other circumstances of risk such as obesity, impaired lipid metabolism and renal function, and hypertension.

DM types 1 and 2 are in part genetically inherited, and both are profoundly affected by diet and daily activity patterns. Biomedical management of DM centers on routine plasma glucose monitoring and the individualization of prevention and therapy. Controlled studies indicate that rigorous management of glucose levels to as near normal as possible diminishes the occurrence and severity of long-term complications such as neuropathies, retinopathy, nephropathy, and other microvascular morbidities. In addition to insulin for DM 1, pharmaceuticals developed in the 1990s improve DM management by amplifying cell response to insulin, overcoming insulin resistance, and decreasing carbohydrate absorption after eating. In recent decades, patient agency has been encouraged, primarily through management of diet. Guidelines emphasize consistent timing and meal size, limiting foods containing simple sugars and saturated fats, and promoting the consumption of complex carbohydrates (starchy vegetables, cereals) and fruits and vegetables (soluble fibers slow or reduce glucose absorption) (National Institutes of Health 2006; World Health Organization 2006). These formal guidelines are augmented by direct-to-patient information from professionals of conventional medicine. Other practitioners and purveyors of products in "health food" emporia and on the Internet offer consumers recommendations for and against a wide array of foods and beverages but represent a varied knowledge base about the physiology of diabetes and its management.

Celiac Disease/Gluten Enteropathy

Celiac disease (CD) is a malabsorption disorder that is characterized histologically by degeneration of small intestine villi in reaction to gluten, an insoluble protein complex of glutenin, gliadin, and other prolamines (proline-rich proteins). The term *celiac* denotes the abdominal cavity, from the Greek *koilia,* "belly." The synonyms *celiac disease, celiac sprue,* and *celiac syndrome* reflect the general knowledge of this condition in the early twentieth century, when CD was simply one of a suite of poorly characterized intestinal malabsorption processes. The contemporary term *gluten enteropathy* (GE) evidences more-specific knowledge of its etiology. It is an intrinsic enteropathy and is distinguished from tropical sprue, which often is associated with enteric infections. Gluten is present in grains (Poaceae), including wheat (gliadin), rye (secalinin) (*Secale cereale* L.), and barley (hordein), and is responsible for the viscoelastic (rising) properties of doughs made with those cereals. Although oats (*Avena sativa* L.) contain no gluten, contamination during processing with other grains is common. The primary autoantigen in GE is tissue transglutaminase. Research has established that gluten toxicity is mediated by the immune system via both humoral factors and T cells, but the mechanisms have not been well characterized (Lutz and Przytulski 2006).

GE has a strong polygenic basis for susceptibility involving both HLA (human leukocyte antigens) and non-HLA genes: 70 percent of monozygotic twins both have GE; 10 percent of first-degree relatives (parent, child, sibling) of GE patients also are affected. It is one of the most common lifelong disorders in the developed world, affecting as many as 1 percent of people in the United States, but is significantly underdiagnosed. In the past, underweight young women presenting with ambiguous symptoms typically were suspected to be anorexic, which significantly delayed diagnosis of GE. Today, standard good practice in U.S. medicine includes screening by biopsy or rapid antibody test (for antigliadin or antiendomysial) for patients who present with irritable bowel syndrome and for infants of high-risk populations. GE commonly is diagnosed in babies when cereals are added to the diet; short stature and anemia may be signs in older children and adults, respectively. Symptoms grade from moderate gastrointestinal discomfort to chronic inflammation, including accelerated intestinal transit and diarrhea, leading to nutrient deficiencies, weight loss, and complications arising from those effects. The cardinal sign is steatorrhea, excess fecal fat. Long-term risks include colon cancer, osteoporosis, arthritis, autoimmune disorders, and birth defects (Young and Thomas 2004; Lutz and Przytulski 2006).

In most cases, GE can be easily managed by excluding gluten, which usually returns the small intestine to histological normal within two or three months. Conventionally, diets were reconfigured by centering on maize or rice. In the past fifteen years, the functional food industry has been promoting gluten-free grains and flours, including products not traditionally used in Western cuisines, such as buckwheat (*Fagopyrum esculentum* Moench, Polygonaceae), sunflower seed (*Helianthus annuus* L., Asteraceae), quinoa (*Chenopodium quinoa* Willd., Chenopodiaceae), amaranths (*Amaranthus* spp., Amaranthaceae), chickpea (*Cicer arietinum* L., Fabaceae), and almond (*Prunus dulcis* D. Webb, Rosaceae). The increasing accessibility of these products makes it easy for individuals to manage GE with fewer medical interventions and less clinical oversight. One outcome of the National Institutes of Health celiac disease awareness campaign, launched in summer 2006, is that some restaurants have begun to offer gluten-free menus. Expanding the variety of food products has the additional benefit of providing a broader spectrum of nutrients.

In contrast to genetic selection for lactose intolerance in some populations, the genetic basis of neither DM nor GE experienced positive selective pressure. Rather, these conditions were *not* selected *against* in early human populations, because symptoms would not have manifested themselves until later, when people began relying heavily on cereals (and later on milled grains) and consuming high volumes of refined sugars.

Lactose Intolerance

Lactose intolerance also describes circumstances of malabsorption and is governed by a single-locus regulatory gene that turns on and off production of the enzyme lactase, which cleaves milk sugar, or lactose, into its constituent simple sugars, glucose and galactose.[6] The early development of all mammalian infants depends on milk digestion, for which lactase is secreted into the small intestine. Enzyme production begins to taper off at the age of weaning (about two years for humans), resulting in lactose intolerance throughout adulthood. Lactase is not inducible, that is, one cannot stimulate the body to produce the enzyme by challenging the intestine with continued ingestion of lactose substrate. When lactose-intolerant individuals consume fresh milk, undigested lactose enters the large intestine, where microfloral fermentation produces gas, cramping, and diarrhea. Among lactose-intolerant individuals, these consequences vary from one dairy product to another, by episode of consumption, and in severity. These irregularities suggest that, beyond genetics, lactose tolerance is further nuanced by metabolic fluctuations, other foods consumed at (or near) the same time as milk, changes in intestinal flora, rates of gastric emptying and intestinal transit, health status, and discomfort thresholds.

Dietary management of lactose intolerance excludes many dairy products, including nonfermented milks and nonaged cheeses. Fermented milk products, in which microflora have already digested the lactose, commonly are tolerated; these include buttermilk, yogurt, cottage cheese, sour cream, and kefir. Butter and ice cream also have low lactose content. Some lactose-deficient individuals tolerate full-cream products better than low-fat products because fat slows gastrointestinal transit, resulting in slower release of lactose from the stomach and small intestine (Sibley 2004).

In a small percentage of the world's people, lactase production continues into adulthood. Before the mid-1900s, virtually all research on lactose tolerance was conducted in populations for whom lactase persistence was common, fostering the impression that lactose tolerance is physiologically normative. Later, through the negative experiences of post–World War II international food aid programs that attempted to distribute milk, Western researchers began to understand the global scale of lactose intolerance. Lactase persistence into adulthood is rare outside of North America, western Europe, the Middle East, and a few populations in Asia and Africa. Human lactase persistence emerged in recent evolutionary history, about ten thousand to twelve thousand years ago, at about the time that animals were domesticated. In dairying populations whose diets centered heavily on fresh milk and milk products year-round, a selective advantage was conferred on lactase-persistent genotypes, who would have enjoyed better nutrition, including improved calcium absorption, and prevention of dehydration. Figures vary and are confounded by individuals who are the products of mixed ethnicities and countries of origin, but common estimates for lactose intolerance are 5 percent among descendants of northern Europeans, 55 percent among Mexican Americans, and 79 percent among African Americans (Enattah et al. 2002).

The cultural constructions of milk drinking in the United States offer insights into interrelations among the American Dairy Association (ADA), the market, and government entities. Whereas *hypo*lactasia is the mammalian template and characterizes at least 75 percent of the world's population, it is medicalized through such referents as "lactase *deficiency*," "*non*persistence," and "*mal*absorption." The message conveyed by the ADA is that lactose intolerance is a treatable disease. For more than one hundred years, U.S. federal and other entities dispensing nutrition advice have promoted milk as "indispensable," "the most complete food," and "nature's perfect food." The idea of a perfect anything is emblematic of an ethos in the United States that depicts industrial production, hierarchical management, and the model of supply and demand converging to define one best way to produce, market, and circulate commodities. National diet guidelines, symbolically sealed in the USDA food pyramid, privilege certain foods, food categories, and foodways (DuPuis 2002)—witness the long-running "Got Milk" advertisements of the National Dairy Council. In the early 1990s, the campaign featured people dealing with dry or viscid foods, with the implication that their circumstances would be relieved by drinking milk. This expanded to include peopleless images of dry cookies, sandwiches missing a bite, and unhappy cats (many of which are lactose intolerant and should not be sad to be relieved of gastrointestinal distress when their humans withhold milk).[7] The more recent advertisements offer consumers milk-mustached images of media, sports, and entertainment celebrities who are powerful, popular, and famous—but neither nutritionally educated nor self-evidently healthy. In 2006, the campaign endeavored to extend the pro-milk ideology to a new demographic. Using several Spanish-language advertisements, including "Toma Leche?" (Drink Milk?), the industry marketed—cynically, one could argue—to populations among whom the rate of lactose tolerance is low. One stimulus of this aggressive marketing of beverage milk is the rapidly escalating competition from soft drinks and bottled waters (see chapter 5), which are not at risk of spoilage and appeal to a wide array of demographics.

History is rewritten by those aspects of the milk campaign that portray drinking cow's milk as an old tradition, part of the "American way" dating to the colonial era. In fact, whatever milk was available early in U.S. history was reserved for butter and cheese production and for cooking. The little that was drunk would have been the fermented by-products of those processes. Nostalgic images about the rural origins of milk drinking conjure up the meme of inevitable increased demand with urbanization and the development of means to deliver the product. This narrative overlooks the keeping of cows and other livestock in towns and that milk drinking began as a *new* foodway in urban centers in the mid-1800s, when it substituted as breast milk for infants and was deemed an appropriate beverage for young children. It also leaves out the history of contamination in early milk production and the association of milk with high morbidity and mortality. Despite this risk, by the mid-1900s, average consumption of milk in the United States had doubled. As DuPuis (2002:6) notes, "The history of milk is not simply a happy reunion with a longed-for past"—it is more a progression of political and other power asymmetries, rural-urban dynamics, and cultural constructions of normative physiologies and perfection. Enlightenment is part of this ethos, based on the idea that "perfection, once discovered, must be taught to the uninitiated" (DuPuis 2002:113). Claims continue to be advanced that "milk is important to the American diet," as if any such homogeneous cuisine were a reality and as if evidence to the contrary were not available.

While intolerance can be readily managed by avoiding dairy products and other foods that contain lactose (see above, in the section on vegetarian diets), several product lines have been developed by the food and nutraceutical industries to respond to what they construct as the "need" for lactose-intolerant people to consume milk. Lactose-reduced and lactose-free milks are readily available, as is lactase enzyme in chewable and liquid forms, including several for pets. These products permit intolerant individuals to dose-regulate to match food type, quantity, and their own physiologic circumstances. The collective (ADA-government) and primary goal is that intolerant individuals will consume across the spectrum of milk products by adjusting to their personal threshold of lactose tolerance. The idea of milk is further reinforced by analog products such as rice, soy, and almond "milks"—although they are, ironically, promoted as "nondairy substitutes." The word *milk* carries significant cachet, which is reinforced through assertive marketing.

These substitutes and nutraceuticals make available digestible foods and beverages for lactose-intolerant individuals who want dairy products in their diet. But the real benefactor is the dairy industry, which has more products to market to more people who have been persuaded that they *should* drink milk. Unpacking the narrative of constructed need illuminates the politicized circumstances of milk promotion in the United States. This includes decades-long ADA advocacy of milk as "the perfect food," recommended for children from infancy through adolescence, for pregnant and lactating women, and to prevent osteoporosis. Among populations whose milk consumption is low, adequate growth rates and bone density and healthy experiences during pregnancy and the postpartum period suggest that these guidelines are not justified. A review of studies published during the past three decades and a three-year investigation of data from National Health and Nutrition Examination Surveys reveal that among U.S. children, there is significant variability in how, when, and whether milk consumption affects height and, in fact, whether increased height is a suitable gauge of health improvements. For example, there is evidence that milk influences height via insulin-like growth factor 1 (IGF-1), a polypeptide hormone that is important in children's growth. Whether the IGF-1 is in the milk itself or milk induces its endogenous production, it is a risk factor for several cancers in later life: it is strongly mitogenic and associated with colorectal and breast cancers (Wiley 2005, 2007).

Surely, for lactose-intolerant individuals, milk is not "a perfect food." It is not necessarily healthful for tolerant individuals either: consumption of medium- to full-fat milk has been linked to obesity, anemia, cancers, asthma, and allergies. Concerns have also been raised about residues of antibiotics and hormones (DuPuis 2002). For the past two decades, the dairy industry has been under the close scrutiny of both consumer and professional dietary and clinical entities. The revised food pyramid locates dairy products in a less prominent position than in earlier iterations of this guide. Nevertheless, as part of its redoubled efforts to encourage milk consumption, the dairy industry recently has been promoting dairy products for weight loss through a "Think about Your Drink Challenge," a twelve-week program[8] through which consumers are offered "free expert help" if they drink twenty-four ounces of milk every twenty-four hours. The 24/24 slogan is more a poster child of advertising than a shorthand formula for success, however. In 2005, the Committee for

Responsible Medicine organized a class action suit against the ADA for trying to persuade the public that "milk and other dairy [products] are the magic bullet to weight control" (Nestle 2006:78). Pro-milk groups demur, backpedaling to say that this and related legal actions are a sign that opposition groups "misunderstood" the message, that the ADA merely wishes to communicate that "adults who get three servings of milk and milk products each day and *follow a reduced calorie diet* are successful at weight management" (Milknewsroom 2008; emphasis added). The subtext is that milk products offer important nutrients that are not readily available in other beverages and foods, which is not the case. That the milk industry has persuaded consumers that milk both promotes growth and helps weight loss seems counterintuitive. It is successful advertising indeed to emphasize constituents or actions that suit the prevailing climate of health concerns. It is even more successful to market using competing paradigms.

Asian, African, Mexican, and other ethnic population–based groups in the United States underscore the paradox of government subsidy of the dairy industry. This iconization of milk in a country whose increasingly ethnically diverse population includes many people who become sick from milk evidences an overarching Euro-Anglo-centric perspective that contradicts the democratic ethos that is projected as representative of U.S. culture and customs. Government subvention is evident in the prominent role that milk plays in public school lunch programs and as the vehicle for delivery of (fortification with) essential nutrients (calcium, vitamins A and D), as well as in the ongoing narrative about the healthful qualities of milk (see chapter 3, the section on proposed fortification of street foods, which is not restricted to one food category). The normalizing subtexts that disregard biological variability in milk metabolism or offer solutions to it "suggest [that] milk's positive symbolism has been overdetermined . . . [and reveal] the entrenched nature of milk in U.S. culinary culture, national identity, and agricultural economy" (Wiley 2004:513).

The connection between calcium and milk was advertised as early as the 1930s, and calcium continues to be the most emphasized nutrient of beverage milk and dairy products generally. Wiley (2007:671) cites Levenstein's observation in *Revolution at the Table* that "the discovery of vitamins and minerals in the 1920s constituted an 'advertiser's dream.'"

These nutrients are advanced as the cardinal rationale for placing milk at center stage in the national dietary guidelines. The language of promotion suggests that milk is the only or best source of calcium and that not consuming milk will eventuate in growth failures and chronic health disorders (Wiley 2007:671).

Milk consumption is expanding beyond the United States and Europe into populations whose traditional foodways do not include beverage milk and who are largely lactose intolerant. The trend is too recent to predict health impacts, but concern about increasing digestive complaints is legitimate. One trend that might be significant is that beverage milk consumption in South Korea and Japan has been diminishing since the mid-1990s. The global dairy industry has targeted China, however, where milk production and consumption have increased more during the past twenty years than in any other country and sales are increasing 25 percent annually. Urban Chinese, the wealthy in particular, associate milk drinking with modernity and health. The popularity of imported products reflects both insufficient domestic supplies and the impression of better taste and safety. Enterprising marketing campaigns similar to those in the United States emphasize milk's purported positive effects on children's growth and extend that to individual and national well-being. Following the example of the United States (or creating its own), China has developed a school-milk program that is sponsored by a joint venture of government and commerce. The goals are to increase milk consumption, energize the country's growing dairy industry, and improve the health of China's people. Drawing on the cachet of celebrity endorsements and Western culture, China's dairy industry seeks to infuse a new generation with the taste for milk and to piggyback on the success of other Western foods, such as McDonald's, which also target children in advertising. In this way, Chinese diets are being transformed by cultural constructions of foods generally, and dairy products in particular, that originate outside of China. In view of the high rate of lactose intolerance, despite government-industry marketing, a reasonable prediction is that the popularity of beverage milk will decline while consumption of fermented, low-lactose products such as yogurt will increase (Wiley 2007).

The example of lactose intolerance underscores the merits of biocultural perspectives that are nuanced by issues of political economy. In this case, we see how culture (subsistence patterns and food choice and preparation) influenced biological evolution (selection for lactose tolerance in some populations) and how that variability has been culturally constructed in the specific context of the United States.

Communities of Circumstance and Metabolic Conditions

Diabetes, celiac disease, and lactose intolerance have been fully characterized bioscientifically (although research still continues), and their dietary management is well understood. Ample information and recommendations are available from many professional health, dietary, and government entities. Influenced strongly by the advent of the Internet, subscribed and informal communities readily circulate information about the incidence and management of these conditions. Diabetes and celiac groups confer identity and praxis for communities of individuals whose circumstances are clinically defined as disorders that have symptoms, prognoses, and management guidelines that have been transposed to the public domain. Individuals with diabetes and celiac disease self-manage their diets, symptoms, and lifestyles. Advocacy and support groups offer information on the etiology of these conditions and on the glucose and gluten content of foods. In the United States, regulations for standardized labeling of nutrient content make the assessment of individual foods easier. I would argue, however, that lactose intolerance is another story, one in which a physiologic condition has been unnecessarily medicalized; much of its dis-easing is related to powerful market forces and the nature of government regulation of a particular food group.

Conclusion

Much attention has been devoted to the foodways of contemporary human populations worldwide. In most of that literature, food sharing is only implicit, and almost none of the circumstances of food sharing are framed by a biocultural perspective. Yet all these cuisines embody rules of inclusion, exclusion, sequence, hierarchy, acquisition, preparation, and distribution. Adhering to these normative conventions cements community and forges identity. Insights into people's history, society, and culture are offered through the language of cuisine, including the lexicon of association, sociability, and food sharing. Further, in keeping with the biocultural perspective that structures this book, the implications of food sharing are written in and on the physical body.

It seems safe to speculate that throughout time, food, beverages, and eating were managed in ways to promote health in the context of diverse explanatory models of nutritional value, disease etiology, and therapeutics. Today, many affluent people in Western societies use their knowledge and resources to fashion diets that have specific health goals. Examples of these diets of association include Slow Food philosophies, low-carbohydrate and vegetarian regimens, and the customs of groups of individuals who adjust food choices to correspond to the physiologic conditions of diabetes, celiac disease, and lactose intolerance.

This chapter spans a long historical perspective, beginning with comparisons of food sharing across diverse taxa and concluding with a discussion of some contemporary diets that reflect health concerns. The next chapter treats a more compressed time frame through examination of the influences of geopolitical expansions on the global circulation of foods and beverages of association.

The Imperial Roots of European Foodways

BEGINNING IN THE 1400s, several traditional plants of association were Europeanized, that is, their production and distribution were extended beyond places of origin as products and people were appropriated to accommodate European tastes and markets.[1] Two particular categories of foods of association affected by this Europeanization include spices (which promote community as emblems of cuisines) and the caffeinated beverages coffee, chocolate/cocoa, and tea (whose histories intersect one another as icons of European expansion). All these foods have significant pharmacologic and nutrient potential; in addition, the activities of expansion and appropriation further influenced health.

The fifteenth through seventeenth centuries of European history are called the "Age of Discovery," "Age of Exploration," and even "Golden Age of Exploration," referencing a phase that expanded the cultural and geographic purview of Europeans (and the world) in a way that was dramatic and extraordinary in commercial and geographic scope. Because the term *discovery* is problematic in its European bias, I must clarify that the bona fide discoverers of places new to Europeans are the earliest travelers to those places. For example, twenty thousand years ago, migrants to the New World crossed the Bering land bridge from Siberia to Alaska and continued southward along the west coasts of North and, later, South America. Similarly, the first migrants to Australia might have reached there forty thousand years ago by traversing a land bridge or by short-distance voyaging from insular Southeast Asia (both dates of first arrival are disputed).

Origins of European Mercantilism

Long before European expansions, China and the Arabic world were powerful mercantile empires, regularly launching commercial enterprises that involved great volumes of commodities and thousands of men. Empires are complex, formed as much by experience and ideology as by the profit motives of the elites. The sociopolitical structures under discussion here advanced imperialist policies. One model of imperialism envisions three structural types: continuous, hybrid, and maritime empires. The Mongol, Russian, and Aztec empires were "continuous," that is, commanding adjacent territories. "Hybrid" empires such as the German Reich controlled both discontiguous (e.g., Africa) and adjacent lands. Maritime empires, such as the European colonial expansions, were "discontinuous" empires in which an imperial core ruled lands that were exclaves distant from the center of power and/or located overseas (Motyl 2001).

Contemporary historians no longer depict the Age of Exploration as one of revolutionary transformations or the accomplishments of a handful of navigators. The voyages and arrogations of that era are more accurately portrayed as the coherence of political, economic, and social forces that had been developing in Europe and beyond since medieval times. The bold vision of sailing masters such as da Gama, Columbus, and Magellan is not disputed: they are judged to have "accelerated the pace of European expansion and helped to determine its character and direction" even as "they built upon or pushed to new limits existing European knowledge, skills, resources and ambitions" (Arnold 2002:58–59). Nor were their efforts unique, for religion, conquest, and trade have served as incentives for long-distance travel during much of human history.

Religion, Conquest, Adventure

Buddhism diffused from India to Southeast Asia by 300 BCE and later spread throughout Asia. During the first 300 years CE, Christianity spread through the Roman Empire; it reached Ethiopia by 400 CE and by 700 CE was established in central and East Asia and India. The later diffusion history of Christianity includes the Crusades (beginning ca. 1095 CE), a series of military campaigns punctuated by elements of pilgrimage. By 700 CE, Islam had come to prevail from the Iberian Peninsula through the southern Mediterranean and Middle East to the borders of China. The discussion that follows reveals that the recurrent theme of religious conversion as moral elevation has been inextricably linked to European conquest and trade from the earliest expansions to the present.

Curiosity and a sense of adventure drove other geographic expansions. Norse settlers reached North America in 1000 CE, Marco Polo traversed Asia in the thirteenth century, and the Islamic scholar Ibn Battuta journeyed through Europe, Asia, and Islamic Africa for almost thirty years of the fourteenth century. During the early 1400s, the renowned mariner Zheng He commanded treasure fleets throughout the South Pacific and the Indian Ocean, reaching East Africa and the Persian Gulf and consolidating Chinese control over much of Asia.

European Extensions

Commerce, which was a more powerful motivation than preemptive geopolitical expansion (empire for empire's sake), drove long-distance travel to secure exotic culinary and medicinal plants and animals, gemstones, fabrics, and other goods. With the domestication of draft animals and refinements in water travel, people developed the ability to transport more and heavier goods over longer distances. As early as 4000 BCE, ancient Mesopotamia in the Middle East was connected in trade with India through navigation of the Indian Ocean and Persian Gulf. Beginning several millennia BCE, Egyptians conducted water trade into the Indian Ocean, connecting with present-day Arabia and Somalia. After 1000 BCE, caravans from the Persian Gulf transported Indian goods to the eastern Mediterranean, from which water and land routes circulated the items throughout the region and beyond. Crusaders returning with heightened tastes for the luxury goods of Asia (re)introduced these products and increased their commercial demand throughout Europe.

The ancient Silk Road, including sea components, spanned a vast area from Asia to Europe for several thousand years. Along its substantial length, luxury goods, primarily fabrics and spices, were conveyed to the Mediterranean, while items that were more mundane were destined for the steppe tribes along the way. Land and sea routes converged to connect Roman, Mediterranean, and Middle Eastern lands with each other and with Asia, peninsular and insular Southeast Asia, and sub-Saharan Africa. Rather than being linear conduits along which goods traveled from point of origin to consumption site, the trade routes more resembled nested networks of direct merchants and the middlemen whose growing numbers raised the price of goods incrementally with each transfer.

The militarization of the Mongol Empire in the first half of the thirteenth century had a more profound impact on long-distance trade in Asian commodities than did European mercantilism. Genghis Khan consolidated many of the tribes of central and northeastern Asia into the largest contiguous empire in the history of the world. His powerful military overthrew regions of China, Russia, Persia, central and eastern Europe, and the Islamic Seljuk Empire. The macrohistorical significance of the early Mongol conquests for long-distance trade included the disruption of trade networks. Later, after consolidation under the Pax Mongolica, trade relations throughout much of Eurasia stabilized. For the first time, Europeans could establish safe and direct commercial contact with Asia, notably China.

The integrity of the Mongol Empire eventually eroded, culminating in Mameluke mercenaries thwarting the Mongol advance in the battle of Ayn Jalut, Palestine, in 1260, which protected the Levant and Egypt. The Mongols dominated most of the Near East for another two centuries. Over the next one hundred years, Mongol command of China also weakened. In 1356, the Buddhist monk Zhu Yuanzhang gained control of Nanking. By 1368, he had defeated rival rebel groups as well as the Mongols and established the Ming dynasty, which governed China for the next three hundred years. The new Ming emperor expelled all foreigners, effectively shutting down both European trade and missionizing. Activity along the once-thriving trade routes of central Asia dropped off sharply; trade continued on a much smaller scale along caravan routes from India to Europe. The Ottoman Turks seized control of northwestern Asia Minor, expanded into sizeable European territories, surrounded the last of the Roman Empire (Constantinople), took control of trade between the Mediterranean and Black Seas, and expanded into the Balkan Peninsula.

During the late Middle Ages, the centerpiece of European trans-Saharan trade with West Africa was gold, which had been an element of transactions for centuries before Arabia took control of North Africa in the late seventh century. Transdesert trade was facilitated by the construction of wells and oases and the introduction of dromedary camels (*Camelus dromedarius* L., Camelidae) into the Sahara region during the last two centuries BCE. From the Mediterranean, traders carried iron, copper, and luxury goods; they loaded on salt from traders at the desert mines.

Northbound caravans moved gold, slaves, hides, ivory, and kola nut (*Cola* spp., Sterculiaceae), the latter not for European consumption (see the sections on Hausa people in chapters 3 and 4). Along caravan routes and at terminal ports, Muslim merchant middlemen inflated the price of trade goods and slaves, who became increasingly important for European economies as forced labor on sugar plantations in Spain, Italy, Cyprus, and Sicily.

During the later phases of the colonial and neocolonial eras, sugar was even more integral to European expansion than were exotic spices and gold. Native to Southeast Asia, sugarcane was under cultivation by the fourth century BCE. Evidence from the following century indicates processing of the cane by boiling, clarification, and crystallization. Sugar spread to the West between 600 and 1400 CE. Arabia traded it with Egypt in the seventh century, and in the twelfth and thirteenth centuries along routes through Persia to the Mediterranean. Earlier, trade in white slaves from the Black Sea and Crimea was fueled by the expulsion of Muslims from Portugal and Spain, in concert with the significant loss of population from European cholera epidemics. A corollary trade in African slaves became part of trans-Saharan commerce. Long before 1600, forced plantation labor—first for the production of sugar, later for tobacco (*Nicotiana tabacum* L., Solanaceae) and cotton (*Gossypium* spp., Malvaceae)—was a glaring icon of European empire and continued to define it through the seventeenth and eighteenth centuries. Individuals who analyze Old World–New World encounters from the perspective of "exchange" (e.g., Viola and Margolis 1991), rather than through the lens of political economy, ignore the asymmetries between those who initiated the encounters and those who were "visited." Imbalances are obvious in the primary direction and volume of flow of resources, who profited, and the accessorial outcomes such as unequal disease burdens, slavery, military actions to seize lands, and missionary campaigns that attempted to erode local cultures. Even the "exchangists" cannot ignore such ironies as the introduction of potato and maize to the Old World. The former provided a carbohydrate-rich food that could be stored easily; it eventually (with improved sanitation and medicine) contributed to a substantial increase in European populations. In a gruesome parallel, maize fueled the growth of African populations, many members of which were forced into plantation servitude in the New World. "Exchange" puts a comfortable spin on what was in reality the inherent European hegemony of those transactions.

By the late thirteenth century, European expansion had come to extend Mediterranean trade down the west coast of Africa and into the Atlantic Ocean. Genoese and Venetian merchants transported Mediterranean and southern products to the Netherlands, Luxembourg, Belgium, and England, where they traded for cloth and wool. Fourteenth-century contact with the Canary Islands proved a disappointment because of the absence of an economic foundation that could support mercantile activities, but eventually sugar became a pioneering crop there. The Madeira Islands, also in the Atlantic, were a source of valuable timber and of land that could support the production of wine (made from grapes, *Vitis vinifera* L., Vitaceae) and sugar, which provided a ready market for West African and Canary Island slaves. Sugar plantations also were established on the Cape Verde Islands.

Portugal's close ties with Genoese merchants, the support of the royal family, and the country's economic expansion cohered as a foundation for commercial expansion during the 1400s. The military expedition that conquered the port city of Ceuta across the Strait of Gibraltar in 1415 secured for Portugal its first foreign possession, punctuating the end of two centuries of efforts to gain a foothold in Morocco. The country's expansion strategy included sustained control of Ceuta and commercial and military advances along the Moroccan coast and was supported by diverse sectors of Portuguese society, including "merchants, would-be pirates, zealous [Christian] crusaders, and adventurous spirits" (Fritze 2002:66).

Although some historians credit technological advances in cartography and navigation as the infrastructural linchpin of early European expansion, the primary drivers were improvements in weaponry and ship design based on technologies developed in Asia and conveyed by Indian and Arabic navigators. Early Portuguese true navigation, moving ships from one location to another out of sight of land, used existing techniques: longitude and latitude estimates, compass, lead-plumb depth measures, charts, and maps. Records of the earliest navigation instruments and advances in astronomical instrumentation are dated to the mid- and late fourteenth century, respectively. These and supporting technologies were not sufficiently refined for reliable navigation until the late fifteenth and early sixteenth centuries; longitude measure was not perfected until the eighteenth century.

For early thirteenth-century Europe, the uncharted coast of Africa carried the reputation of adverse ocean currents and winds and uninhabited wastelands. Muslim merchants reinforced these dangerous images as part of a strategy to retain a monopoly on trans-Saharan trade. After at least fifteen attempts, in 1434 a member of Portugal's royal household rounded Cape Bojador beyond the Canary Islands; he reported his success upon his return with a spray of shoreline rosemary (*Rosmarinus officinalis* L., Labiatae). Three years later, Portugal waged unsuccessful military actions in Tangier, losing control of already-captured commercially strategic Moroccan territory. In the years that followed, Portugal resumed expansion farther along the African coast. So began that nation's direct trade in West African slaves, which the Portuguese rationalized as fair exchange because they offered their captives "eternal salvation" through forced conversion to Christianity (Fritze 2002:85). By 1448, the Portuguese had reached what is today Guinea-Bissau. After losses of personnel during encounters with well-armed Africans, they shifted their strategy from raiding to trading for slaves and gold. In addition to commercial interests, antipathy toward Islam and conquest of Islamic regions were recurrent themes in Portuguese expansion in Africa. King Alfonso V (1432–1481) redoubled military efforts and by 1471 had regained control of the northern coast of Morocco. Along-shore advances continued south, reaching Gabon by 1473; between 1482 and 1488, the Portuguese rounded the Cape of Good Hope and reached the Indian Ocean, the gateway to trade with the East.

The New World and Beyond

After decades of unsuccessful forays into the Atlantic, the next significant advances in European expansion were the voyages of Christopher Columbus (1451–1506). Promoting his family's Genoa-based wool business, he developed a proficiency for navigation and by the 1480s had begun to contrive a plan to reach Asia by voyaging across the Atlantic. This speculation was theoretically underpinned by two widely held, but flawed, fifteenth-century understandings of geography: first, that the

Asian landmass extended much farther east and was considerably larger than it actually is; second, that the circumference of the earth was about 25 percent smaller than in fact it is. Together these assumptions suggested that westward sailing to Asia would be a substantially shorter trip than it proved to be. By then a resident of Portugal, Columbus sought support from but was rebuffed by the ruling family and later by the monarchs of France and England. Finally, he engaged the royalty of Spain, who were persuaded in the context of expanding mercantile ambitions and the anticipation of great economic gain. Instead of discovering what everyone anticipated, however—a few islands along the seaway to the treasures of Asia—Columbus's four voyages (1492–1503) revealed to Europe many islands, some of which were sizeable, and a landmass spanning two continents.

Early Spanish efforts to colonize Hispaniola to establish commercial centers in the Caribbean were not successful but instead were fraught with chronic "instability, insubordination and conspiracy . . . and increasing enslavement of [indigenous] peoples" to work the largely nonproductive gold deposits (Fritze 2002:149). Later, Spain gained a substantial presence in the New World, fueled by the desire to expand empire and commerce and by considerable Christian zeal. The brutal conquests of Mexico, the Yucatán, and Peru brought substantial wealth to Spain in gold, silver, chile (*Capsicum annuum* L., Solanaceae), cacao (*Theobroma cacao* L., Sterculiaceae), and other prized items. Spain's aggressive search for gold underlay both the speed and the voracity of New World conquests between 1520 and 1550. Silver played an even more important role, providing Europe with the capital to purchase Asian silk and cotton fabrics, spices and, later, tea (*Camellia sinensis* Kuntze, Theaceae).

In 1497, John Cabot (born in Italy as Giovanni Caboto, ca. 1450–1499) was funded by Bristol merchants for a trans-Atlantic voyage. The ship landed first in Newfoundland, then explored hundreds of coastal miles without landing again before its return to England. This exploration and other efforts to cross the Atlantic suggest that Columbus's intentions to reach Asia by traveling west were part of a "general ferment of geographical ideas . . . [that gained] momentum during the late fifteenth century in Europe" (Fritze 2002:122). Like Columbus, Cabot thought he had reached Asia, and King Henry VII and his English subjects enjoyed speculation that London would come to rival the Egyptian seaport of

Alexandria as a spice-trading center. The bleak Newfoundland landscape did not provide England with an incentive for settlement, however, particularly in the light of Spain's difficulties in colonizing Hispaniola and the eventual realization that the Americas were not Asia but instead a solid obstacle to reaching that land of abundant resources and trade infrastructures.

Although Portuguese navigator Bartolomeu Dias (1450–1500) navigated around the Cape of Good Hope and provided evidence of a sea route to India in 1488, a sea expedition to Asia was not mounted until nine years later. This delay in Portugal's expansion has been attributed to political and social vicissitudes, paramount among them military engagements with Morocco, the influx of migrants who strained national resources, and uncertainties of royal succession. Although eager to develop a trade foothold in the East, advisors to King João II (1455–1495) noted that the sea route was dangerous and no less costly than Mediterranean travel and land routes across the Middle East. Instead they encouraged, for the short term, expansion of existing trade relations with Africa.

Despite continued domestic opposition, João's successor Manuel I (1469–1521) revived exploration of both the sea route to India and extension into the Atlantic. In a move resonating with the themes of expansion outlined above—trade, religion, and conquest—navigators were commissioned to forge commercial relations and to introduce Christianity, forcefully if necessary. In 1497 (and again in 1502 and 1524), Vasco da Gama (1469–1524) traversed the sea route to India; in 1500, Pedro Álvares Cabral (1467–1520) explored Brazil; in 1505, Francisco de Almeida (1450–1510) was appointed the first viceroy (Portuguese representative) of India; and between 1503 and 1515, Afonse de Albuquerque (1469–1521) secured a Portuguese monopoly of sea routes through the Persian Gulf and Indian Ocean. Diplomatic and trade relations were cemented with China and the Persian Empire. These developments secured Portugal's empire and generated considerable wealth through trade, notably in spices.

In the early sixteenth century, explorations of the Italian merchant Amerigo Vespucci (for Spain) and other navigators established that, rather than reaching Asia, Columbus had encountered two continents previously unknown to Europe. Excursions into rivers and bays and thousands of miles of shoreline travel eventually characterized the coastlines and gave Europe some sense of the size of the New World and its distance from both Europe and Asia.

Portugal and Spain

During the 1500s, Portugal and Spain spearheaded European mercantile and colonial expansions. Their empires were "conferred" by the Treaty of Tordesillas (1494), which divided the non-European world along a north–south line, stretching 1,100 miles off the West African coast, with territories to the west assigned to Spain and those to the east to Portugal. Commerce prospered along sea routes that eventually connected both countries across the Pacific between East Asia, via the Philippines, to Mexico; and across the Atlantic to the New World. The Spanish rapidly conquered much of Central and South America and large areas of North America. Later, the Dutch, French, and English colonized Caribbean islands and lands in New England, Louisiana, and the New York tristate area (then known as New Netherlands).

After charting the sea route to India, Portugal pursued trade possibilities and expanded into an empire that comprised small, militarily fortified seacoast settlements. Islamic polities along the East African coast were subjugated or destroyed. In the Indian Ocean, the Portuguese located the archipelago Socotra and the islands of Madagascar, Mauritius, and Ceylon. By establishing widely dispersed trade stations in Nagasaki, coastline Macau (China), Malacca (Malaysia), Goa (India), and Maluku (the Spice Islands, eastern Indonesia), Portugal controlled trade not only between Europe and Asia but also among regions of Asia. Although it had an important impact on commercial transactions in the Indian Ocean, Portugal did not significantly alter or monopolize trade practices. The appreciable wealth generated by trade was offset by the costs of maintaining the trade fleet and outposts, as well as by middlemen. In the New World, shortly after Cabral's landing in Brazil, Portugal's temporary settlements formed a nucleus for trade in brazilwood (*Caesalpinia* spp., Fabaceae), the source of a highly prized red dye for luxury fabrics.

The 1513 Spanish expedition of Vasco Núñez Balboa (1475–1519) included traversing Panama and seeing (for the first time by European eyes) the eastern aspect of the Pacific Ocean ("the Great South Sea"), which he claimed for Spain. This is the same sea that indigenous peoples of the

Caribbean had described for Columbus a decade earlier. The depletion of human and other resources on Hispaniola eventuated in the conquests of Puerto Rico (1508), Jamaica (1509), and Cuba (1511), which were similarly exhausted of resources within a decade. Juan Ponce de León (1460–1521) sailed from Puerto Rico in 1513 in search of uncharted territories and tradable goods, as well as a fountain of youth (see chapter 5), and is on (European) record for having discovered Florida, although the hostility of native residents suggests that other Europeans had reached Florida and the Yucatán first. Three years later, de León's explorations took him to Mexico, and in 1519 Alonso Álvarez de Pineda (1494–1519) charted the Gulf of Mexico to record maps that documented the lack of a water connection between the Atlantic and Pacific Oceans.

Following earlier attempts to find such a channel, the Portuguese Ferdinand Magellan (1480–1521) accepted the challenge under Spanish sponsorship. Venturing out in 1519, he navigated an eccentric course along the West African coast, then across the southern Atlantic to evade Portuguese ships that plied the North Atlantic to intercept competitors. Magellan's fleet followed the east coast of South America and eventually passed through what was later named the Strait of Magellan. From there, his ships continued north along the west coast of South America and then across the great expanse to Asia. When they reached the Philippine archipelago in 1521, the Spaniards acquired considerable wealth trading their goods for gold and other local commodities, even as Magellan's evangelical efforts were criticized by officers eager to reach Maluku. Magellan led what was essentially the first circumnavigation of the globe: he died in battle in the Philippines, but his two remaining ships reached Maluku in late 1521, and one returned to Spain nine months later.

The fact of circumnavigation accelerated growth in European knowledge and mercantile ambitions: the relative proportions and shape of the globe and the reality of the Pacific Ocean were confirmed, and aspirations to control trade in luxury goods of the East grew exponentially across Europe. Spain was well positioned to compete in this arena, in view of its military campaigns and the strategic vantage of its extensive empire. Spain's second Pacific expedition sailed in 1525, but after sixteen difficult months, only one ship reached Maluku, where the crew learned of a more substantial Portuguese presence than had been expected. The two European powers and their respective indigenous island allies engaged in a war whose outcome, despite its small scope, had the potential to determine control of "the world's richest islands and the fate of empires" (Sherry 1994:74). In 1527, Spain launched an expedition of reinforcement to Maluku from Mexico. The crew of this beleaguered fleet assessed the struggle between Portugal and Spain and for the next two years attempted to return to Mexico for reinforcements. Unsuccessful, they returned to join the "little war" and participated into the next decade. Their failures are ironic, because the Spanish king, not cognizant of the struggle, in the meantime had sold "his" Spice Islands claim to Portugal.

At the same time, Portugal began a more systematic colonization of Brazil, including mounting defenses against French and other incursions. The establishment of permanent trading posts encouraged the plantation production of sugar, which depended on indigenous American (and later, African) slaves. Portugal's empire was in ascendancy until the sixteenth century, when it could no longer compete with the Dutch, English, and French. Despite the breadth of its expansion, Portugal's influence did not rival the expanse and depth of Spain's New World empire, and the continued European conquest in Asia was not Portuguese but Spanish, with control of the Philippines.

Euro-wide Expansions

Although Portugal and Spain were primary players in maritime expansion, the campaign was pan-European. The dynamic nature of geopolitical borders and cultural or national identities supported relatively easy shifts in the affiliation and service of navigators, merchants, and military forces. One effect of the loosening of structural constraints was the dissemination of an expanding knowledge base among the polities of Europe. Examples of the broadcasting effect of enhanced personal mobility are the contributions of the Italian Columbus and the Portuguese Magellan, both of whom served Spain. Further, the Age of Expansion overlapped Johannes Gutenberg's introduction of printing from movable type (1455). From that time forward, a growing abundance of pamphlets and books recorded and circulated knowledge gained about navigation, the destinations and peoples reached, and the resources located.

The participation of France and England in global explorations was insubstantial until the 1520s, when representatives of these nations searched for a route to Asia around the southernmost tip of South America. In 1523, France commissioned Giovanni de Verrazano, who sailed north to the coast of today's North Carolina, where he mistook the open water that separates the barrier islands (today's Outer Banks) from the mainland as a route to Asia. From there, he staked out what he thought were lands with great trade potential as "New France," and he explored coastal New England. Other navigators of the east coast and estuaries of North America who sought a transcontinental strait (Northwest Passage) include Spain's Esteban Gómez in 1524, England's John Rut in 1527, and France's Jacques Cartier in 1534, 1535, and 1541 and Jean François de la Roque in 1542. Later expeditions to locate a Northwest Passage were led by England's Martin Frobisher in the 1570s, John Davis in the 1590s, and William Baffin in 1612, 1615, and 1616.

The Dutch also entered the competition late: subjects of Spain from the 1560s until 1648, their ambitions for empire were not put in motion until the late 1500s. In the early 1600s, the Dutch East India Company made major commercial inroads into the Indian and Pacific Oceans, where they captured trading posts from Portugal and Spain and staked out new ones. Dutch ascendancy over these two powers is explained by better navigation skills and instrumentation and more-effective financing. Further, the Dutch were a lesser evil for indigenous peoples, whom they did not try to subdue through religious conversion and whose governance they did not disturb. By 1607, the company had centralized its commerce in Java and rapidly developed trade along routes that included posts on India's Malabar (southwest) coast and in Maluku, Taiwan (then known as Formosa), and Japan. By 1610, the Dutch had set up trade in the Amazon and Guiana, in the center of Spain's New World lands. In that same year, the company hired Henry Hudson (1570–1611) to explore a Northwest Passage, and Dutch fur trade flourished in the valley named for him.

As the likelihood of a Northwest Passage dimmed, continued efforts to establish trade links with Asia envisioned a Northeast Passage. In the early 1500s, Norse and Russian navigators failed to find passage through the waters of the North Pole. By the mid-sixteenth century, English sailing masters had reached the archipelago Novaya Zemlya, "New Land," in the Arctic Ocean north of Russia and Archangel in northern Russia. The Dutch also sought a navigable northern route, as did Russia during the early 1600s.

Supported in part by the royal houses of Portugal, Spain, and England, Italy's contributions to western European expansion included knowledge and technical competence—in particular, cartography and navigation skills that were refined in the Italian Mediterranean. During the Middle Ages, Italy was the only European polity that had a significant colonial presence. From the eleventh century forward, commercial and colonial interests were established in the Levant by merchants of Genoa, Venice, Pisa, and later Florence and southern Italy. By the beginning of the twelfth century, Pisan and Genoese merchants had established along the length of the Iberian coastline commercial posts that depended on long-distance sea trade. Italy also infused intellectual and cultural advances of the Renaissance, notably, knowledge imparted by rediscovered classical texts of geography and other subjects.

Italy had an economic impact on western European expansion as well, including control since the late Middle Ages of trade settlements in North Africa, the Iberian Peninsula, and the western Mediterranean. In the 1400s, as control of the Black Sea and caravan trade was taken over by the Ottoman Turks, Genoese trade was forced out of a geographically defined key position at the juncture of long-distance trade with Asia and Africa; this trade moved to the western Mediterranean and Atlantic islands. Merchants of Genoa and other Italian cities provided indirect financial support for some of the early Portuguese and Spanish New World explorations and, in return, profited smartly from the substantial trade in sugar, spices, and silver. Despite navigation of a sea route around the Cape of Africa, the spice trade along the land route to the East had regained much of its early activity by 1520. Venice again became a major player in the spice trade, but political discontinuities kept Italy from competing with the expanding successes of Portugal and Spain. More challenges came from northwestern Europe, where the Netherlands and England were strong contenders.

Slave trade was a grim, ever-present feature of expansion, pioneered by the Portuguese and joined later (1562) by the English, who embarked on a lucrative trade between Africa and the Caribbean islands. The Dutch proved to be a more significant threat to traffic in forced labor: in the 1630s, the Netherlands captured Portugal's West African trade settlements and eventually took control of the "Gold Coast" (Ghana). The late 1700s and early 1800s comprised an era of decolonization during which

New World colonies gained independence, irrevocably loosening Portugal and Spain's economic potency but leaving the Netherlands, England, and France in strong positions as they redirected expansion to the Old World, principally Southeast Asia, India, and Africa.

The economic incentive for later (that is, nineteenth-century) expansions would be industrialization and attendant efforts to secure markets for European-produced goods. But during the 1400s and 1500s, those commodities were not prized, or even much appreciated, in Africa and Asia, for the fabrics in those regions were more luxurious, gemstones more plentiful, and spices unparalleled in abundance and diversity. Rather than focusing on export during the fifteenth and sixteenth centuries, European merchants sought resources that could be absorbed into their own markets. Beginning in the seventeenth century, a restructuring of European economies was characterized by a phase of compression, the last vestiges of the transition from feudalism to capitalism that replaced Baltic and Mediterranean commercial ventures with those of the New World. In the context of these transformed Europe-other world relationships, global patterns of commerce were both broadened and intensified. "The . . . accelerating current of overseas trade [that] swept the infant industries of Europe with it . . . , [in some] cases . . . *creating* them, was hardly conceivable without this change" (Hobsbawm 1968:51, quoted in Mintz 1985:66). This transformation depended on three sets of interrelated circumstances: developing a European market for nonluxury (everyday) overseas goods, which could be expanded as trade in those products came to embrace larger volumes and lower costs; conquering lands whose resources and people would serve European commercial and other needs; and establishing in those lands economic systems, such as plantations, to produce goods for European consumption. Increasingly, the shift in European economies privileged Britain at the expense of the Baltic and Mediterranean trade networks.

Health Consequences of European and Other Expansions

The demographic impacts of European expansion include significantly increased morbidity and mortality associated with the physical and psychological conquest; intensification and creation of political asymmetries and armed conflicts among indigenous peoples; imposition of rigid and authoritarian systems of revenue and labor; disarray of existing systems of production, including conversion of forest and other land and labor to cash cropping; the diversion of labor to nonsubsistence activities such as plantations and mining; depletion of resources to accelerate profits; control of local markets; forced labor and migration; malnutrition; and disease introductions and exacerbations. The impact of infectious diseases was especially dramatic in the New World, Pacific, and African continental interior, regions in which there had been little prior contact with Old World peoples and their infections. Native populations suffered high morbidity and mortality from introduced infections for which they were immunologically naive; measles, smallpox, plague, and influenza presented major challenges. For many peoples in the developing world, the intersection of these processes resulted in diminished dietary quality—notably, protein and calorie deficiencies.

In addition, European introductions of non-native animals and plants transformed landscapes in detrimental ways: feral pigs overran many Caribbean islands, lands once devoted to food production were converted to pasture for herds of cattle and horses, and indigenous subsistence regimens were irreparably damaged. Forests were depleted of valuable dye and timber trees; additionally, making space for European trading posts, residences, and other constructions further eroded biomass and diversity. Although mercantile expansions had (and still have) the potential to increase variety in diets worldwide and also to circulate advances in agricultural and production technologies, most of the impacts on diets in the developing world have been negative. The global diffusion of plant and animal species that were native to particular regions includes several foods and beverages of association; of particular interest to this discussion are spices and caffeinated beverages.

Spices

An interesting perspective from which to launch a more specific discussion of European and other expansions is the spice trade, which has been mentioned several times in the preceding discussion. I include spices among foods of association in view of the iconic role that they play in cuisines, making them vehicles of identity and community. These botanically diverse species serve a variety of functions. In all the world's cuisines, they impart flavor and color to foods; many also preserve foods. Throughout history, spices served as currency in commercial transactions and were included among luxury tributes demanded by ruling classes. As perfumes and cosmetics, spices disguise the taste and smell of unpalatable foods, places, and people. They are burned as fumigants and incense for funerary and religious ceremonies (see chapter 4). They mediate life-cycle transitions by marking individuals (e.g., priests, newborn babies) with color and scent. In many cultures, sorcery and witchcraft are mediated by aromatics, among which volatiles offer both tangible and metaphoric essences. As signal prints for foods and beverages of association, they distinguish the cuisines of ethnically diverse peoples and, within groups, mark social asymmetries through varied combinations, applications, and the frequency and volume of consumption of a spice.

Pungent and aromatic substances have dressed the world's cuisines for thousands of years, during much of that time as localized flavorings. The accelerated regional circulation and eventual globalization of spices is intimately linked to European expansions. Records from the third century BCE note that Maluku clove (*Syzygium aromaticum* Merr. & Perry, Myrtaceae) and Indian black pepper (*Piper nigrum* L., Piperaceae) were trade items in China and the Middle East, respectively. The luxury commodities that moved across North Africa into the Iberian Peninsula in tandem with Muslim commercial expansion include clove, black pepper, and cinnamon (*Cinnamomum zeylanicum* Blume, Lauraceae) from India, as well as Maluku mace and nutmeg (*Myristica fragrans* Houtt., Myristicaceae). Other, more affordable, spices of commercial interest included Mediterranean cumin and coriander (*Coriandrum sativum* L., Apiaceae) and—curiously, in view of today's costs—saffron (*Crocus sativus* L., Iridaceae) from Greece.

Much of European navigation during the later centuries centered on the quest for sea routes to spice-producing lands in the East. Venice's command of the medieval European spice and drug trade was usurped by Portugal in the 1400s. By the middle of the next century, centers of commerce had shifted from the port cities of Egypt and Italy to those in Portugal and Spain. By that time, Europe had again secured an overland (caravan) spice trade with the East, and the pace and volume of spice commerce increased significantly. For example, the million pounds of black pepper that traversed traditional trade routes through the eastern Mediterranean each year was less than 20 percent of the volume of all spices that reached Europe via Spanish and Portuguese ports. The lucrative spice trade was a strong incentive for European expansion throughout the fifteenth and sixteenth centuries. Their transit punctuated by political and social instabilities, luxury commodities moved along trade networks from Asia to Europe beginning in Roman times. Trade in Asian silk eventually was eclipsed as Europe began to produce its own luxury fabrics, but there was no substitute for the highly valued Asian spices. During the next few centuries, military hostilities among European states were driven by rivalries for control of spice-producing lands. One corollary was great suffering among indigenous populations forced into plantation spice production to supply European markets. By the end of the fifteenth century, the Dutch had driven Portugal and England out of the Maluku and established monopolies in clove, mace and nutmeg, black pepper, cinnamon, turmeric (*Curcuma longa* L., Zingiberaceae), and ginger (*Zingiber officinale* Roscoe, Zingiberaceae) (Toussaint-Samat 1992; Dalby 2000).

Today, spice production and commerce are no longer centralized but include many countries in the tropics and several in the temperate zones. Jamaica is an important source of ginger and allspice (*Pimenta dioica* Merr., Myrtaceae), Brazil is a major producer of black pepper, and Europe and North America produce substantial quantities of parsley (*Petroselinum crispum* A. W. Hill, Apiaceae), sesame seed (*Sesamum indicum* L., Pedaliaceae), basil (*Ocimum basilicum* L., Labiatae), and other herbs. In the past several decades, the United States has been the world's primary spice consumer (Davidson 1999).

Spices and Health

Spices, widely used in cuisines and in preventive and therapeutic medicine, collectively embody substantial pharmacologic potential. Many of those actions are attributed to allelochemicals, which have been bred out of other domesticated species but continue to be selected in spice plants, whose physiologically active metabolites provide the very scents, tastes, and activities that meet culinary and medicinal objectives.

Although they are botanically and chemically diverse, groups of spices can be linked through classes of phytochemical constituents or similar physiologic effects. For example, pungent compounds improve digestion by stimulating liver bile production, increasing absorption into the blood from the intestines, and stimulating digestive enzyme secretion and peristalsis. They also influence regulation of metabolism through hormones and the nervous system, and they increase body temperature, heart rate, peripheral circulation, and lipid metabolism. Pungent constituents include capsaicin in chile pepper, piperine and chavicine in black pepper, zingerol and shogaol in ginger, diallyl sulfide in onion (*Allium cepa* L., Liliaceae), and allylthiocyanate in horseradish (*Armoracia rusticana* P. Gaertner, Brassicaceae) and mustard (*Brassica nigra* Koch, Brassicaceae). Many spices have antimicrobial and antioxidant effects attributable to constituents such as curcumin in turmeric, vanillin in vanilla (*Vanilla planifolia* Jackson, Orchidaceae), and allicin in garlic. Stronger and more broad-spectrum antimicrobial activity occurs in volatiles and pungents and in phytoconstituents that include hydroxyl (-OH) and aldehyde (-CHO) groups (Etkin 2006a:ch. 3, appendix).

In the places of origin of spices in China and Southeast Asia, ancient texts reference the use of spices as medicines and to preserve foods. Thousands of years ago, Egyptians embalmed the dead with spices such as cumin, cinnamon, and thyme (*Thymus vulgaris* L., Labiatae). Borrowing from Arabic medicine, Europeans regarded spices, individually and as a class, as virtual panaceas. Coriander and mint (*Mentha* spp., Labiatae) preserved milk and meat in early Rome and Greece. Similarly, for centuries in the West, spices have been used in general medicine and as specifics for a wide range of infectious disorders. It is not possible to establish how important knowledge of antimicrobial activity is in the design of cuisines, but one should not assume that it signifies only when disease explanatory models include a specific etiology and a specific cure, such as with "germ theory."

The antimicrobial activity of spices generally leads to conjecture about the role of spices in food safety. A popular belief is that in places where, and during times that, refrigeration and other technologies are not available, spices mask the taste of already spoiled foods. This overlooks the fact that historically, and in contemporary developing countries, various methods such as drying, salting, and fermenting ensure food safety. Perhaps more salient is that consuming spoiled food poses observable health risks and that spices not only impart flavor but also enhance existing tastes—including, one would predict, the sensation of decomposition.

Biological scientists have speculated on this issue as well. Taking into account the ubiquity and antiquity of spice use, Sherman and colleagues invoked an evolutionary trajectory of adaptations to the risk of food spoilage (e.g., Sherman and Flaxman 2001). Spice use was inferred from cookbooks, a questionable methodology that is flawed further by referencing only whatever cookbooks the researchers collected, without knowledge of how representative the recipes are and how often particular foods would be consumed. They predicted that more (and more antimicrobially potent) spices correlate with warmer climates and that within a country, meat recipes are more heavily spiced than are vegetable recipes. The researchers' hypotheses were substantiated through this indirect exercise. They proposed that enhancing the palatability of foods is only a proximate reason for spicing; the ultimate explanation is that spices inhibit or kill food-spoiling microorganisms. Distinguishing proximate from ultimate explanations does not serve scholarship. A more productive approach would be to underscore the complementary and complex goals that underlie food choice and preparation. A biocultural perspective helps us to understand that the cultural construction and physical substantiation of cuisine are informed by pharmacologic activity, learned tastes, aesthetics, and other cultural constructions.

It is important not only to record discrete activities for singlet spices but also to contextualize pharmacologic action to actual use. In this regard, an interesting point for consideration is the physiologic implications of the synergistic effects among spices and between spices and other foods and beverages. Synergies are interactions that influence the potency and bioavailability of companion phytochemicals. Consider *shichimi tôtgarashi* (Japanese seven-spice), literally "seven chile peppers," although not all the constituents are chiles or peppers. The mixtures vary regionally, combining chile, flower pepper (*Zanthoxylum zanthoxyloides* Lam., Rutaceae), orange peel (*Citrus sinensis* Osbeck, Rutaceae), nori seaweed (*Porphyra tenera* and other *Porphyra* spp., Bangiaceae), and seeds of sesame and poppy (*Papaver somniferum* L., Papaveraceae). Constituents of flower pepper inhibit tumors and have antioxidant activity, citrus oil monoterpenes are antifungal and antimicrobial, and sesame oil is anti-inflammatory. Papaverine in poppy treats gastrointestinal spasm and improves circulatory function through vasorelaxation. Dry nori is a good source of minerals and fiber, stimulates immune function, and is anticarcinogenic (more pharmacologic data for nori appear in chapter 3 in the discussion of the Hawaiian street food musubi; see also Etkin 2006a:ch. 3, appendix; Yamasaki et al. 2007). The range of physiologic activities among these individual constituents is compounded when they occur together and with other pharmacodynamic foods and beverages.

Two Peppers

Although black pepper and chile belong to botanically discrete taxa at the species, genus, and family levels and have different growth forms and fruit, the histories and even identities of these two pungents are interlocked. Black pepper is a climbing, broad-leaved vine that bears small, round fruit on thin, densely clustered flower spikes. The hard fruit (a drupe) is collected just before it is ripe, fermented via phenoloxidase oxidation of tannins, and dried; it can then be ground into a powder. Chile is a shrub bearing fleshy red, yellow, or green fruit. It or its seeds are used fresh or dry, intact or extracted, and powdered. That chile is not a pepper at all but was so named by Columbus is a defining theme in the history of European expansion (see above).

Black Pepper

Piper nigrum is native to the forests of the Malabar Coast and has been used in food and medicine for at least three thousand years. The term *pepper* is derived from the Sanskrit *pippali*, "berry," which refers to long pepper (*Piper longum* L., Piperaceae), while *maricha* names black pepper. Transposition of the root word *pippali* to black pepper can be traced first to ancient Greek merchants, who thought that black pepper was a variety of long pepper and transliterated the root word to *peperi*, which became the Latin *piper* (*pipor* in Old English and near-homonyms in other European languages). Centuries later, Columbus compounded the confusion by giving the name to the completely unrelated plant chile.

Whereas long pepper had been an integral part of spice commerce since Greek and Roman times, western Europe had little knowledge of black pepper before the Middle Ages. Long pepper, which is more aromatic and less hot than black pepper, suited the early medieval European palate for the "sweet pot," in which savory and sweet ingredients were hearth-cooked in a single vessel. This manner of preparation favored spices such as clove, ginger, mace, nutmeg, and cinnamon. Introduction of the stove, for those who could afford one, permitted separate cooking of savory and sweet dishes. Black pepper was preferred for savories; during the Middle Ages and Renaissance, it was greatly prized by wealthy Europeans, who used it as a food seasoning and preservative, as well as for medicine. Spices generally, and other strong acidic and sweet flavors, were used abundantly in medieval haute cuisine, emulating a link to "the sophisticated Mediterranean world" (Mennell 1996:53). Muslim culinary arts were translated to European recipe books that exaggerated exotic ingredients and emphasized rich and sweet tastes. This transmutation forged a homogeneity in which foods were vehicles for spices and the tastes of dishes were largely undifferentiated. On the most elite tables, spices were served separately from prepared foods and beverages and were distributed on a gold or silver compartmented platter, from which diners selected spices, still in large volumes. Later, during the late medieval and Renaissance eras, the social contests of western Europe included kitchen imperatives to create more dishes. One overall effect was to reduce the number of spices per dish to augment natural flavors and to individualize the tastes of dishes.

Spices generally moved fluidly between the categories "food" and "medicine." Their commerce was transacted not only by spice merchants but also by grocers, physicians, and apothecaries. Reflecting the important role of pepper, the terms *pepperer, spicer,* and *apothecary* (and European-language counterparts) were used interchangeably. Black pepper was so valuable that it served as currency, and in the mid-1500s its price in the trade port Antwerp was a gauge of the general health of European commerce. Thus, the quest for other, less expensive sources of black pepper was a key incentive for European expansions. Enter chile.

Chile

Chile is a New World native that originated in an area that extended from present-day Brazil to Bolivia, from which it was dispersed by birds throughout Central and South America. Wild chile was an essential component of diets in southern Mexico and the Yucatán Peninsula. This "bird fruit" also was integral to the religious life of the Inca, Maya, and Aztec peoples: chile consumption was forbidden when fasting to propitiate deities; certain avian taxa were regarded as both dispersers of chile seed and conveyors of knowledge about the plant (Nabhan 2004); and Inca origin narratives (cosmogonies) designated the holy chile as one of the four brothers sent by the god Viracocha to instruct humankind.

Chile had been domesticated by the third millennium BCE; by 500 CE, at the height of the Aztec Empire, thirty varieties or more had come to be cultivated and widely used in food and medicine and as currency. Columbus encountered chile on the island of Hispaniola. So strong was his conviction that he had reached the East, he was surprised (instead of instructed) when the indigenous peoples he encountered did not recognize the black pepper and other spices demonstrated by his crew. Resolute, he unwittingly created ethnographic and botanical confusion by (re)naming the indigenous peoples Indians and by calling chile (the *other* pungent spice) "pimiento," after the Asian Indian black pepper, "pimienta," which he so desperately sought. *Chile* was transliterated by the Spanish from the Nahuatl (the language of the Aztec in central Mexico) *chilli* and came to be known outside its areas of origin as "chile pepper" (Andrews 2003).

Thereafter, the pungent chile rapidly diffused east, from Central and South America to Europe and Asia, in about fifty years. This contrasts with the stuttering and slow adoptions of potato, tomato, squash (*Cucurbita* spp., Cucurbitaceae), and other New World foods. Chile was transported along ancient spice routes from Europe to Asia and Africa, even as merchants of the real (black) pepper endeavored mightily to impede its growing commercial and aesthetic appeal. In addition, three chile cultivars that were developed on India's Malabar Coast were exported to Europe along established routes through the Middle East and along the new Portuguese route around Africa. By the late 1400s, chile and other items of commerce had begun to be circulated through two Mediterranean trade theaters. The Spanish dominated western Mediterranean trade, while Venice, at the center of European spice commerce, negotiated Asian commodities with Ottoman merchants who traded goods from Portuguese posts on the Persian and Malabar coasts. Between 1535 and

Hausa girls in Hurumi, northern Nigeria, sit beside a dish of *barkono*, "chile pepper," which their mother will use preparing *miya*, "soup." *Tuwo*, or porridge with miya, is the centerpiece of at least one of three daily meals. Barkono is the signature spice of Hausa cuisine. Taxonomists' and historians' chronicles of New World origins notwithstanding, Hausa, like many other peoples, consider barkono to be a traditional element of their food and medicine since earliest times.

1585, chile was traded in markets throughout Europe, but it became a signature spice only in the Balkans and Turkey (Andrews 2003).

Portuguese merchants introduced the spice to Southeast Asia and Japan; thereafter, seed dispersal by birds established chile throughout insular Southeast Asia and inland areas not accessible to human travel. Chile and other New World foods also were introduced via overland spice routes that connected the Middle East to India, Burma, and China. Chile trade thrived in the Middle East and Asia and eventually in the New World, after Spanish merchants established a Manila-Acapulco trade route. Chile was introduced to North America considerably later—to the English colony Virginia in 1621 (Ho 1995; Andrews 2003).

Since introduction outside of its native tropical America, chile has become a prominent, even signature, spice in many cuisines worldwide.

Historians' and taxonomists' chronicles aside, many cultures regard chile as not only an intrinsic but also a timelessly traditional culinary flavor and medicine. This transfer is not an appropriation of tradition but an example of how extant, even key, foods and flavors are substituted for and replaced by new items and how new products are assimilated. Chile resonated with existing palates that had been contoured by pungent spices. Its fluid assimilation contrasts markedly with the adoption of cacao into European cuisines (see below). Further, through a syncretization of tastes, chile amplified the complexity of those cuisines. It was rapidly absorbed into foodways and pharmacopoeias characterized by pungent spices such as clove, ginger, and the various peppers—black, long, African melegueta (*Aframomum melegueta* Schumann, Zingiberaceae), and flower. In other words, the diffusion of chile into cuisines around the world reflects the convergence of phytoconstituents and their organoleptic apprehension and activities. In some languages, depending on which pungent was supplanted, the terms for those spices were transferred to the overall category "chile."

Chile and these other spices are characterized by pungency, a quality that, like taste, depends on the composition and concentration of essential oils. The acid amide structural group (R-CO-N-R-R) defines the pungent constituents in chile (capsaicin) and black pepper (piperine, chavicine). The pungency of these constituents is perceived as hot, which diffuses through the mouth, compared to sharp pungent principles that stimulate the nasal and oral mucous membranes, such as allyl-thiocyanate (isothiocyanate group: R-N-C-S) in horseradish and mustard. The facility with which chile became a substitute for another spice or was assimilated applies especially to black pepper, a luxury and key catalyst of European expansions, an engine of the spice trade, and a commodity that Columbus (and after him, Europe) confused with chile.

Peppers and Health

Wherever black pepper and chile were adopted into a diet, their therapeutic traditions were circulated and new applications were developed as the peppers were physically and culturally reconstructed in new places. Black pepper and chile remain common elements of many contemporary pharmacopoeias. While some medicinal uses are overtly ideational, when these species are contextualized through a biocultural perspective, we observe a rich pharmacologic potential that overlaps diverse preventive and therapeutic objectives.

Pharmacologically active constituents of black pepper include â-bisabolene, camphene, eugenol, myristicin, phellandrene, pinene, piperidine, piperine, and safrol. These account for actions that range among diverse activities: antibacterial, antifungal, expectorant, hypotensive, diuretic, carminative, anti-inflammatory, and antioxidant. Chile too is pharmacologically remarkable, containing capsaicin, capsanthin, capsicidin, capxanthin, carotene, ferredoxin, solanine, and scopoletin. Variably and in combinations, these are responsible for an array of actions: antibacterial, antiulcer, antioxidant, and anti-inflammatory, as well as lowering serum triglycerides, stimulating lipid mobilization from fat tissue, increasing blood flow, diminishing cluster headaches, acting as a carminative, and serving as a counter-irritant for rheumatism, arthritis, neuralgia, and lumbago (Etkin 2006a:ch. 3, appendix).

Caffeinated Cordials

The intersecting sociopolitical histories of coffee, cacao/chocolate, and tea also are emblematic of European expansion, as they demonstrate global commodification and economic interdependencies (Simpson and Ogorzaly 2001; Trang 2003). Rather than being considered foods and beverages proper, these traditionally were stand-alone items whose consumption was grounded in other than nutritive features. These are "cordials" in the broad sense of that term and collectively are rich in pharmacologic, social, and historic implications.[2]

Coffee

The fruits of wild coffee (*Coffea arabica* L., Rubiaceae) were chewed in Ethiopia, perhaps as early as the sixth century CE. For hunting expeditions and other sustained travel, green coffee fruits were mixed with fat and consumed, presumably so that caffeine would mitigate fatigue and hunger while fat fueled the body. Beverage coffee appeared later, reaching Yemen in medieval times and Istanbul and Cairo in the 1500s, and shortly thereafter being adopted in the Mediterranean and England. The word *coffee* entered English in the late sixteenth century via the Italian *caffè* and the French *café*. These, and the German *kaffee* and Dutch *koffie*, are derived from the Turkish *kahve* and can be traced further to the Arabic *qahwa*, which is truncated from *qahwat al-bun*, "wine of the bean." Evidence that an alcoholic coffee-fruit beverage predates the one made by infusing the roasted ground seeds in water has led to speculation that infused coffee substituted for alcoholic beverages, which are proscribed by Islamic custom (Weinberg and Bealer 2001).

Coffee and Sociability

First in the Near East and later in Europe, coffeehouses flourished as sites of association in leisure for wealthy men and served as emblems of "bourgeois masculinity, [and] serious, purposive and respectable" socializing (Goodman 1995:132). In the early sixteenth-century coffeehouses, sociability was manifest in the circulation of, and drinking from, a common cup (Hattox 1985). In London, the first coffeehouse was established in 1652; many more followed in rapid succession, some serving also as mailing addresses for regular patrons. By 1700, London coffeehouses had become common, and many catered to a specialized mercantile, artistic, political, or social patronage. English café society became so cultivated that the coffeehouses were characterized by conversational themes: "gallantry and entertainment . . . [at] White's; poetry [at] Will's; foreign and domestic news [at] St. James's; and learned articles [at] the Grecian." In later decades, tea, chocolate, and sherbet were added to the menu. By the mid-eighteenth century, however, "the traditional London coffeehouse was dead. No longer was it the favored men's forum for transacting business, reading newspapers, [and] exchanging ideas about art, science, and manners." Coffeehouse proprietors turned instead to selling alcoholic beverages to boost profits. By 1815, the number of London's dedicated coffeehouses had diminished, perhaps to fewer than twelve: in only 150 years, the coffeehouse phenomenon had ebbed, but as a result of its currency, coffee, tea, and to some degree chocolate had become customary beverages (Weinberg and Bealer 2001:171, xv).

The popularity of coffeehouses diffused rapidly through Europe and later America. For a hundred years they flourished, as they had in England, as the heart of urban life, a cultural phenomenon that drove political, scientific, literary, and fiscal change. As European consumption of beverage and medicinal coffee increased rapidly during the eighteenth century, plantations were established in Indonesia, Réunion in the Indian Ocean, Brazil, and Martinique and Hispaniola in the Caribbean. By the early nineteenth century, merchants and investors had begun to entertain the prospects of selling coffee to European and Muslim countries, which comprised roughly one third of the world's population (Trang 2003).

In the West, the coffeehouse is no longer the site of socializing adults but has instead become a place of mixed demographics, including children. Of these, the multinational Starbucks is iconic. Retail cafés feature coffees, and now teas and fruit beverages, in great varieties of preparations. They also sell pastries and more-substantial foods, as well as branded equipment, clothing, and accessories. Starbucks and its aspirants typify "mass class and leisure-time entertainment marketing strategies" (Trang 2003:433). In the United States, the current popularity of branded coffee shops can be traced to the espresso and pastry emporia established by Italian immigrants in major urban centers, notably, San Francisco's North Beach, Manhattan's Little Italy, and Boston's North End. The most contemporary analogues or revivals of the coffeehouses of old are dedicated coffee emporia, including cybercafes where people socialize on- and off-site (Weinberg and Bealer 2001).

Coffee and Health

The tonic and stimulant actions of coffee were recognized in Islamic medicine beginning as early as the eleventh century. England's and Europe's first coffeehouses promoted the medicinal, not culinary, qualities of coffee to mediate the humors as a cold and dry medicine: to aid digestion, improve temperament, soothe sore eyes, and cure dropsy, scurvy, and gout. The stimulant effects of coffee are attributed primarily to the alkaloid caffeine, the production of which evolved as the plant's defense against herbivory and bacterial and fungal infection (table 2.1). Antimicrobial actions are evident against human pathogenic microflora as well (Almeida et al. 2006). The health implications of methylxanthines are more fully explored in the discussion of cacao pharmacology, below.

Caffeine reduces fatigue, increases motor activity, stimulates the senses, and shortens reaction time. Consumption of 200–500 milligrams

TABLE 2.1. Caffeine and theobromine in beverages of association

Beverage	Caffeine (mg)	Theobromine (mg)
Coffee, 8 oz brewed	135	0
Coffee, 8 oz instant	95	0
Coffee, 8 oz decaf	3	0
Starbucks Coffee Grande	259	0
Tea, 8 oz leaf or bag	50	trace
Tea, 8 oz green	30	trace
Tea, 8 oz white	15	trace
Cocoa, 8 oz	8	250
Milk chocolate, 1 oz	6	130
Dark chocolate, 1 oz	20	390

Sources: CSPI 1997; Apgar and Tarka 1999; Mayo Clinic 2005.
Note: Published figures vary; phytochemistry is influenced by cultivar type and blending, plant maturity, harvest and fermentation conditions, and beverage preparation.

can make individuals irritable and nervous. The popular image of coffee drinking among high-energy, "Type A" individuals is that caffeine contributes to "stress" and, by some logic of extrapolation, to cardiovascular disease. To the contrary, a growing number of studies reveal that there is no association between coffee consumption and cardiovascular disease. One prospective cohort study on long-term (twenty-year) habitual coffee consumption concluded that there was no evidence that coffee consumption contributes to cardiovascular disease among study participants, comprising 84,488 women and 44,005 men (Lopez Garcia et al. 2006a). Similarly, a shorter (ten-year) prospective study in Finland demonstrated that habitual coffee drinking is not a risk for cardiovascular disease among 20,197 women and men (Kleemola et al. 2000). Other researchers have reported that consumption of both caffeinated and decaffeinated coffees is inversely related to markers of inflammation and endothelial impairment (Lopez Garcia et al. 2006b). High levels of antioxidants (e.g., pyrroles, furans, and maltol) in beverage and green coffee fruits suggest pharmacologic benefit for cardiovascular and other diseases; such antioxidants have been linked to protection against DNA damage and promotion of immune resistance against bacteria by augmenting lysozyme activity and increasing the concentration of immunocompetent cells (Fredholm 1995; Apgar and Tarka 1999; Nawrot et al. 2003; Ramanavièiene et al. 2003; Abraham and Stopper 2004; Yanagimoto et al. 2004). Recent research has reported in vitro inhibitory effects of beverage coffee on tumor growth and proliferation (Miura et al. 2004). Dose-dependent diminished risk of Parkinson's disease among ethnically diverse populations suggests that protective effects play some role in the complex, multifactorial etiology of this disease (Evans et al. 2006). The literature is inconsistent about an association between caffeine consumption and pregnancy loss. A recent study of 2,407 pregnancies with a 10 percent rate of miscarriage concluded that there is little indication of potential harmful effects of caffeine during pregnancy and that the recorded 10 percent might be attributed to overreporting or misclassification of caffeine exposure and a heterogeneity of pregnancy losses, which was not measured (Savitz et al. 2008).

Cacao/Chocolate

The source material for beverage cocoa and solid chocolate are the seeds ("beans") of the cacao tree, to which the eighteenth-century botanist Linnaeus assigned the genus name *Theobroma*, "food of the gods," leaving no question about how his palate received this New World native. Indigenous to the area that stretches from southern Mexico to the northern Amazon Basin, cacao was domesticated in the first millennium CE by Mayan peoples in ancient Mesoamerica, in what is now the Yucatán and Guatemala. The term *cacao* has been traced linguistically to the Mixe-Zoquean *kakaw*, while the suggested etymology of *chocolate* is the Aztec *xocoatl*, "bitter water," or a conflation by the Spanish of Maya *chocol*, "hot," and Aztec *atl*, "water." The Maya made a hot beverage by mixing the seed extract of *T. cacao* with chile and maize, which was poured from one vessel held high above another to create a much-prized froth. Recent archaeological evidence suggests that a cacao alcoholic beverage might have preceded the unsweetened chocolate drinks. Archaeologists John Henderson and Rosemary Joyce note that the unique flavor of chocolate beverage emerges only when cacao seeds and the watery pulp of the fruit are fermented together and the seeds are ground to yield chocolate. Noting that this is not an intuitive process, the authors suggest that the experience of fermenting to make alcoholic beverages preceded making cacao beverages. Their speculation is supported by evidence of theobromine, the signature phytoconstituent of cacao, in potsherds that date from 1100 to 1200 BCE. The pots yield no evidence of chile, with which Mesoamericans flavored cacao beverages, and the oldest vessel is a long-necked bottle that could have contained a cacao alcoholic beverage but would not have accommodated frothing the drink (Hecht 2007). Cacao could not be cultivated in other parts of Meso-america and was widely traded, serving for some duration as currency. By late Maya times, cacao had been introduced by long-distance trade to western Mexico and the Aztec Empire, where it became an important source of wealth. The Aztec also drank cacao as a frothed, but cold, beverage that they commonly flavored with honey (Young 1994; Coe and Coe 1996; Davidson 1999).

Cacao was a key ceremonial item for the Olmec, Maya, and Aztec: it propitiated the deities, was a centerpiece of celebratory feasts and an item of reciprocity among the aristocracy, and was emblematic of the Mayan and Aztec fertility gods. Its images were depicted on sacred temples, and the tree and fruit were woven through origin narratives that connected heaven and earth. Bowls filled with cacao were included among grave goods buried with the nobility and warriors, and cacao was served to celebrate marriages, puberty rites, and other life-course transitions.

Like the consumption of other beverages of association, cacao drink-ing traditionally was reserved for immediately after a meal, rather than during it (Young 1994; Davidson 1999). This marks cacao as an integral element of cuisine whose consumption signaled sociability rather than nutriture.

Flavors added to cacao beverages varied with social context. For Aztec nobility, the most common addition was earflower petals (*Cymbopeta-lum penduliflorum* Baill., Annonaceae). Others include Mexican tarra-gon (*Tagetes lucida* Cav., Asteraceae), vanilla, flowers of rough leaf pep-per (*Piper amalago* L., Piperaceae), and seeds of sapote (*Pouteria sapota* H. E. Moore & Stearn, Sapotaceae), *Ceiba* spp. (Bombacaceae), and annatto (from the lipstick tree, *Bixa orellana* L., Bixaceae) (Coe 1997). The importance of individuals, families, and occasions was marked by adjusting the amount of chile added to the beverage, increasing with rank. Cacao drinking was marked by age, social status, and gender: its consumption was intended for adult men who represented the aristoc-racy, held a military or a high government office, or were members of the decorated warrior class or priesthood, as well as individuals designated for ritual sacrifice (Dillinger et al. 2000).

Cacao in the Old World

Although Columbus returned from his last New World voyage (1502) with cacao seeds, he and his crew had no knowledge of cacao beverages and generated no interest in the product in Europe. When Hernando Cortés and his Spanish troops invaded the Yucatán two decades later, they gained a better understanding of the economic value of cacao when they witnessed vast stores of seeds in the Aztec capital, Tenochtitlan. The Spanish troops also learned the cultural importance of beverage cacao in the context of Aztec banquets, where men of nobility and authority consumed large quantities served in gold goblets. Cortés returned to the Spanish royal court carrying not only trunks of cacao seeds but also instructions for preparing beverage cacao (Young 1994).

Cacao's reputation preceded its availability in Europe. The first official shipment of seeds reached Seville as late as 1585, by which time the Spanish royals were flavoring the beverage with cinnamon, sugar, citrus water, and vanilla. Wherever cacao was adopted, chile spice was assimilated into existing palates and cuisines (see above). But unlike chile, cacao and cocoa were not inserted into European discursive categories and flavor complexes. Europeans, first in the New World and then in the Old, embraced Mesoamerican taste and beverage aesthetics (Norton 2006). Patterned on Mesoamerican customs, cacao drinking (like tea and coffee) was reserved for after the meal in Europe. Spanish control of Mesoamerican agriculture and trade established a world monopoly on cacao production, but despite the Spanish efforts to keep secret the production of cacao and preparation of beverage cacao, within a century its culinary and medicinal uses had diffused to France, the Netherlands, and Italy and later to England, where it was named "cocoa" (Young 1994; Davidson 1999).

Chocolate houses quickly became fashionable, frequented by the wealthy aristocracy, artists, the literati, and politicians. These sites reproduced the culture of coffeehouses on which they were modeled and replicated the classed and gendered customs of Mesoamerican cacao consumption. The popularity of cocoa drove affiliate commodities such as chocolate services that included trays, pots, and frothing whisks made from silver and other expensive materials. Beverage material culture proliferated throughout the eighteenth century as the context of cocoa consumption, like that of coffee and tea, shifted from public to domestic. The classed and gendered aspects of cocoa drinking eroded as domestic consumption became more common, but cocoa still was identified with the more affluent classes until widely affordable cocoa powders became available in the early nineteenth century (Young 1994).

Through commercial expansions, cacao became a pantropical crop, and its production took on the character of other plantation-based, forced-labor enterprises that exploited local populations for European markets. From Mesoamerican traditions through the Spanish colonial era in Mexico, cacao was consumed in beverage form. During the early European experience with cacao beverages, foundation liquids included beer, wine, water, and coffee. The addition of sugar to cacao (and to coffee and tea) created a fusion that was a centerpiece of mercantile capitalism and colonial expansion around the world. In the 1720s, the English began to blend cacao with milk, thus creating the cocoa (hot chocolate) favored in the West today (Goodman 1995). By the mid-1700s, the use of cacao had begun to extend beyond its beverage form; a century later, inexpensive technology to extract cocoa butter (actually cocoa oil, or fat) increased the availability of both the beverage and solid confectionary forms of chocolate (Bixler and Morgan 1999). Since then, the diversity and number of cacao products have expanded enormously, including solid chocolate confections that have in the United States and Europe become iconic of holidays such as Saint Valentine's Day and Easter. Until recently, beverage cocoa was a less transformed cacao product, but over the past two decades, it too has found a niche among designer commodities as variably flavored and otherwise dressed-up beverages.

Cacao and Health

The use of cacao as medicine predates its consumption as a beverage of association. For the Aztec, Olmec, and Maya, beverage cacao served as a primary medication as well as a vehicle for other medicines or to offset their bitter taste. Although its social beverage role marked demographics, medicinal cacao was status-, gender-, and age-neutral. Cacao leaves, flowers, bark, and oil also had medicinal applications. In Mesoamerica, cacao was commonly used to treat gastrointestinal disorders, encourage weight gain, and stimulate the nervous system. Instructions for the preparation of medicinal cacao were transposed to Europe, where physicians recommended it for a wide spectrum of conditions; applications included general tonics and specifics for typhoid, tuberculosis, and gastrointestinal disorders. As in Mesoamerica, the European medicinal uses of cacao during the sixteenth through nineteenth centuries were democratic, while the social contexts of beverage cocoa remained gendered and privileged. Despite its medicinal importance in earlier eras, Europeans in recent years have come to project a view more like that of U.S. consumers, who regard cocoa and chocolate as confections that taste good but are not nutritive or otherwise healthful (Lupien 1999; Dillinger et al. 2000).

Cacao Pharmacology

The methylxanthines theobromine, theophylline, and caffeine have been well characterized with reference to structural chemistry and physiologic effects. All suppress sleepiness by antagonizing receptors of adenosine, an endogenous drowse-inducing chemical; in addition, they stimulate heart muscle and the central nervous system, are diuretic, and relax smooth muscle (notably, in the bronchial airways). However, the site and strength of methylxanthine activities vary. For example, the effects of caffeine are more apparent in the brain and skeletal muscle, while theophylline exerts more effects in the heart, bronchia, and kidney (see table 2.2). Vasoconstriction by caffeine and theobromine may be responsible for methylxanthine relief of hypertension-associated headache, although abrupt withdrawal of caffeine also causes headache by dilating cerebral blood vessels. Unlike other fatty acids, stearic acid—the predominant fatty acid in cocoa butter—does not increase blood cholesterol and is not associated with increased risk of coronary heart disease. Large-sample studies of dietary saturated fatty acids and risk of cardiovascular disease in the United States concluded that cacao is not an important contributor to total saturated fatty acids or stearic acid intake. In fact, a cholesterol-neutralizing effect has been demonstrated in humans through controlled studies with chocolate-enriched diets. Cacao contains high levels of cardioprotective minerals such as copper, magnesium,

TABLE 2.2. Sites of action and relative strengths of methylxanthines

Organ system	Caffeine	Theobromine	Theophylline
Skeletal muscle	strong	weak	moderate
Brain	strong	weak	moderate
Heart	weak	moderate	strong
Kidney	weak	moderate	strong
Bronchia	weak	moderate	strong

Source: Apgar and Tarka 1999.

calcium, and potassium; additionally, reduction of phytate content during the fermentative processing of cacao seeds increases mineral availability. On a per-weight basis, the flavonoid content of cacao products (as much as 10 percent) is higher than that found in most plant-based foods, which may promote cardiovascular health through antiplatelet and antioxidant actions that reduce inflammation, delay thrombosis, and improve vascular endothelial function. Evidence suggests that cacao flavonoids inhibit human colonic cancer and diminish tumor growth in other cancers (Jardine 1999; Keen 2001; Carnesecchi et al. 2002; Hannum et al. 2002; Kris-Etherton and Keen 2002; Rios et al. 2003; Serafini et al. 2003; Steinberg et al. 2003; Hermann et al. 2006). A comprehensive review of the literature (Rogers and Smit 2000) confirms that the impression is widespread among the public that chocolate contains psychotropic chemicals, but that review concludes that those actions as well as the purported addictive potential of cacao are at least grossly exaggerated and probably not true.

Tea

The history of tea (*Camellia* spp.) is more than five thousand years old in China, where it has been cultivated for at least two thousand years. The earliest reliable written record of beverage tea is a dictionary written by the scholar Kuo Po in 350 CE. *Ch'a* was described as a bitter medicinal beverage made from roasted green tea leaves boiled with citrus, ginger, and onion and used to treat diverse symptoms including poor eyesight, lethargy, distemper, and gastrointestinal disorders. From Mandarin *ch'a*, *chai* was adopted into many languages: for example, Russian, Turkish, and Swahili. Hokkien *te* from southern China is the etymological root of *tè* (Italian), *thé* (French), *te* (Swedish and Norwegian), and *tea* (English) (Anderson 1988).[3]

Early Szechuan tea was prepared with ginger, flour, and salt; later additions include fruit peel, scents, and flowers. Along the western and northern borders of China, pastoral groups added salt and milk, or butter. In the sixth century CE, social tea drinking became popular among monks and the upper classes; after 780 CE, when the tea classic *Cha Jing* was published, tea producers learned methods for improving tea quality. Farmers of the Tang dynasty (618–907) were encouraged by these more flavorful teas to designate small plots for tea production, which eventuated in a class of wholesalers who purchased tea from the peasants and set up a system of regional reserves. Tribute teas were developed for the imperial court, where tea ceremonies were elaborated. Buddhist monks extended tea cultivation throughout China, and roasted and boiled tea leaves with a bit of salt became the national beverage for people of all social strata. During the Ming dynasty (1368–1644), a cultural renaissance returned attention to tea and its ceremonies. Green tea and the steeping process were introduced. By refining the fermentation process, tea producers of the Qing dynasty (1644–1911) developed many varieties, increasingly for export, including the tea trade that began between China and Europe in the 1800s.

Regions of origin and production methods distinguish tea varieties. White tea is made from immature leaf buds that still bear fine white hairs, while green tea is made from mature leaves that are steamed and dried directly after harvest. For black tea, mature leaves are bruised, fermented, and dried. Oolong (brown) tea is made from a large-leaf *Camellia* that is partially fermented. Of the more than two thousand tea varieties that are commercially traded, five hundred are produced in China. Other leading producers are India, Indonesia, Sri Lanka, Kenya, and Malawi (Anderson 1988; Manchester 1996).

A political ecology perspective helps us to understand that the later history of tea commerce is one of asymmetrical access to products and processing. Tea figured heavily in Dutch and English expansions in Indonesia, India, and Sri Lanka, where much land and many local human resources were appropriated to establish plantations and supply Europe's growing taste for tea. China's small-plot production could not compete with the economies of scale of Europe's colonial plantations. Tea also played a role in the nineteenth-century Opium Wars: to offset the cost of Chinese tea, English merchants appropriated large tracts of agricultural land for the production of opium poppy in their Indian colony and smuggled the opium into China, where its high profitability balanced England's trade deficit. One outcome was the imposition of unequal terms of trade onto China. In the eighteenth century, the monopoly of the East India Company was cast into bolder relief by government taxes that made tea too expensive for commoners. Their continued demand for tea encouraged smuggling and adulteration,[4] which the population supported in order to afford tea and other expensive resources. Underscoring the classed nature of tea drinking, used leaves were purchased from servants of wealthy homes. Tea also was at the heart of disputes between England and its North American colonies: England's 1773 Tea Act, an effort to manipulate trade, precipitated the Revolutionary War (Simoons 1991; Weatherstone 1992; Manchester 1996; Davidson 1999; Moxham 2003).

Tea and Sociability

Traditionally not a part of Chinese meals, tea was served before and after; although all classes drank tea, its patterned consumption became increasingly ritualized as social status rose. Teas marked occasions such as religious rituals, business exchanges, and marriage. During the Sung dynasty (960–1279), teahouses were established in garden and pastoral settings. Although tea was drunk there and snacks might have been consumed, teahouses were primarily sites of association. Like their coffee and chocolate counterparts, teahouses were places whose patrons were devoted to discussions of writing, painting, and music. Gender asymmetries (in this case, marked by the presence of more men than women) were most apparent in upscale establishments. Strict rules of etiquette guided Chinese tea drinking until the thirteenth-century invasion of China by nomadic Mongols, for whom the nuances of tea and its ceremonies did not resonate. Tea remained China's national beverage, but it was no longer held in such high esteem. Formerly the purview of the learned and wealthy, teahouse patronage had come to be extended to all classes by the beginning of the Ming dynasty. Later, sociability via tea extended from the public teahouse to the domestic sphere, where status was gauged by the caliber of tea and tea service and how much space was devoted to entertaining tea-drinking guests. Although they shed some of their polish and formality, teahouses were popular in China until the 1940s, when the Communist government disapproved of this leisurely socializing (Anderson 1988; Simoons 1991; Manchester 1996).

Tea and Health

As in China, tea became a valued medicine in Europe, where dry and beverage teas were used as general tonics and as specifics for gastrointestinal disorders, obstructed breathing, and a variety of other symptoms (Weinberg and Bealer 2001; Lu 2002). Teas have a high content of flavonoids (discussed above in the section on cacao pharmacology, as are methylxanthines; see tables 2.1 and 2.2). Epigallocatechin in green tea promotes apoptosis (cell death) in cancers and prevents tumor growth. Consumption of beverage green tea is related to reduced risk of coronary heart disease, high blood pressure, and elevated cholesterol. Polyphenols in black and green teas may protect against cancer. Other healthful characteristics of tea include that it is antimicrobial, anti-ulcer, hypoglycemic, and anti-inflammatory; in addition, it lowers risk of osteoporosis and protects against stroke and liver disease. Tannins in tea can bind and inhibit the absorption of iron, leading to speculation that consumption of large volumes of tea with meals could lead to iron deficiency. On the same principle, tea can mitigate iron accumulation and in this way protect against organ damage and cancers. Consuming tea with meals reduces iron absorption in individuals who have thalassemia (a hereditary anemia in which destroyed red blood cells spill iron into the circulation system), hemochromatosis (inherited elevated absorption of iron), and other disorders (Gomes et al. 1995; Maity et al. 1995; Halder and Bhaduri 1998; Kaltwasser et al. 1998; Hegarty et al. 2000; Mukhtar and Ahmad 2000; Anderson and Polansky 2002; Kris-Etherton and Keen 2002; McKay and Blumberg 2002; Sabu et al. 2002; Zhen 2002; Kamath et al. 2003; Siddiqui et al. 2004; Mbata et al. 2006).

Conclusion

Long-distance maritime exploration was not a phenomenon born of the Age of Expansion; long before this era, Polynesians, Chinese, Indians,

Arabs, and Vikings had engaged in transoceanic travel. European voyaging in the 1400s–1600s was distinguished by the connection of the world's oceans "into a single system of navigation and the ways in which this mastery of the sea became the basis for the eventual extension of European influence into every inhabited continent" (Arnold 2002:xi). By seizing already established sea-land trade networks in the Indian Ocean and Asia and by negotiating new trans-Atlantic and trans-Pacific routes, Europeans created a navigation of expansion that was foundational for a worldwide system of Europe-controlled trade. The influx of products from lands conquered and explored fueled Europe's economies, setting a trajectory of entrepreneurial expansion for centuries to come.

That expansion resonates a political economy perspective that identifies a significant negative impact on the lives of non-European populations, people whose health was diminished by introduced infections, forced labor and other brutalities, and compromised nutritional status that resulted from food shortages created by converting food-producing lands and labor to cash-cropping and by moving farmers to other occupations. In the abstract, however, expansion had a positive influence in circulating foods and food technologies globally and increasing the potential for dietary diversity. But this abstract good was and is offset, often and in the extreme, by structural asymmetries that eventuate in uneven access to resources. These consequences are apparent in the histories of the pharmacologically dynamic foods and beverages of association described in this chapter: the spices that are emblematic of expanding trade, including chile and black peppers; and the caffeinated cordials, cacao, coffee, and tea.

CHAPTER 3

Street Foods and Beverages

STREET FOODS INCLUDE a fascinating array of comestibles that are sold by ambulant vendors from wagons, pushcarts, and motorized conveyances; others are purveyed from stalls, cookshops, and other stationary structures. These are ready-to-eat and ready-to-drink items that are prepared or sold in public places and consumed at or while moving from the purchase site. They may be ready-transported from the place of preparation or cooked and further modified at the vending site. Of course, all these foods can be taken home or to another location, but I have selected examples that, in their traditional presentation, fit my more narrow definition of street foods. Typically, these are simple foods and drinks that can be dressed up or down depending on vendors' marketing strategies. Some street foods are sold and consumed as full meals (see section on Plate Lunch, below); many are consumed without utensils; and in the developed world (and increasingly elsewhere), virtually all are presented in disposable containers. Public foods have been described as offering "environmental proximity" that does not involve consumers' "anticipation or planning" (Simopoulos and Bhat 2000:ix), but I offer examples that, in contrast, illustrate that street foods embody identity and other meanings, they meet people's expectations, and their consumption is only sometimes spontaneous and more commonly deliberate. While people who eat or drink public consumables overlap in time and space, a social entity of consumption may be episodic, even abstract, and its membership fluid.

Where they are consumed regularly, street foods are integral to the diets of people representing a broad array of social and economic circumstances. Particularly in the developing world, these items command a sizeable percentage of household food budgets, with smaller and poorer families spending more on street foods and beverages; by contrast, in the United States, larger families are more likely to consume fast (including street) foods (Tinker 1997). In this chapter, street foods are distinguished from those sold in restaurants, cafés, and other dine-in establishments.

The purchase and consumption of street foods may be in the moment, but these are not fast foods in the conventional sense of enclosed restaurants that have walk-in, drive-through, and sit-in components and also have more infrastructure. Street foods and their purveyors are not branded or standardized to nearly the extent that fast food chains are; still, individual vendors may be widely recognized and may have large patron bases. Throughout the world, public foods and beverages tend to be easily accessible, inexpensive, short-cut options to traditional dining and drinking customs. In many communities, the rhythm of daily activity patterns is timed by public foods that may be available throughout the day or coincide with certain hours, seasons, or occasions.

Street foods from different world cultures—including skewered and roasted meats, hand-held sweets, savory pastries, noodles and soup, hot and cold drinks, fresh or preserved fruit, and infinite variations on fillings contained by bread or its analogues—illustrate recurrent metaphors and presentations. In addition, particular foods have specific contextual histories, social roles, and health impacts.

A History of Street Foods

The concept of cooking and serving food from portable containers is ubiquitous and integral to the evolution of cuisines worldwide. In the cities of Europe, the purchase of cooked foods has a long history that can be traced to several institutions, none of which corresponds to the restaurant's combination of food and beverage varieties and social functions. The cookshops of medieval cities were artisanal, small-scale enterprises where individuals could send their meat to be cooked and their bread baked, as well as select from a wide range of hot dishes. These establishments were important for the lower classes, whose modest living circumstances and furnishings could not accommodate cooking fires. During the early Roman and medieval eras, street foods and beverages also were sold in markets and at sports events, fairs, theaters, and other gatherings. Because street foods filled a practical—rather than social—function, the clientele of food stalls was demographically inclusive, rather than socially stratified (Mennell 1996).

During the 1700s and 1800s, the number of street vendors in western European cities declined, but they continued to be important in the periurban margins, where distribution networks for foods and other goods were not well developed (Matalas and Yannakoulia 2000). In the industrial era, street foods filled working people's needs for portable, fast, and inexpensive nourishment at convenient locations. As workplaces became more concentrated, laborers had to travel farther from home, and when women joined the workforce in larger numbers, they were no longer at home during the day to prepare meals, even if their men were able to return at midday.

Street Foods around the World

Throughout the developing world, street foods represent long-established traditions that are part of complex trade networks. The ways in which street foods are culturally constructed and circulated in different societies embody both enormous variety and similarities that bear on available ingredients, technology, structures of cuisine, consumption patterns, and, of course, borrowing. In the past, more street foods were available in developing countries, including in touristic areas. Exceptions to this general pattern include such places as highly developed Hong Kong, which continues a strong tradition of outdoor foods, and other cities whose immigrant populations use these foods as a vehicle to forge identity in the diaspora. In recent decades, globalization has come to result in exchanges of "ethnic" foods that become readily available in Western and developing-world urban centers. Conventional wisdom argued that when societies reach a level of economic development that coheres around large-scale commercial exchange, "small-scale vending . . . decline[s] spontaneously" (Matalas and Yannakoulia 2000:1). However, in the modern era, worldwide, accelerated migration from rural to urban areas is accompanied by an increased trade in street foods as lifestyle adjustments embrace abbreviated meals and mobile consumption. Expendable incomes and growing curiosity about food are contributing factors.

The Agorae of Greece

When public foods made their appearance in Greece in the sixth century BCE, the only one sold in *agorae*, or marketplaces, was lentil soup (*Lens culinaris* Medikus, Fabaceae), which was consumed on-site because ambulant eating was not acceptable. During the seventeenth and eighteenth centuries, mobile "round about professionals" offered *koulouri*, a small ring-shaped barley bread; *boyatsa*, custard pie; *chalvas*, honey cake; baked carrots; and coffee. The diversity of street foods expanded over the next two centuries and today includes variations on koulouri; *boureki*, meat pie; *kefte*, fried meatball; *tzieri*, fried liver; *kebab* and *souvlaki*, grilled skewered meat; *gyros*, sliced pork or beef; *strayalia*, chickpea; *pilav*, rice; *pastelli*, sesame dessert; and *karythato*, walnut cake (*Juglans regia* L., Juglandaceae). Hot beverages include *salepi*, prepared with the boiled root of the purple orchid (*Orchis mascula* L., Orchidaceae). New World domesticates were not integrated into Greek street foods until the twentieth century. Sunflower seed, tomato, and groundnut (*Arachis hypogaea* L., Fabaceae) also were incorporated into domestic and restaurant cuisines, but the fire-roasted cob prepared by street vendors is the only way that maize has been used until very recently, having been cultivated primarily as animal feed (Matalas and Yannakoulia 2000).

Greek street foods are inexpensive and high in calories and are commonly sold at sporting events, train stations, and wherever else there is substantial foot and vehicular traffic. In the past, the consumption of core street foods such as koulouri, boureki, and gyros corresponded to people's daily activity patterns, meeting expectations for the availability of certain items at particular times of day. Today, that regularity has eroded (Kochilas 2001), inviting speculation about how the meanings of food and cuisine might have shifted.

Greek street foods lack social function and prestige: people representing a full spectrum of demographic and economic circumstances consume a broad spectrum of products, from the simple *kollyrio*, or roasted maize kernels, to elaborate pita-wrapped souvlaki. However, today's health regulations have both classed and gendered the sale of street foods. The licensing of vendors privileges low-income and otherwise disadvantaged individuals, for example, those who are physically handicapped or support large families. In contrast with the developing world, where women play a prominent role in the preparation and vending of street foods, Greek vendors are predominantly men, an artifact of regulations enforced in the 1980s that prohibit selling foods prepared in the home, the realm of women (Matalas and Yannakoulia 2000).

The Sidewalks of New York

Unlike the traditional vending of Greek and many other street foods, New York City practices were historically gendered and classed, as well as nuanced by ethnicity: street trade was the domain of the lower class, primarily men, as both consumers and vendors.[1] This hierarchy reflects that many of the vendors were immigrants whose language and other skills precluded some forms of employment and whose social mobility was further restricted by the city's dominant culture. In the late nineteenth and early twentieth centuries, immigrants tended to segregate themselves into neighborhoods, where pushcart-vended foods provided some economic security at the same time that they served as short-radius, but ambulant, sites for cultural identity.

Throughout its history, the regulation of New York City street vending has been controversial; today, it embodies some of the most restrictive local laws in the United States. Seventeenth-century ordinances curtailed street vending to prevent competition with markets and restaurants and to reduce congestion. In the early decades of the nineteenth century, commercial trade expanded, drawing middle- and upper-class consumers into enclosed specialty shops, further sharpening class differences in street food vending and consumption. In the 1930s, in advance of the 1939 World's Fair, the city imposed additional restrictions on street vending, which declined significantly over the next few decades.

New York's first street foods represented the cultures of early immigrant communities of the time, predominantly from Italy, Ireland, Germany, and Russia. Today, the pushcart is once again a prominent signature of the city, with an estimated ten thousand vendors of food and merchandise (Baker 2005). The growing heterogeneity of the city is reflected in today's most popular street foods: pizza, bratwurst, egg roll, gyro, burrito, Navajo fry bread, Indian *samosa*, and many more. As the variety of street foods expands, their consumption is no longer demographically scaffolded, although their vending still is the domain of individuals with limited economic resources.

In aggregate, the diversity of public foods fuels New Yorkers' self image as a "melting pot," a term coined in the early twentieth century for the high-density, Lower East Side immigrant neighborhoods. Today, this metaphor is invoked across the U.S. mainland as a celebration of blending across ethnic heterogeneity and resonates in other, primarily coastal, metropolitan centers such as San Francisco, Washington, D.C., Boston, and Chicago. Across the country, confluence emerges from dishes such as New England clams with Chinese sausage, Virginia wild duck with basmati rice, and Bavarian *lumpia*. But the melting pot metaphor more appropriately applies to fusion cuisines proper (see chapter 1, section on Slow Food movement), foodways that deliberately combine components from two or more temporally or spatially discrete cuisines into new, perhaps temporary, normative structures. Similarly, the burgeoning worldwide trend since the 1970s for innovative restaurant cuisines includes variations on Western and pan-Asian or Pacific Rim fusions that do not simply hybridize or homogenize tastes but coalesce into a unique mix not only of ingredients and seasonings but also of presentation styles and restaurant decor. One could argue that, unlike restaurant fusions, many of the street foods of New York and elsewhere still mark discrete, parallel lines of identity. Even suggested substitute terms for *melting pot—quilt, mosaic,* and *jigsaw puzzle*—do not capture the identity-forging role of culture-specific public foods.

Alimentos de la Calle

Most of Mexico's urban street foods are based on the tortilla, a thin unleavened bread made from finely ground maize cured with lime (calcium hydroxide). In Mexico City alone, more than 30 million tortillas are sold each day (Muñoz de Chávez et al. 2000), their consumption bridging class, gender, and other demographics. Tortillas are folded or rolled into tacos or other forms that vary in size and presentation: tamales are cooked in maize husks or banana leaves, quesadillas are made with thicker tortillas, flautas are fried and rolled. Fillings include meats, vegetables, flowers, mushrooms, nopal cactus (*Opuntia* spp., Cactaceae), avocado (*Persea americana* Miller, Lauraceae), and chile pepper. Regional street foods reflect different ecologies and ethnicities: beef production in the north and the availability of seafoods along the coasts color the availability of street foods. Vendors on the streets of Mexico City sell *esquites*, or maize kernels cooked with epazote (*Chenopodium ambrosioides* L., Chenopodiaceae), chile, and lime (*Citrus aurantifolia* Swingle, Rutaceae). All over Mexico, fresh fruit and fruit cocktails include mango (*Mangifera indica* L., Anacardiaceae), pineapple, watermelon (*Citrullus lanatus* Matsum. & Nakai, Cucurbitaceae), and cucumber. Crystallized fruit and *aguas frescas* (fruit beverages) also are popular (Muñoz de Chávez et al. 2000; Long-Solís and Vargas 2005). At least two hundred insect species are eaten in Mexico, many of them as street foods. In the diaspora—in such cities as Chicago, Houston, and Los Angeles—and in the transformed landscapes of Mexican resort towns, people enjoy street foods that appeal to their ethnic identity, including *insectos de la patria* (DeFoliart 1997). Interesting transpositions that grew out of colonial experiences include, in Pachuca, the sweet or savory *paste* named after the Cornish pasty, a baked meat- and vegetable-filled pastry introduced to Mexico by English mining engineers. Another English introduction in northern Mexico is *ginyabre*, or gingerbread cookie (Muñoz de Chávez et al. 2000).

Street Foods in Hawai'i

Hawai'i has one of the most diverse culinary heritages in the United States. The cuisine was shaped first by voyaging Pacific Islanders from the west, in the first century CE (or perhaps earlier, as dates vary). What more sociable gesture could there have been than to prioritize an assemblage of plants that friends and family would carry literally into the future, to new places that would be infused with community and identity? The foods catalogued in table 3.1 were included among *nâ meakanu o ka wa'a Hawai'i kahiko*, the phrase referring to "canoe plants" that voyagers of long ago carried with them as seeds, fruit, cuttings, and whole plants.

Beginning in the 1700s, the arrival of European mercantile capitalists and missionaries ended Hawaii's relative isolation. Early in the next century, whalers began to make regular stops in the islands. The first large influx consisted of Chinese immigrants, arriving initially as nineteenth-century entrepreneurs, later and in larger numbers as sugar and pineapple plantation workers. Since the last half of the 1800s, Hawaii's land and people have been impacted by other immigrants destined for plantation labor and beyond—from Japan, Portugal, Puerto Rico, the Philippines, and Korea. Later influences include arrivals from Mexico, other Polynesian islands, and Southeast Asia. Unless otherwise referenced, descriptions of street foods in Hawai'i are drawn from Laudan 1996, Clarke

TABLE 3.1. Polynesian botanical canoe foods

Hawaiian	English	Parts eaten	Genus and species	Family
ʻApe	giant taro	corm, leaves	*Alocasia macrorrhizos* G. Don. f.	Araceae
ʻAwa	kava	root for beverage	*Piper methysticum* Forster	Piperaceae
Kalo	taro	corm, leaves, leaf stalk, flower/inflorescence	*Colocasia esculenta* Schott	Araceae
Ko	sugarcane	stem juice	*Saccharum officinarum* L.	Poaceae
Maiʻa	banana	fruit, pseudostem ("trunk") heart, leaf bud	*Musa* spp.	Musaceae
Niu	coconut	water, fruit	*Cocos nucifera* L.	Arecaceae
ʻOhe	bamboo	shoots, seeds	many genera and species	Poaceae
ʻOhi ʻa ʻAi	mountain apple	fruit	*Syzygium malaccense* Merr. & Perry	Myrtaceae
ʻOlena	turmeric	rhizome	*Curcuma longa* L.	Zingiberaceae
Pia	Polynesian arrowroot	starch from rhizome	*Tacca leontopetaloides* Kuntze	Taccaceae
ʻUala	sweet potato	tuber, leaves	*Ipomoea batatas* Lam.	Convolvulaceae
Uhi	yam	tuber	*Dioscorea* spp.	Dioscoreaceae
ʻUlu	breadfruit	fruit	*Artocarpus altilis* Fosb.	Moraceae

Sources: White 1990; Krauss 1993.

Note: Other *nâ meakanu o ka waʻa o Hawaiʻi kahiko* were valued for medicine, dyes, construction, fiber crafts, cordage, and religious and other customs (Krauss 1993).

1997, Japanese American National Museum 1997, Namkoong 2006, and my own observations on and interviews with residents of Hawai'i during the course of my research on the intersections of food and medicine (e.g., Etkin 2003, 2004).

Historically, women of these diverse ethnic groups prepared the simple plantation foods that were exchanged among field-workers when they gathered for their midday break. Japanese rice and tofu joined Chinese *cai xin* (or *choy sum*), cabbage (*Brassica rapa* L., Brassicaceae); Hawaiian *lomi-lomi*, salmon (diced with tomato and onion); and Portuguese *chor
iço*, pork sausage. The tolerance, and eventual adoption, of others' foods—and by extension the acceptance of the others themselves—was expressed in the social context shared by these laborers.

In Hawai'i, a local identity emerged from exchanges of all kinds— food, language, medicine, and other knowledge. These shared cultural traditions reinforced the structural underpinnings of local identity. At base, the working-class status of plantation laborers connected these diverse ethnic groups, at least insofar as they occupied a diminished social position vis-à-vis predominantly Caucasian businessmen and plantation owners. I do not imply a sustained association that was seamlessly carried forward from the plantation era. Indeed, shifting political, social, and economic circumstances shaped different meanings and content for this panethnic culture. During the early plantation years, workers lived in ethnically segregated camps that encouraged the maintenance of unique cultural traits, while the shared place and experience of labor encouraged connections. In the 1940s and 1950s, local identity was energized by the unionization of plantation laborers and Democratic Party efforts to marshal political strength. During the next decade, local identity was cast into bolder relief in juxtaposition to the rapid expansion of the tourist industry and increased immigration from Asia, the Pacific, and the U.S. mainland. Since the 1970s, the emergence of Native Hawaiian political entities that cohere around indigeneity has nuanced, but not eroded, the meaning of "local" (Aoude 1994).

The intersection of diverse culinary influences forged the East-West-Pacific style called "Local Food," a cuisine created by lunch-wagon cooks, small entrepreneurs, and homemakers. For the most part (see section on Plate Lunch, below), its preparation, vending, and consumption are not gendered or classed; the clientele ranges among laborers, students, and downtown bankers. However, although Local Food attracts a diverse patronage, it maintains a working-class ethos. Today, its symbolic value is stronger than in the past, projecting an image of being "all working class; this is what laborers eat" (Construction Worker 2006). At least for food choices, it unites as local or *kamaʻaina* ("children of the land") what were historically disparate ethnic groups, distinguishing them from outsiders. Local Food represents multiethnic convergences of foods and cuisines that later accompanied former plantation labor families to urban areas.

Local Food has been compared to Hawaiʻi Creole, a language spoken by many Hawaiʻi-born residents. It originated as a means of communication between native and nonnative English speakers, taking the place of the pidgin Hawaiian that had been the vehicle of communication on the plantations and elsewhere. Hawaiʻi Creole has been influenced by the languages (lexicon, syntax, pronunciation) of all of Hawaii's immigrants; in its present form, it is an evolved creole language with an expanded grammar and lexicon. Like Hawaiʻi Creole, cuisine in the islands is characterized by a unique syntax and vocabulary. Also like Hawaiʻi Creole, Local Food first appeared in public, not in the domestic sphere, where ethnic cuisines still predominated.

Plate Lunch

The centerpiece of Local Food is Plate Lunch, inspired by the cold *bento*, or segmented-box lunch, that Japanese plantation workers carried for the midday meal. Entrepreneurs of the World War II era or perhaps earlier translated this into a hot meal sold from homemade wagons to rotating shifts of waterfront and other war-effort laborers. Today, Plate Lunch is sold from both fixed and mobile sites. Although customers represent the demographic spectrum, the size of the meal attracts active people with heartier appetites, including blue-collar laborers and sport enthusiasts.

Plate Lunch is quintessentially local, a fusion of items drawn from different cuisines. This inexpensive full-meal street food is structured by two scoops of rice; a sizeable portion of chicken, beef, pork, or fish (Mixed Plate contains two or more meats); and one scoop of macaroni salad. The foundation of this U.S. mainland salad is macaroni dressed with mayonnaise; common additions are sweet pickle, grated carrot, and hard-cooked eggs. Plate Lunch garnishes might include *kimchi* (see below) or other shredded cabbage (*Brassica oleracea* L.), pickled daikon (giant radish, *Raphanus sativus* L. var. *longipinnatus* Bailey, Brassicaceae), and other vegetables. Foods representing different cuisines may be incorporated: Korean *kalbi*, grilled beef; U.S. mainland baked ham; Chinese *cha shao*, pork ribs (see below); Hawaiian *kālua puaʻa*, pork or pig traditionally slow-cooked in an *imu*, or underground pit oven, and wrapped in leaves of ti (*Cordyline terminalis* Kunth, Agavaceae) or banana. Regardless of additions, the basic architecture of the meal remains the same: patterned on the bento, Plate Lunch is served on segmented paper plates or in foam clam-shell boxes; one plate division each is devoted to rice, macaroni salad, and meat. Like dishes and meals in general, in all cuisines this spatial patterning meets consumers' expectations and affirms local identity. Plate Lunch now is sold in some restaurants as well. One local chain has expanded to more than one hundred U.S. mainland locations, where it markets this meal as "Hawaiian barbecue."

Plate Lunch is convenient and affordable. It is also a large volume of food, as noted by the film crew of a television food program, who weighed a four-pound meal (Blanco 2005). This substantiality and the familiarity of structure and integration of diverse cuisines all contribute to its appeal. In a state where obesity and cardiovascular disorders are significant health problems, Hawaii's Plate Lunch is in no one's imagination a healthy meal. The anatomy of Plate Lunches (outlined in table 3.2) reveals calorie-, fat-, and protein-dense foods. Other calculations demonstrate a high percentage of saturated fat, little fiber, and few vitamins. For example, the nutrient composition of a Mixed Plate that combines five ounces each of barbecue beef, chicken, short ribs, and macaroni salad (and not taking into account the rice) is estimated to be 1,690 calories, or 85 percent of the Dietary Reference Intake (DRI 2008): this consists of 98 grams of fat (151 percent DRI), including 33 grams of saturated fat (165 percent DRI); 109 grams of carbohydrates (36 percent DRI); and 94 grams of protein (188 percent DRI). Salt-rich meat marinades and sauces, and the ubiquity of soy sauce seasoning, contribute to high sodium content (Blanco 2005). Some of the garnishes do contribute to nutritional health, although they add substantially less bulk to the plate lunch than other ingredients do. Kimchi, for example, is a Korean fermented vegetable product made predominantly with Chinese cabbage and daikon; minor

TABLE 3.2. Hawaiian Plate Lunch nutrient values

Plate Lunch[a]	Amount	Calories cal. (% DRI)	Fat g (% DRI)	Protein g (% DRI)
Mahimahi				
with 2 scoops of rice and	7 oz. fish, 1.5 cups rice	650 (33)	12 (19)	46 (92)
* macaroni salad, tartar sauce	0.75 cup salad, 3 T tartar sauce	1,153 (58)	58 (89)	49 (98)
* macaroni salad, no tartar sauce	0.75 cup salad	933 (47)	34 (52)	49 (98)
* tossed salad, French dressing, tartar sauce	1 cup salad, 3 T dressing, 3 T tartar sauce	1,035 (52)	50 (77)	47 (94)
* tossed salad, French dressing, no tartar sauce	1 cup salad, 3 T dressing	815 (41)	27 (42)	47 (94)
tossed salad, no dressing, tartar sauce	1 cup salad, 3 T tartar sauce	880 (44)	35 (54)	47 (94)
tossed salad, no dressing, no tartar sauce	1 cup salad	661 (33)	12 (19)	47 (94)
Chicken Katsu[b]				
with 2 scoops of rice and	9 oz. chicken, 1.5 cups rice	1,105 (55)	48 (74)	60 (120)
* macaroni salad	0.75 cup salad	1,356 (68)	68 (105)	63 (126)
* tossed salad, French dressing	1 cup salad, 2 T dressing	1,237 (62)	61 (94)	61 (122)
* tossed salad, no dressing	1 cup salad	1,104 (55)	48 (74)	61 (122)
Teriyaki Beef[c]				
with 2 scoops of rice and	5 oz. beef, 1.5 cups rice	790 (39)	23 (35)	52 (104)
* macaroni salad	0.75 cup salad	1,093 (55)	47 (72)	55 (110)
* tossed salad, French dressing	1 cup salad, 2 T dressing	982 (49)	41 (63)	53 (106)
* tossed salad, no dressing	1 cup salad	798 (40)	23 (35)	53 (106)

Source: Adapted from Shovic 1994:28. Nutrient values were computed for average weights of each item on the plate and are averages of 7–9 dishes from 5–8 plate lunch vendors.

Notes: Abbreviations: T = tablespoon; g = gram; % DRI = Dietary Reference Intake. Dietary Reference Intake is based on a diet of 2,000 calories, 65 grams of total fat, and 50 grams of protein daily (DRI 2008).

[a] High-salt items are designated by an asterisk.

[b] Breaded (coarse bread crumbs and egg), oil-fried boneless chicken.

[c] Beef marinated in teriyaki sauce (soy sauce, ginger, garlic, and sugar), grilled or broiled.

ingredients include carrot, cucumber, and *Allium* species. Fermented fish sauce is important to provide enzymes to drive fermentation and add flavor. Chile, garlic, ginger, and salt impart flavor and control populations of microflora, to promote those that aid fermentation. The B vitamin content of kimchi doubles during fermentation, carotene content is high, and nitrate and nitrite titers decrease. Protein defensins in daikon are antifungal; antimutagenic and antioxidant activities have been reported as well (Nakamura et al. 2001; Takaya et al. 2003). The enhanced nutrient value of fermented foods and beverages is discussed below (see the section on *nono*).

Drinks and Street Fruit

Plate Lunch and other Local Foods typically are accompanied by canned commercial fruit-flavored juices and carbonated drinks, which also are ubiquitous stand-alone snacks. It is so long a stretch that it would be inaccurate to suggest that these beverages have even a remote connection to traditional Hawaiian fruit drinks. Coconut (the milk of which was used for cooking), banana, and mountain apple have no beverage history; moreover, sugarcane extract did not sweeten traditional beverages (see table 3.1). Early fruit introductions following European contact include orange in the 1790s, mango in the 1820s, pumpkin (*Cucurbita* spp., Cucurbitaceae) in the 1840s, and macadamia nut (*Macadamia integrifolia* Maiden & Betche, Proteaceae) and pineapple in the 1880s. Local adoptions of other fruit reflect both immigrant palates and colonial influences such as missionaries, trans-Pacific commerce, development of the agricultural sector, and growth of the tourist industry. Today, only a small fraction of street beverages are made with fresh fruit. The sources of those drinks, as well as street fruit, include home and school gardens, open-air markets and stalls, and, with some luck, arboreta, parks, and hiking trails. Today's popular street fruit include mango, coconut, mountain apple, papaya, pomegranate (*Punica granatum* L., Punicaceae), star fruit (*Averrhoa carambola* L., Oxalidaceae), passion fruit (*Passiflora* spp., Passifloraceae), guava (*Psidium guajava* L., Myrtaceae), avocado, lychee (*Litchi chinensis* Sonn., Sapindaceae), jackfruit (*Artocarpus heterophyllus* Lam., Moraceae), Surinam cherry (*Eugenia uniflora* L., Myrtaceae), tamarind (*Tamarindus indica* L., Fabaceae), and citrus species (family Rutaceae) such as lemon (*Citrus limon* Burm.f.), tangerine (*C. reticulata* Blanco), and pomelo (*C. maxima* Merr.).

A phenomenon related to street fruit is POGs, a game using cardboard milk caps that originated in Hawai'i in the early 1900s and later gained popularity on the U.S. mainland and internationally. The acronym stands for passion-orange-guava, a popular juice bottled by the same dairy (Haleakala Dairy, Maui) that branded its milk as "POG" in the 1970s. POGs were repopularized in the 1990s, when a Honolulu schoolteacher introduced the game to her class; the caps became collectables. The media and market frenzy that ensued fueled mass appeal and commercial circulation of myriad versions of plastic and metal pogs featuring elements of popular culture such as sports, celebrities, and films. Brand extension into clothing, newsletters, and other commodities piggybacked on this phenomenon until the fad waned in the mid-1990s. Earlier, in the domestic arena, families imitated the dairy juice by blending their own combinations of bottled orange, guava, passion fruit, and other juices. Today, syrup-based low-fruit-content versions of these early juices are still popular at parties, picnics, and other informal congregations.

A review of just a few studies underscores the range of pharmacologic activities of local fruit plants, some of which also are used medicinally. Bromelain in pineapple reduces inflammation, fibrinolysis, thrombosis, and edema; it has immunomodulatory activity and is antimetastatic (Maurer 2001). Pomegranate flavonoids are antimicrobial and antioxidant and inhibit cardiovascular disorders, including atherosclerosis (Rosenblat et al. 2006; Seeram et al. 2006); their polyphenols may have chemopreventive and adjuvant therapeutic applications in human breast cancers (Kim et al. 2002). Star fruit is antioxidant (Luximon-Ramma et al. 2003) and inhibits increased plasma glucose by suppressing the decomposition of fats and carbohydrates in the intestine (Arai et al. 1999). Passion fruit is antimicrobial (Agizzio et al. 2003) and has anxiolytic activity (Dhawan et al. 2001). Papaya seeds and fruit extract are antibacterial against common wound microorganisms (Dawkins et al. 2003). Surinam cherry is hypotensive (Consolini et al. 1999) and antimicrobial (de Souza et al. 2004). Tamarind is a good source of zinc; has antioxidant, laxative, and carminative properties; and is active against fungi, bacteria, and schistosomes (Etkin 2006a:appendix). Its enhancement of aspirin bioavailability (Mustapha et al. 1996) suggests additional pharmacologic potential. All these fruits offer the advantage of fresh preparation, low or no fat, and substantial amounts of vitamins, minerals, and fiber: lychee, mango, and papaya have high levels of vitamin A and potassium; all citrus fruit, guava, and papaya are good sources of vitamin C.

Musubi

Musubi is a snack of Japanese origin that traditionally served as journey or lunch food or as an offering for the dead. The early musubi was a ball or flattened triangle of unseasoned or vinegar-flavored rice. In the center might be embedded soy-seasoned tuna, pickled daikon, or pickled *ume* fruit, a sour apricot locally glossed as "plum" (*Prunus mume* Siebold & Zucc., Rosaceae).[2] Later, musubi were fully wrapped or striped with roasted nori seaweed. The simple musubi is affirming in its visual consistency and taste: salty, dark green nori is positioned against bland, white rice, with limited variations in form; ume and other pickles impart a small amount of color and a salty, tart taste. During the early plantation years, hand-formed musubi were made at home and consumed in public during work or while socializing. In later decades, musubi paraphernalia made possible in-home production in larger quantities. Adaptations of sushi culture offered uniformly sized sheets of nori, Plexiglas or wood molds and presses, and bamboo (Poaceae) rolling mats. Expanding into the public domain, musubi were sold from stands and stalls at food fairs and other public events and were popular at social gatherings. In this way, they were transformed from a simple fill-me-for-a-short-time food to a substantive item of positive affect.

The volume of production and consumption increased during the 1980s when technology was developed to automate production of triangular musubi. The most recent commercial iterations offer rolled and triangular musubi for which nori is wrapped in cellophane independent of the rice. Directions on the packaging instruct how to open the still-dry nori and wrap it around the rice. This presentation compounds the snack's appeal by juxtaposing the crisp nori against the moist rice and filling. Today, commercial musubi are available in a wide array of convenience and grocery stores.

Evolving from its modest presentation in Hawai'i plantation culture, and accumulating elements of both historical and contemporary food cultures, musubi has been transformed into a variety of shapes and sizes: bars, spheres, logs, triangles, and cones. *Temaki* (meaning "hand roll") are loosely structured and commonly filled with cucumber and other vegetables, fish, and avocado, the latter a California influence. *Futomaki* logs are about 1.5 inches in diameter and 3 inches long and commonly contain these ingredients: carrot, cucumber, shiitake mushroom (*Lentinula edodes* Sing., Marasmiaceae), the sweet pink codfish powder *oboro*, *kampyo* (bottle gourd, *Lagenaria siceraria* Stand., Cucurbitaceae), and *tamago*, or sweet sushi egg omelet. *Inari*, or cone sushi, is made with vinegared rice stuffed into *aburage* pouches made from oil-fried, fermented soybean curd. Whole musubi of various shapes often are wrapped in nori seaweed; *furikake* (a mixture of toasted sesame seed, flaked seaweed, and MSG) might be mixed into the rice. Over the past few decades, musubi fillings have appeared in larger volume and in combinations and have become even more diverse and substantial. Today's common fillings include crab salad, avocado, ume, pickled vegetables, egg, cucumber, bright yellow daikon, fish roe, salmon, and tuna.

Spam musubi is a local cultural icon in which the "filling," a slice of the tinned pork product, sits atop a rice block and is secured by an inch-wide strip of nori. This configuration retains the structure and clean lines of the musubi. Because of its simplicity, many people assume that Spam musubi has been in existence for a long time, but a loose consensus among people who have given the issue of Spam musubi more thought is that it became popular as late as the 1980s. Another reason that this musubi has been mistakenly aged is an artifact of Spam's long history and ubiquity in the Pacific. In the 1940s, the U.S. military introduced Spam as part of ready-to-eat meals that are fat-, protein-, and calorie-dense; are easily shipped and stored; and have a long shelf life. Environmental, political, and social upheavals created by the circumstances of colonialism and World War II continued into the postwar and contemporary eras. Where traditional protein sources were depleted or became prohibitively expensive for many Pacific peoples, Spam filled culinary niches throughout the region, spanning the Pacific Rim to Hawai'i.

Spam acquired a positive affect among many western Pacific island peoples, for whom it became a metaphor for power. This attitude carried over to Hawai'i, where locals do not associate it with a blue-collar consumer base and are not as ambivalent or negative about Spam as are residents of the U.S. mainland. Spam was first aggressively marketed in the 1930s, when its manufacturer (Hormel), located in Minnesota, drew on the cachet of middle America to promote this "wholesome" food. During World War II, consumption rose as people were encouraged to limit beef consumption as a gauge of their contribution to the war effort, and more than 100 million pounds were provided as military rations in Europe and the Pacific. In the ensuing decades, Spam lost much of its appeal as its affect shifted to simplicity and "innocent-but-hokey pride and patriotism" (Lewis 2000:87). For many Americans, the irony has been revealed: not only is Spam not healthful, it is a caricature of both middle America and poor-quality food. Today, Spam is emblematic of U.S. popular culture. Fueled by irony and an object of derision and jokes, its image sells countless products, ranging from tennis balls to clothing to license plates. The metaphor is no more strongly expressed than in the term for junk e-mail: "spam." Whether or not one eats this street food, Spam musubi spearheads the genre. In Hawai'i, generations of locals re-create its history through memories of their experiences: When did this become my lunch food or after-school snack? When did Auntie begin to make Spam musubi for our family, and later the whole soccer team?

Some contemporary presentations of musubi use "sticky" (glutinous) rice; these may have a multicomponent or singlet filling surrounded with nori, with rice packed around that (and no exterior nori). This inside-out roll, with a parallel in futomaki, is commonly cut into slices, offering the consumer a colorful display that violates the simplicity of the original musubi but not the structure, which is retained in mirror image. More recently, upscale and more creative preparations only approximate the traditional musubi. In many, the filling overshadows the rice. The chef of one of Honolulu's catering businesses, "an architect of musubi mutations" (Shimabukuro 2002) fills a musubi with tuna *poke*—raw fish chunks marinated with seaweed and seasonings such as soy sauce, sesame oil, seaweed, and *kukui* nut (*Aleurites moluccana* Willd., Euphorbiaceae). To this he attaches barbecued beef with a strip of nori; the now very dressy musubi is topped with sliced octopus. Other variations center on caramelized salmon or *mochiko* chicken (deep fried in seasoned rice flour and egg marinade), in which the rice block is slightly smaller than the meat. The transformation to gourmet musubi introduces combinations that infuse noise into what had been a clean food, adds calories and fat, alters the structure, and erodes its character as an affirming, reliable snack. The most recent elaborations of the musubi suggest its mutation into a protein- and calorie-dense food that shares some of the health risks of Plate Lunch; these rich restaurant analogues of the traditional musubi exaggerate what used to be minor health risks.

On a positive note, transmutations of musubi introduce nutritional diversity and pharmacologic complexity. A substantial literature documents antitumor activity for lentinan in shiitake mushroom; cholesterol-lowering, glucose-reducing, and antimicrobial effects are reported as well (Shouji et al. 2000; Hassegawa et al. 2005). Nori is a red macroalga that turns green when toast-processed into the dry sheets used in many foods, including several discussed here. Like all seaweeds, it is a rich source of zinc, calcium, potassium, iodine, and fiber; in addition, it has a higher content of bioavailable vitamin B^{12} than do many other seaweeds (Takenaka et al. 2001; Urbano and Goñi 2002). One of the principal components of nori is porphyran, an acidic, sulfated polysaccharide that stimulates immune function by enhancing antioxidant enzymes and scavenging free radicals (Zhao et al. 2006). It activates macrophages; antiallergy activity is suggested by its inhibition of contact hypersensitivity reactions in mice (Ishihara et al. 2005). It has antitumor activity, is antimutagenic, and prevents chemo-induced hepatocarcinogenesis (Ichihara et al. 1999; García-Solís and Aceves 2005). There is speculation that iodine and selenium, both of which occur in high titers in seaweeds, act synergistically to prevent development of breast cancer (Cann et al. 2000). Musubi commonly are garnished and spiced with the Japanese horseradish, wasabi (*Wasabia japonica* Matsum., Brassicaceae), which is prepared by shredding or grating the rhizome into a green paste that is so strongly pungent and lachrymatory that it is used only in small quantities by first-time or early users, who gradually build tolerance. Even when consumed sparingly, wasabi's strong antimicrobial, anti-inflammatory, and cancer-suppressive actions (Shin et al. 2004) might be realized, as it is ingested regularly with a variety of foods, including sushi and sashimi.

Manapua

These steamed (less commonly, baked) buns are made with lightly sweetened, yeast-raised wheat dough and are filled with vegetables and meats.

Manapua is a Hawaiian term for bun, or Chinese *bao*. Although its etymology is disputed, the most common local understanding is a contraction of *mea ʻono*, "cake" (literally, "delicious thing"), and *puaʻa*, "pork." This snack food also emerged from plantation food culture. The Chinese "Manapua Man" sold from bamboo containers that were balanced by a stick on his shoulders. Later, vendors operated from stalls and mobile trucks.

Like musubi, manapua now are sold in convenience stores and restaurants. They also appear in dedicated bakeries and (fresh or frozen) in grocery stores. The white steamed or golden baked bun that contrasts with the colorful filling is visually appealing. As an example of re- or ultralocalizing foods, some manapua are made with the flour of taro (*Colocasia esculenta* Schott., Araceae), the centerpiece of the creation narrative as the first offspring of Sky Father and Earth Mother. Some vendors distinguish varieties of manapua by dotting the tops with colors that correspond to the different fillings. Over time, manapua increased in size and the fillings expanded to include chicken, turkey, *la chung* (Chinese sweet pork sausage), shrimp, spicy eggplant (*Solanum melongena* L., Solanaceae) and other vegetables, sweetened adzuki bean (*Vigna angularis* Ohwi & Ohashi, Fabaceae), curries, sweet potato, and hot dog. This evolution of fillings is an amalgam of local tastes infused with outside influences and reflects consumers' interest in improvising on what are still physically, structurally, and cognitively familiar and simple items.

Despite its evolution, manapua remains relatively low in calories and fat, and its still typically singlet fillings offer a variety of nutrients. The original preparation of manapua had a filling of marinated, red shredded roast pork, *cha shao*—not "barbecued pork," as this is commonly described. In the lexicon of Cantonese dim sum,[3] manapua would be *cha shao bao*. Cha shao is pork marinated in a mixture of Hoisin sauce,[4] salt, sugar, honey, sesame oil, and Chinese cooking wine. Recipes vary, for example, adding ginger and dark soy sauce or omitting the sugar. The marinade also includes Chinese five-spice powder, a fragrant, pungent, hot, and somewhat sweet composite that is prepared from equal parts of clove, flower pepper, cinnamon, star anise (*Illicium verum* Hook.f., Illiciaceae), and fennel (*Foeniculum vulgare* Miller, Apiaceae).[5] Five-spice powder resonates with the symmetries in ways of knowing the world. The five Chinese tastes have cognates in these five-kind domains: elements, cardinal points, colors, smells, and more. The number five derives from the Taoist concept of five evolutions, or five elements, and has played a key role in Chinese cosmology since antiquity. On the theme of food and medicine, the five smells are fragrant, rancid, scorched, putrid, and rotten; the five tastes are sweet, sour, bitter, salty, and piquant. Constituents of five-kind domains must be carefully balanced, both among themselves and with cognate domains. This assures the consolidation of cooking, medicine, social life, and other activities and brings harmony and balance to the universe to confer symmetry on human circumstances (Anderson 1988).

These five spices are pharmacologically versatile. For example, all are antimicrobial and carminative; cinnamon is antipyretic and antithrombotic; clove is anti-inflammatory and cancer-suppressive; and flower pepper is antioxidant and inhibits tumors (Etkin 2006a:ch. 3, appendix). This range of activities invites speculation about whether and how even the small amount of five-spice present in one cha shao manapua might affect the consumer physiologically.

Traditionally, the red color of cha shao was imparted by polyketide pigments in Chinese red yeast rice, *hong qu mi*, a nonglutinous rice onto which the filamentous fungus *Monascus purpureus* Went (Aspergillaceae) is cultivated. It also colored other foods, for example, wines, red rice vinegar, fish, and pastries. It contributes a subtle, pleasant taste to foods. In much of China and the diaspora today, red food coloring has replaced natural colorants.

Hong qu mi also is a traditional Chinese medicine for improving blood circulation (Ma et al. 2000). In animal models, the polyketide metabolite monacolin K contributes to the total cholesterol-lowering activity of hong qu mi. Monacolin K is a 3-hydroxy-3-methylglutaryl coenzyme A (HMG-CoA) reductase inhibitor that blocks an enzyme involved in cholesterol synthesis. Hong qu mi also reduces triglyceride levels and "bad cholesterol" (low-density lipoprotein [LDL]) and increases "good cholesterol" (high-density lipoprotein [HDL]) (MedlinePlus 2006). The plasma glucose–lowering effect in both diabetic and normal rats is attributed to increased circulating insulin and c-peptide (Chang et al. 2006). In human studies with hong qu mi, total cholesterol, LDL, and triglycerides decreased while HDL increased (Li et al. 1998; Heber et al. 1999; Ma et al. 2000). Another polyketide, citrinin, is bactericidal against gram-positive bacteria but may be nephrotoxic in mammals. Commercial production of hong qu mi selects strains of *M. purpureus* that do not produce citrinin. Hong qu mi also can be prepared in domestic contexts using leftover red rice as a starter culture (Shimizu et al. 2005).

Hong qu mi is produced as whole dry grains, ground powder, or pasteurized wet aggregate. Some (locals report very few) recipe adaptations substitute other natural dyes, such as annatto or cochineal, or commercial dyes. Annatto is produced from the red pulp that surrounds achiote seeds (lipstick tree, *Bixa orellana*). Its traditional uses in South America include flavoring (see chap. 2), food and textile dyes, cosmetics, and medicine. Cochineal is derived from a red scale insect (*Dactylopius coccus* Costa, Dactylopiidae) which shares a mutualistic relationship with prickly pear (*Opuntia* spp., Cactaceae) and was used by the Aztec and Maya as a dye for textiles, as tribute, and for body decoration.

By the end of the eighteenth century, the cochineal trade had come to circle the globe. That little is recorded about the medicinal and food uses of cochineal before the modern era (Donkin 1977) might be an artifact of its playing such a prominent role in early Central American commerce and the imposition by the Spanish of the *repartimiento* colonial credit system. Whereas indigenous Central Americans had been cultivating (primarily foods) for their own consumption, repartimiento encouraged them also to produce *grana cochinilla* for export. Their profits from this trade were part of a complex suite of survival strategies under colonial rule (Baskes 2000). Red carminic acid, with which the insect defends itself against predators, is the essential constituent of the extracted dye (Eisner et al. 1980). Cochineal extract prevents carcinogen-induced DNA damage in experimental animals, enhances IgM production, and is antibacterial, estrogenic, antithrombotic, and immunomodulatory (Kuramoto et al. 1996; Takahashi et al. 2001; Rojas et al. 2006; Etkin 2006a:appendix).

Saimin

The soup-noodle dish *saimin* (the Cantonese term; in Mandarin, this is referred to as *ximian*) was developed in Hawai'i during the plantation era, patterned on Filipino *pancit* (a pan-fried dish), Chinese *mian*, and Japanese *ramen* noodles, with influences from Korean and Hawaiian cuisines. The name compounds the Cantonese words *sai*, "thin," and *mein*, "noodle." The soft wheat noodles contain egg, which makes them crinkle when cooked, and are suspended in hot stock (*dashi*) made from Japanese-style broth prepared with bonito or other fish, dried shrimp or scallops, pork, or chicken. Among the most popular garnishes are scallion tops (*Allium fistulosum* L., Alliaceae), Chinese mustard cabbage (*Brassica juncea* Czern., Brassicaceae), baby bok choy (*B. rapa* L.), Chinese cha shao, steamed fish cake, Spam, egg, dry nori, and Portuguese *linguiça*, which is pork sausage seasoned with onion, garlic, and paprika (*Capsicum annuum* L., Solanaceae). Saimin is an inexpensive, light meal substitute enjoyed at any time of day. It offers in one dish a diversity of food sources and nutrients representing all food groups: meat and fish, egg, grains, and vegetables.

In its earliest form, saimin vending was one of the easiest businesses to start. Everyone knew how to prepare saimin, and little infrastructure was required beyond a pushcart with two burners (one to cook noodles, the other to assemble the saimin ingredients) and permission to park at a street corner, empty lot, or gas station. Saimin began appearing in cookbooks from the 1930s and may be one of the first foods to be characterized as local.

As public food, saimin is available today at fairgrounds, sporting venues, and small shops and stands. In Chinese and other Asian and Southeast Asian cultures, noodles symbolize continuity and longevity. Increasingly, this local comfort food also is available as a healthy alternative in the public schools and in restaurants that grade from modest to high-end. Capitalizing on the popularity of saimin in Hawaiʻi, McDonald's serves its own version of saimin (some locals eschew this), which has become one of the chain's best-selling items. In a similar vein, island outlets of McDonald's and Burger King offer white rice, Portuguese sausage, and Spam with eggs or in croissant and biscuit sandwiches.

Street and Market Foods in Rural Nigeria: "Abincin Hanya da Kasuwa"

Exploration of street foods in a rural context offers interesting parallels to the foregoing, largely urban examples. For this discussion I offer insights from my research on Hausa food and medicine in northern Nigeria, including previously unpublished findings. Since 1975, colleagues and

I have conducted research on traditional medicine (*magani*) and food (*abinci*) in Hurumi (a pseudonym), a rural village southeast of Kano City on the Nigerian savanna. The larger region is the Sahel, the boundary zone between the Sahara Desert to the north and, to the south, the more fertile Sudan area. The Kano Close-Settled Zone comprises dispersed settlements punctuated with urban centers. For hundreds of years, it has been an area of intensive land utilization and high population density. All activities and circumstances are strongly influenced by the sharp seasonality of rainfall (for issues of aridity and water, see chapter 5).

Although changes in infrastructure and connections to the global economy continue to evolve, circumstances in Hurumi fall between traditional and cosmopolitan ends of a modernity continuum. The subsistence base is intensive, primarily nonmechanized agriculture that centers on *dawa*, sorghum; *gero*, millet (*Pennisetum* spp.); *rogo*, cassava (*Manihot esculenta* Crantz, Euphorbiaceae); *gyada*, groundnut; and *wake*, cowpea (*Vigna unguiculata* Walpers, Fabaceae). This production is supplemented by the collecting of wild plants; year-round riverside garden cultivation of foods and medicines such as chile pepper/*barkono*, tomato/*tumatir*, garden egg/*yalo* (*Solanum melongena* L., Solanaceae), and leafy greens/*ganye*; small-scale livestock management; cash-cropping, primarily of groundnuts; and trade in locally produced items such as leather goods and fiber mats (made of Poaceae or Arecaceae species), and in exotic commodities such as medicinal plants and salt. A small percentage of Hurumi residents generate income as Islamic scholars, barbersurgeons, medicine specialists, and traditional birth attendants (see chapter 4). (For details of the methodology and scope of the larger study and the fuller ethnographic context of Hurumi, consult Etkin and Ross 1994, 1997; Ross et al. 1996; and Etkin et al. 1999.)

Compared to urban sites, village layout and infrastructure offer a different, but equally compelling, venue for street foods. Many of the same public foods are sold in the towns and cities of Nigeria, where they compete with a growing array of commercially produced snack foods and beverages. In earlier times, commercial foods accompanied colonial cadres and other expatriates; later they were imported from the West; and today many are produced by Nigerian firms and, through market networks, reach rural villages. The *hanya*, "streets," of Hurumi consist of the open, common spaces in the nucleated village center, as well as narrow

In a public area in Hurumi, the author encounters a group of Hausa women and children. They sit in the shade of a *madaci* tree (African mahogany) and engage in *hira*, or conversation.

lanes that separate *gida,* "compounds," from one another. Vendors position themselves in, or move through, areas of high foot traffic. Hanya include other locations where people come together in leisure or to discuss community affairs, such as in front of the village chief's residence, a shaded area adjacent to the primary well, and several *kasuwa,* "markets," in the vicinity of Hurumi.

As part of Muslim customs, Hausa married women practice *kulle,* "purdah," which is in-home seclusion that deliberately segregates them to avoid the gaze of (unrelated) men, with only occasional ventures out to visit family in the same or neighboring villages. Unmarried, including widowed, adult women are not constrained by kulle but do not socialize outside their own or others' compounds except to exchange brief greetings.[6] The gida interior is the domain of women and includes a discrete sleeping hut, or *daki,* for each adult woman, as well as children's daki, animal shelters, and structures for food storage, preparation, and cooking. Adult men's leisure and business activities occur outside the compound; they do not enter one another's residences except in special circumstances, such as assisting in emergencies or joining ad hoc work teams, for example, to raise a roof. Children of both genders fluidly go between the inside and outside domains, conveying goods and news in both directions. As boys mature, during their early teens they too are restricted from compound interiors other than home. In that transition, girls become the primary conveyance of goods and news until they marry, in their late teens to early twenties.

Gender segregation extends to street foods, of which men and older children are the primary customers, while married women are the preparers and usually only indirect vendors. Purdah nuances street trade to include foods and beverages sold door-to-door, usually by the preparer's children. Some in-compound venues also exist; unmarried women and children can enter these to make direct purchases. Although husbands and children purchase street foods for them, women in purdah eat fewer of these items simply because they are not at the sites of sale. Most of Hurumi's street foods fall under the rubric of *kayan kwadayi* (*kaya* are goods/products, and *kwadayi* connotes keen interest or desire). These include luxuries or delicacies that one eats in small quantities that are insufficient for, but can be part of, a meal (see chapter 4, section on Hausa).

Tsire

Hausa street foods include one meat item, *tsire*, which consists of small pieces of meat, or *nama*, that are skewered, seasoned with the groundnut condiment *karago* (see below), and roasted. This is the only food, including street foods, whose preparation and vending does not include women. Sheep and goats are confined inside compounds during the farming season from early June through September; during the rest of the year, they typically spend only the night inside. Cows, which are owned by only about 10 percent of households, are tethered outside the compound exterior wall. Chickens and guinea fowl wander in and out. Women contribute to animal tending for all livestock inside the compound but do not butcher or dress out larger animals (see chapter 4).

Tsire is prepared with beef, goat, and sheep but not chicken, guinea fowl, or fish. Because the small size of Hurumi's population does not support in-village-only sales, several butchers prepare the skewers and roast tsire prior to walking twenty or thirty minutes to a kasuwa, while other vendors do most of their preparation and roasting at the market. Individual skewers include mixed flesh and organ meats or are organized by and priced according to the meat quality of each stick. Some tsire sellers walk about the market to ply their wares, or *tallata*, while others cluster around a fire where potential customers congregate to socialize. Although much of the tsire is consumed on-site, suggesting that it is a snack whose consumption is gender- and age-limited, it is a commonly requested from-market snack by women.

Beverages in Hurumi

The only traditional street beverage sold in Hurumi is *nono*, a lightly sour fermented cow's milk. Hausa, the traditional sedentary agriculturalists of northern Nigeria and southern Niger, have for generations intermarried and blended cultures with Fulani nomadic cow pastoralists from the Niger-Nigeria region. In Hurumi today, Fulani women from cattle-owning households predominate among milk vendors. In a departure from preparers of other Hurumi street foods, these women also sell in regional markets but otherwise conform to the customs of kulle. Although milk is not a seasonal commodity, more nono is sold during the dry season, when Fulani from farther north in Nigeria and Niger move south to find water and grazing for their cattle. These seasonal migrants swell the ranks of local nono vendors.

Nono is prepared from *madara*, fresh milk to which is added a small amount of *kindirmo*, "curdled milk." Fermentation occurs over one or two days; when fully curdled, the kindirmo is shaken in a capped *buta* (bottle gourd), until *man shanu*, "butter," is separated and floats to the top. Adding water to fermented nono produces *tsala*, a diluted product that also can be used as a fermentation starter. *Kuka*, or baobab fruit pulp (*Adansonia digitata* L., Bombacaceae), is added to improve taste and expand volume (*auki*), and its low pH (3.2) contributes antimicrobial properties to the final product (Bankole and Okagbue 1992). *Malaiduwa*, or grape ivy (*Cissus populnea* Guill. & Perr., Vitaceae), accelerates fermentation but might impart an undesirable slimy (*yauki*) texture. Nono is consumed sparingly as an expensive street beverage. Like the full-fat kindirmo, it also is consumed with porridges and other grain-based foods for celebrations (see chapter 4 for health implications).

Foods Made with Cowpea

Cowpea is the foundation for several Hausa street foods. *Dan wake* (literally, "son of *wake*, or bean") is made from cowpea flour alone or, more commonly, with equal parts of cassava and sorghum flours. Three-quarter-inch balls of flour paste are seasoned with *kanwa*, a culinary sodium carbonate salt; *man gyada*, groundnut oil; *gishiri*, commercial sodium chloride salt; barkono; and crumbled *karago* (see below). *Karkashi*, wild sesame or benniseed (*Sesamum radiatum* Schum. & Thonn., Pedaliaceae) fruit, can be substituted as an alternative source of oil or to vary taste. Dan wake are boiled in water. The portion size is around ten pieces, served in clay or metal bowls that are returned to the vendor when empty.

Alala is made from cowpea flour paste (the beans are first soaked and the seed coat removed) and seasoned with the composite spice *yaji*. Included among *kayan kanshi*, "things that smell good," yaji contains barkono along with *citta maikwaya*, melegueta pepper; *cittar aho*, ginger; *fasakwari*, flower pepper; *kanumfari*, clove; *kimba*, guinea pepper (*Xylopia aethiopica* A. Rich., Annonaceae); *kulla* (*Thonningia sanguinea*

Young Hausa men share freshly prepared *kosai,* or cowpea fritters, in the shade offered by a *Ficus* tree and an outer compound wall made of guinea-corn stalks. Shehu serves himself *kunu,* "gruel," with a calabash spoon.

Vahl., Balanophoraceae); *masoro,* Benin pepper (*Piper guineense* Schum. & Thonn., Piperaceae); and gishiri. Tumatir also may be added to the paste. In its traditional preparation, the alala mixture was poured into four-ounce condensed milk tins lined with *man ja* (oil from the red palm, *Elaeis guineensis* Jacq., Arecaceae), and steamed. Over time, other molds have been substituted, yet cooking still involves steaming and roughly the size and the single-portion serving are the same. For *kosai,* the same cowpea flour paste and seasonings are formed into pieces and deep-fried in groundnut oil to yield 1.5-inch-diameter fritters. These are dusted with gishiri and barkono and are sold in portion sizes of six to eight, served into clients' bowls or ones provided by the vendor.

"Nuts," Roots, Fruit, and Wild Plants

Other Hausa street foods include *aya* (tiger nut, *Cyperus esculentus* L., Cyperaceae) and groundnuts roasted in hot sand or over fire in metal containers. Prior to roasting, aya and gyada might be soaked in salt water, or sugared, and sun-dried. Groundnuts also are roasted and sold in the shell. Aya and gyada are sold in fixed volumes; a typical portion of shelled nuts corresponds to a four-ounce condensed milk tin, from which the nuts are simply transferred to the client's hands. Sliced boiled or roasted cassava is another snack food that is commonly seasoned with barkono and karago (see below). *Dakuwa* cakes are made of roasted and hand- or machine-ground millet, groundnut (about 40 percent each), and tiger nut (20 percent). Water is added to adjust the consistency of the paste, which is formed into 1.5-inch round confections that are flavored with yaji, additional barkono, and sugar or gishiri. The portion size is one or two dakuwa.

Karago is an oil-fried groundnut press cake prepared from lightly roasted groundnuts ground to a paste consistency (called *tunkuza*) and further processed to express most of the oil. The now-more-viscous paste residue is shaped into one-inch spheres that are fried in groundnut oil. These press cakes are sold intact (with three to five cakes per portion) or crumbled to garnish snacks such as dan wake, cassava, and tsire.

Hausa consume *gurjiya* (Bambarra groundnut seeds, *Vigna subterranea* Verdc., Fabaceae), fresh or boiled after drying. The plant is far less abundant than groundnut, whose production as a cash crop has been encouraged since the first decade of the twentieth century, when England established colonial control of Nigeria. Hurumi residents remark on the similar growth form of gyada and gurjiya but are otherwise ambivalent about the latter. There is little understanding of its medicinal potential and nutrient value.[7]

Goro (kola nut, *Cola* spp.) is a common item of sale and exchange in all public spaces and is described in more detail in the next chapter. Hausa street foods also include local seasonal fruits such as *aduwa*, desert date (*Balanites aegyptiaca* Del., Zygophyllaceae); *mangwaro*, mango; *goba*, guava; *gwanda*, papaya; *dabino*, date (*Phoenix dactylifera* L., Arecaceae); *tsamiya*, tamarind; and garden egg, the only fruit among those named here from an herbaceous plant (and not sweet). All trees are owned individually, usually but not necessarily corresponding to ownership of the land on which the tree grows. Yields from most of these generally exceed what the tree owner's family can consume. Although dabino and tsamiya can be dried and have an extended period of saleability, the others have no local tradition for preservation and are sold ripe as

Hausa boys remove red seed coats from roasted groundnuts in preparation for their mother's production of the press cake *karago*. Married women who observe *kulle*, "purdah," typically do not sell products directly, from their compounds or otherwise. These boys vend karago for their mother from in front of the compound entrance and itinerantly through the village.

TABLE 3.3. Terms for semiwild fruit in Hurumi

Vernacular[a]	Taxonomic identification
aduwa, desert date	*Balanites aegyptiaca* Del., Zygophyllaceae
baure, fig	*Ficus* spp., Moraceae
danya, marula	*Sclerocarya birrea* Hochst., Anacardiaceae
giginya, palmyra (fan) palm	*Borassus aethiopum* Mart., Arecaceae
kokiya, monkey orange	*Strychnos spinosa* Lam., Loganiaceae
kurna, Christ's thorn	*Ziziphus spina-christi* Willd., Rhamnaceae
tamba, finger millet	*Eleusine corocana* Gaertn., Poaceae
zaki banza, spiny amaranth	*Amaranthus spinosus* L., Amaranthaceae

Source: Adapted from Etkin and Ross 1994, which contains a full list of sixty-one semiwild medicinal food plants.

[a] The first term is in Hausa; the second is in English.

street foods. Because these fruits ripen synchronously and are perishable, their sale does not yield much profit.

Over the past two decades, producers of commercial canned chutneys and pickles have been approaching tree owners, primarily owners of mango trees, to secure purchase of the entire green or ripe harvest. These buyers-on-speculation are from urban centers such as Kano, where chutneys and related condiments are popular among people who migrated from or trace ancestry to the Indo-Pakistani subcontinent. Rural Hausa are not familiar with these condiments and regard full-tree and, remarkably, green harvest as peculiar. Although more lucrative than selling individual ripe fruit, futures purchase of anticipated yield is not part of the Hausa trade aesthetic. It cancels people's anticipation of certain seasonal fruit and likely has an impact on the availability of nutrients provided by those species.

Wild foods (see chapter 1) are not vended and are regarded as *abincin yara*, "children's foods." Groups of boys and girls consume these items opportunistically at the site of collection while at play or walking between home and school or market. These wild foods include several species of birds, which are cooked and shared on the spot, as well as the fruit of species itemized in table 3.3, some of which (e.g., *tamba, zaki banza*) also are cooked.

The Nutritional and Pharmacologic Potential
of Hausa Street Foods

Hurumi's street foods are protein- and calorie-dense and provide nutritional breadth. Their consumption includes significant potential for physiologic action. Cowpea and groundnut are high-protein legumes that the Hausa regard as healthy because they influence the quality and circulation of blood (*jini*). Cowpea increases blood flow (*karin jini*) and treats anemia (*fara*), which is linked to several symptom complexes of varied and overlapping etiology that can phase into one another. These complexes cohere around anemia, fatigue, wasting, comorbidities, and failure to thrive: *shawara*, *bayamma*, and *mayankwaniya* are the primary complexes and are grave concerns for young children (see chapter 4). Wake is also part of composite medicines that encourage disease egress to treat *maruru*, abscesses; *rauni*, wounds; and *kaluluwa*, axillary or inguinal lymph gland inflammation that occurs in the presence of an infected lesion on the proximal limb. These medicines might take advantage of the antiviral and antifungal proteins in cowpea seed (Ye et al. 2000). The strengthening food value of wake is reflected in its use for *maganin karfi* (a preventive medicine against arrow and gunshot) and for *sammu* (sorcery). Groundnut treats blood stasis, which is consistent with Hausa understandings of disease etiologies that include accumulations of bodily substances such as blood and phlegm (*majina*). The stilbene resveratrol is a defensive allelochemical in gyada, produced in response to fungal challenge. It diminishes risk of cardiovascular disease by mediating platelet aggregation and lipoprotein metabolism, and it is antioxidant and antimutagenic (Nepote et al. 2004; Yen et al. 2005). Flavonoids in *Vigna* species have cardioprotective, cancer-suppressive, and antioxidant activities (Lattanzio et al. 2000).

Benniseed also contributes to nutrient and pharmacologic potential. It contains high levels of protein and potassium; in addition, aqueous extracts are hypotensive, acting via cholinergic receptors to effect vasorelaxation and cardiodepression (Oshodi et al. 1999; André et al. 2006). Hausa take literal advantage of its yauki texture for other foods such as *miya*, or soup; to facilitate *nakuda*, or difficult childbirth; and in complex medicines for *farin jini* (literally, "white blood"), or popularity, the essence of which extends to domains of interpersonal and business relations.

Red palm oil is rich in carotenoids; vitamin E (primarily tocotrienol) accounts for cholesterol-lowering, anticancer, antioxidant, and antiatherogenic effects (Sundram et al. 2003). Danya and kuka contain high levels of vitamin C and iron (Eromosele et al. 1991); malaiduwa demonstrates anti-sickling activity in individuals with hemoglobin S (Moody et al. 2003). Tiger nut is rich in starch, oil, and sugars and is cholesterol-free. The antimalarial and antimicrobial sesquiterpenoids (Thebtaranonth et al. 1995; Ohira et al. 1998) in aya are consistent with the common use of this aromatic plant against spirit-caused illness. Like other fermented foods and beverages, nono improves constituent availability, adds vitamins and amino acids, preserves milk, and is antimicrobial (Etkin 2006a:ch. 4).

The individual components of yaji as well as their synergies are anti-inflammatory, antimicrobial, carminative, antioxidant, and vitamin-rich (Etkin 2006a:ch. 3, appendix). Hausa fruits offer soluble fiber and various micronutrients and physiologic activities. Mango is analgesic, antioxidant, immunomodulatory, anti-inflammatory, and high in vitamin A (Garrido et al. 2005); guava is antimicrobial, antioxidant, and antidiarrheal (Martínez et al. 1997; Qian and Nihorimbere 2004); date is antioxidant and antimutagenic (Vayalil 2002); and yalo is hypolipidemic and antioxidant (Sudheesh et al. 1997, 1999).

Wild species generally expand the range of available nutrients and increase the likelihood of consumption of pharmacodynamic constituents, many of which have been eliminated from cultigens through domestication (Etkin 1994a, 1994b, 2002). Aduwa has cytostatic constituents (Pettit et al. 1991), danya is antidiarrheal and antioxidant (Braca et al. 2003), baure is antimicrobial (Ogungbamila et al. 1997), kokiya has anti-tryposomal constituents (Hoet et al. 2006), giginya and zaki banza are anti-inflammatory (Santetropicale 2003; Olajide et al. 2004), and kurna is antidiarrheal and hypoglycemic (Glombitza et al. 1994; Adzu et al. 2003). The dietary and medicinal meanings of Hausa street foods, and their pharmacologic potential, are amplified on in chapter 4.

Logically, individuals from wealthier residential units have more diverse and nutritionally sound diets. From the perspective of society and political economy, it is interesting to note that consumption of Hausa street foods can contribute to nutritional differences among children within the same compound. The household head (*mai gida*) is the patriarch; he superintends his wife or wives (*mata*) and children (*yara*). The domestic units of mai gida's married sons also are under his physical and social jurisdiction but constitute semidiscrete entities of people who "eat from the same pot." Daily food preparation responsibilities rotate among co-wives, commonly in three-day sequences. Every husband is responsible for feeding (and clothing, gifting, and educating) all his wives and children equally, including the three daily meals—morning, midday, and evening—and snacks. Women, who do not share these obligations, typically use their personal reserves only for their own children, commonly to expand and improve children's nutrition. Street foods and other between-meal kayan kwadayi are typical supplements for children's foodways. This fosters the potential for, and sometimes the reality of, nutritional differentials among children living within the same compound: children of mothers who are wealthier in their own right are more likely to be nutrient healthy.

Street Foods and Health

A Way Forward?

Despite their important role in the diets of many people, street foods and beverages are commonly ignored in diet surveys at all levels—national, regional, local. Failure to take into account street food and beverage consumption reflects, in part, their great variety, but it ignores what is increasingly an important proportion of daily consumption. Worldwide, these foods represent a significant proportion of aggregate annual incomes, and the percentage of labor forces involved in these microenterprises is sizeable. The U.S. Department of Agriculture (USDA 2006) reports that foods eaten outside the home—including street foods—tend to be fat-, cholesterol-, and sodium-dense with low fiber, vitamin, and mineral content, but the foods that are so characterized are not specified. The conflation of street foods with fast foods implies the nutrient deficits of the latter, whereas careful observation of consumption and content, as outlined above, reveals numerous benefits of street foods. From an economic perspective, the street-food sector is complex and large and offers income-generating opportunities. Infrastructure, start-up and managing costs, and training to the profession all are modest investments. Earnings can contribute to individual and family health via improved access to nutritionally diverse and pharmacologically active foods as well as income for health care and other resources.

Because of the enormous variety and complex mix of ingredients in street foods, it is difficult to say much about the nutrient potential of street foods. The few studies that have systematically documented street foods reveal their variety: more than two hundred items in Bogor, Indonesia, and in Iloilo, Philippines; more than three hundred in Ife-Ife, Nigeria, and in Chonburi, Thailand (Tinker 1997). One can generalize the category to highlight fresh ingredients prepared in relatively small batches; additionally, the versatility of sources and preparations translates into nutrient diversity. The foods and beverages itemized for Greece, New York, and Mexico provide, particularly for lower-income people, good-quality animal protein; omega-3 and omega-6 fatty acids in fish and seafood; a wide range of phytochemicals in vegetables and seasonings; antioxidants and vitamins in fruit and fruit juices; and significant sources of protein, energy, calcium, and fiber (Simopoulos and Bhat 2000). In Bogor, inexpensive meals provide almost 50 percent of daily protein and calorie needs and more than 50 percent of iron and vitamins A and C (Tinker 1997). Typically cuisines, or at least their central elements and food behaviors, are transported to new places; national cuisines historically have been very stable. In the home, familiar foods offer comfort and continuity: "the immigrant's refrigerator is the very last place to look for signs of assimilation" (Pollan 2006:295). Street foods that are marketed in mixed-ethnicity neighborhoods publicize and further cement identity in the diaspora. Indirectly, and immeasurably, this contributes to health through emotional well-being.

Risk Assessment

International, local governmental, and NGO entities concerned with the safety of street foods tend to focus on microbial and other contamination and perishability, on the theory that risk permeates open-air environments, where potable water, refrigeration, refuse collection, and other infrastructure might be inadequate. Common foodborne pathogens represent a broad spectrum and include *Escherichia coli*, *Salmonella*, *Listeria*, hepatitis A, *Shigella, Staphylococcus, Clostridium botulinum*, and *Bacillus cereus* (FDA 2007). In many cases, outbreaks of acute gastrointestinal disorders attributed to public foods have not been investigated with sufficient epidemiological rigor to identify the source of microorganism infection (e.g., Mensah et al. 2002). In fact, research demonstrates that, despite theoretical risk, the incidence of street food contamination is low—not higher than in restaurant foods (Tinker 1997; Umoh and Odoba 1999; Simopoulos and Bhat 2000). Studies that report contamination by listing the microorganisms isolated from foods or their places of preparation and sale leave out the important datum of contaminant titers, including what levels of particular microorganisms are tolerable. In other words, the very presence of pathogenic microorganisms does not necessarily constitute risk. Regulation thresholds established by the Food and Drug Administration and analogous entities elsewhere vary and should be established in species- and context-specific circumstances rather than painting all street foods with the same brush of contamination. For example, Cardinale and colleagues (2005) tested street-vending sites and foods in Dakar, Senegal, and reported that 20 percent of 148 sites and 10 percent of the poultry dishes sampled contained *Salmonella* species, one of the most common causes worldwide of gastrointestinal disorders. Given its prevalence, the presence of *Salmonella* does not surprise, but the authors have not established relative titers of the microorganism or levels of risk.

The safety of street foods is supported by anecdotal accounts and the experiences of seasoned travelers, anthropologists, and others who conduct research in urban and remote field settings. Fearless eaters stress that it is typically easier to monitor the preparation and further handling of street foods and beverages than their restaurant counterparts. The assumption that developing world peoples know less about food and beverage spoilage is illogical; a lack of refrigeration, expensive cooking fuels, and inadequate water supplies all contribute to high vigilance of something so critical to well-being as food and drink. In small communities, it is generally common knowledge whose food handling does not conform to local understandings of hygiene, which in most locations are very similar to those in the West. Reputation goes a long distance in influencing which vendors will continue to have a clientele. A general strategy to apply in selecting food vendors is to patronize establishments that are popular among locals, where turnover is rapid, and where one can observe how foods and beverages are handled. There is an unsubstantiated assumption that in the developing world, street foods are a relatively new phenomenon, an artifact of urbanization that contributes to poor knowledge of food safety. To the contrary, as the Hausa example illustrates, rural peoples have their own versions of street comestibles; moreover, rural and urban populations both have centuries of experience with the proper handling of foods and beverages, street and otherwise. Public foods are a vibrant, not ephemeral, sector of local economies. Further, regulatory entities have not paid much attention to what specifically is contained in these diverse foods and beverages, how they are prepared and stored, and their nutrient value and pharmacologic potential. It is not productive to generalize this category out of context.

Fortification

Food fortification is a common means of uniformly and inexpensively delivering micronutrients (e.g., iron, iodine, vitamins) to target and to general populations; it has been used successfully in developed and developing countries to improve health from both preventive and therapeutic perspectives. Street foods have not been included among the many items that serve as vehicles for fortification, however. Beginning a decade ago, many health and nutrition entities seized on the importance of street foods to consider them as vehicles for nutrient fortification. The rationale is that these foods are available, inexpensive, integral to diet, and consumed regularly across all social strata, especially by lower-income individuals, including children (Green et al. 2005; Haas and Miller 2006).

Recommendations include programs that would identify commonly consumed street foods in culture-specific contexts and consider fortification according to a denotation that conflates the United Nations Food and Agriculture Organization's (FAO) definitions of "fortification" (adding a nutrient to a food item that does not ordinarily contain that nutrient) with "supplementation" (increasing the amount of a nutrient to a significant level) (FAO 2007). Fortification may be ingredient- or food-based. The feasibility of fortifying public foods is challenged by the complexity of street food sectors, their variable cultural constructions, and the diversity of street foods and beverages in any given location. Note that these proposed fortifications apply across a spectrum of food and beverage categories, which contrasts with the U.S. government- and industry-supported fortification of milk (see chapter 1, section on lactose intolerance).

An exception to the received wisdom on the importance and safety of street foods is the work of Tinker (1997:3), who founded the Equity Policy Center (EPOC), a think tank based in Washington, D.C., to study improving street vendors' incomes and the safety of their products, with a special focus on the asymmetrical impact of development on women. EPOC studies have influenced the FAO to conduct its own research on street foods, to stand back from earlier efforts to enforce "unrealistically high food safety standards" (Tinker 1997:4) for street vendors, and to document the trade and identify the most serious health issues that might be addressed by municipal governments. EPOC and FAO studies contribute to our understanding of (micro)regional variations in street foods and beverages and emphasize how important for these microenterprises is the role of water in both preventing contamination and spreading disease (see chapter 5). An important practical outcome of EPOC's work is insight into how vendors' and government efforts can intersect, including the establishment of street food vendors' associations.

Conclusion

How shall we better understand street foods and beverages from the perspectives of their physiologic implications, cultural constructions, and meaning-generating contributions to cuisines? Inattention and generalizing have not been instructive. More-systematic and otherwise rigorous research might explore, from very local perspectives, the physiologic, demographic, and economic implications of public food vending and consumption. How do these foods influence diet quality, and how do they impact the larger context of cuisine and health? To what extent, and to what specific end, should public foods be regulated? How practical are suggestions that these foods be fortified or otherwise serve as vehicles for improving diet diversity and nutritional health? Much research remains to be conducted on these important everyday elements of diet in the developed and developing world.

CHAPTER 4

Foods and Beverages of Occasion, Circumstance, and Ceremony

This chapter is devoted to consumables that mark occasions joyful and sad, sacred and secular, routine and transformative. All evoke expectations for items that are specified by both mode of preparation and presentation, and all have physiologic as well as meaning-centered implications. Rather than single events, ceremonies typically are streams of occasion that offer opportunities to include diverse foods and beverages. In the discussion that follows, the primary focus is on the foods themselves; ritual and celebratory customs provide context. The caffeinated beverages coffee, cacao, and tea are also used in religious and other ceremonial contexts (see chapter 2).

Some foods of occasion—such as eggs, meat, blood, grain, honey, fruit, and alcoholic beverages—have near-universal significance. Eggs and meat specifically have been the subject of extensive study that overlaps folklore, religion, and ritual. Geese and other birds that lay golden eggs are common throughout European and African folklore. The Hausa *fufunda* story, for example (which may have been borrowed and transformed from an Arabic tale), starts with a king who sent Ataru, a poor man, to learn where the sun originates. He set off on a horse and after one month reached *kasan babba da jaka* (*kasan*, "the place of"; *babba*, "large ones with"; *jaka*, "pouch"), the land of the storks, who recognized him and gave him directions through a place where a river of silver flowed. Finally, he reached a large tamarind tree, where he saw the fufunda, Sarkin Tsuntsu—the king of birds—who, after creating the world, sat on his one egg, which will not hatch until the last day of the living. Reputable people will come under its shadow, while the morally repugnant will only see the shadow and be scorched by the sun (Tremearne 1970).

In centuries past, divination customs (including ovamancy, ooscopy, and oomantia) employed eggs, often at times of transition such as the new year, at Halloween (when spirits walked), and when seasons shifted. Meaning emerged from patterns created by breaking eggs into water, watching how white and yolk flow across hard surfaces, and many other iterations. Chicken and duck eggs are central images in Chinese folk religions. Simoons (1991) described two forms of egg divination in ancient and modern customs. In one instance, the egg is drawn upon, blackened, or painted and subsequently boiled or roasted. Meaning is interpreted from patterns in how the shell cracks or in the appearance of the yolk and white after the shell is removed and the egg cut. In other practices, the egg is thrown; predictions depend on whether the shell shatters and where the egg lands.

Eggs figure prominently in origin narratives worldwide and are key metaphors in traditional customs of renewal. For example, early Greeks described the universe as a formless, chaotic egg. In Macedonia and Serbia, colored Easter eggs are buried in vineyards to encourage good harvests, while in Slovakia, eggs are mixed with seed wheat and an egg is rolled across the newly seeded field to encourage growth (Newall 1971) (see explanations of seder and Naw Ruz eggs, below).

In China, eggs are part of the ceremonial bath for brides and are later shared among the wedding guests. For many occasions, eggs are dyed red, which symbolizes happiness, good fortune, and protection against spirits; at engagement and wedding occasions, they are gifts or part of the wedding feast. Two red eggs are moved across a bride's bodice and into her lap to encourage fertility. White or red eggs are given to a newborn and the baby's mother and are placed in the water of the newborn's first bath. Hard-cooked eggs also are gifts for these and other life-cycle transitions. White eggs carry the wish that the child will reach an advanced age and have white hair. Chinese preserved eggs are extraordinary in appearance, taste, smell, and texture. Most are conserved by salting: eggs are soaked in brine for twenty to forty days (or are brined for one week), then are coated with an earth-salt-chaff mixture to prevent them from sticking together, placed in a large earthenware jar, and rearranged every three days for fifteen days; the jar is sealed for another thirty days. Although these eggs are called "thousand-year-old," "Ming dynasty," or "one hundred-year-old," the duration of preservation is typically measured in months (Simoons 1991).

For most of the world's people, meat is a highly valued food but is not consumed in the same amounts as plant foods, in part because hunting and producing meat are more expensive in time, labor, and land and, in the case of hunting, not as reliable in results (see chapter 1). These circumstances justify reserving meat, or the best cuts, for the elite and for marking special occasions. Meat is also the only single class of food that is commonly proscribed by certain cultures and religions. Those taboos might reflect the emotional and closer physical relationships that people have with animals, compared to plants. Pork is proscribed by Seventh Day Adventist, Jewish, Ethiopian Orthodox, Hindu, and Muslim peoples, although this prohibition is irregularly enforced among some groups. Temporary food avoidances intersect fasting customs, the most important of which in medieval Christianity was Lent, during which period (between Ash Wednesday and Holy Saturday) meat and other animal products were disallowed. Fridays, Ember Days, and other occasions also were marked by meat proscriptions (den Hartog 2003).

While eggs, meat, and other universals are rich in imagery, they also affect us physiologically by providing concentrated nutrients—protein, fat, vitamins—which in some cases contribute to, or are the foundation of, their meanings. (The physiologic implications of honey consumption are described later in this chapter.) In some ways, alcoholic beverages are an exception among these nutrient-rich universals: their detrimental effects have been amply documented. But in traditional contexts, these beverages are produced in relatively small volumes at the household level and have low ethanol and relatively high nutrient values. For example, traditional beers produced by contemporary populations contain only 1–2 percent ethanol, unsprouted grains, and natural sugars. Since the popularization of the "French paradox" in the early 1990s, alcoholic beverages (wines, at least) have become associated with heart health. The phytoalexin resveratrol, which is abundantly present in grape skin and seeds (produced in response to fungal infection), has a broad spectrum of pleiotropic physiologic effects, including anticancer activity, slowed senescence, and kidney-, brain-, and heart-protective actions. It improves post-ischemic indices of myocardial function; this is in part explained by its antioxidant properties, although it has no effect on pre-ischemic heart function (Mokni et al. 2006; Goh et al. 2007). Whereas I understand some lay incentive to claim "healthful" properties for alcoholic beverages, the continued focus of bioscientific research on resveratrol in wine strikes me as a twisted logic, since this phytochemical also occurs in *non*fermented grapes, other berries (e.g., blue-, sparkle-, and cranberries; *Vaccinium* spp., Ericaceae), groundnuts, and other foods.

Food in Celebration and Devotion

Throughout this book, I examine ways in which meaning-centered behaviors both impact and are informed by physiologic processes: this is particularly evident in the case of foods and beverages of celebration and devotion. Foods of association are versatile and powerful vehicles for the construction of community. Some circumstances of their consumption are integrative, democratizing participants who eat and drink the same things at the same time. Items of commemoration also can be constructed around asymmetries, for example, when elevated status is conferred on the convener or on other consumers in order of their rank.

Feasting customs are an interesting theme in historical and contemporary foods of occasion. Contributors to Dietler and Hayden's *Feasts* (2001) demonstrate that feasts are "extremely widespread, if not universal; . . . extremely persistent, probably dating back to the Upper Paleolithic, if not before; and . . . in many instances require years of preparation and surplus accumulation, extending even into future, debt-ridden years due to the deficit of financing feasts" (Hayden 2001:25). Feasts are discussed as occasions for alliance, means by which to mediate political and social status, vehicles for redistributing resources, occasions for labor mobilization and exploitation, and contexts for ritual and symbolism. Although the contributors employ different definitions of feasting (for example, varying in the number and hierarchy of participants), the collective perspective of this volume underscores the magnitude of accumulations and consumption. The discussion that follows includes feasts but concentrates on more-modest customs that occur on smaller scales and with more regularity.

Some foods and beverages are regarded to be sacred because of intrinsic characteristics. For example, in Brazilian Candomblé, fish are consecrated by virtue of their connection to Iemanja, goddess of the sea. Throughout Central and South America, *santo grasia nal*, "sanctified and compassionate maize," is a gift from the gods and a key element in creation narratives. Rather than recognizing intrinsic qualities, other religious customs sacralize ordinary foods and beverages, and those who eat them. In some cases, foods and beverages are marked linguistically with special spellings or inflections, or mundane items of consumption are designated as holy for the duration of a particular practice. In Christian traditions, for example, bread and wine become the body and blood of Christ, sacralized for the duration of a weekly worship service or religious observance. The disassemblage of the whole into parts consumed by individuals in the group aggregates the collective.

The seder (meaning "order," referring to the way in which foods are arrayed in a fixed order of service) is a ritually sequenced meal at the end of the eight-day Jewish Passover, which commemorates and re-teaches the Israelites' flight from Egypt. The otherwise common foods that are marked for this occasion include unleavened bread, representing the haste with which the Israelites fled, with no time to allow bread to rise; bitter herbs, commonly horseradish or chicory (*Cichorium intybus* L., Asteraceae), to remind participants in the meal of the bitter times of slavery; a green vegetable such as parsley, marking new growth, that is dipped in salt water representing tears; a roasted whole egg, serving as a metaphor for offerings brought to temple festivals in early days, as well as being iconic of the cycle of life; a lamb bone, symbolizing animals sacrificed by the slaves before their flight; a fruit and nut paste, connoting the mortar the Israelites used in building the Egyptian pyramids; and wine. A symmetry with the injunction that bread must be unleavened is the prohibition against foods made with spelt (common bread wheat, *Triticum aestivum* L., Poaceae), wheat, rye, barley, and oats that have been in contact with water after harvest, which could start the fermentation process (Davidson 1999; Kirshenblatt-Gimblett 2003).

An underlying principle for gifting deities is that offerings should be enhanced in volume or embellished in variety and presentation. In Bali, women construct large and elaborate fruit and flower arrangements in baskets that they carry to temples. For Greek Orthodox Easter, *prosforon* (offering breads that are a yard wide and circular) are baked in village homes, decorated with marigolds (*Tagetes* spp., Asteraceae) and other flowers, and carried by procession to the monastery.

In insular Southeast Asia, women are responsible for the daily task of cooking, but men prepare religious and other festival foods, following conventions that are different from ordinary cooking and knowledge of which is kept secret. Similarly, among the Iteso of Kenya, for whom *roasted* meat is the centerpiece of religious feasts, men are responsible for its preparation, *outside* the residence. Otherwise, cooking is the domain of women, who *boil* meats, *inside* cooking houses (Kochilas 2001; Luard 2001). This gendered and sited cooking of meat and other special foods is a metaphor for social relations in many cultures, including Hausa in Hurumi. Tsire (see chapter 3) and other roasted meats are prepared by men outside the compound, in public domains such as the village commons and at markets, while women cook foods, including soup meat, in pots suspended over hearths, inside the compound. Some cooking in Hurumi is further interiorized within cooking huts, which are dedicated, rain- and animal-protected discrete units within the larger compound. Public/private and exterior/interior metaphors also mark the preparation of meat for women during postpartum (see section on *mai jego*, below).

For Christians, Easter marks the resurrection of Christ and coincides with the beginning of spring, which invokes birth and renewal. Like other Christian celebrations, this holiday incorporates some folk religious elements, including eggs and breads inscribed with or contoured as metaphors such as crosses, fish, lamb, and circles or cylinders (signaling continuity, god's eternity, and regeneration). The French bake *agnaeu pascal*, "Easter lamb," biscuits in the shape of a recumbent lamb, with a meringue topping that resembles wool. In Greece, *lambrópsomo* is an egg-rich bread whose surface is shaped into flowers or leaves and is decorated with red eggs, signifying both the blood of Christ and the rebirth of flora and fauna; clover-shaped breads evoke the Trinity. Germany's *osterkarpfen* is a fish-shaped loaf topped with almonds that resemble scales. *Colomba*, "dove" (representing the holy spirit), is an Italian bird-shaped bread topped with sugar, while *pignola* bread includes raisins, lemon zest, pine nut (*Pinus* spp., Pinaceae), and candied orange peel. Baking in a milk pail ensures a round shape for *pääsiäisleipä*, a Finnish wheat bread enriched with butter, eggs, and cream and flavored with raisin, almond, cardamom (*Elettaria cardamomum* Maton, Zingiberaceae), and lemon zest. For Easter, Russian Orthodox priests bless *yaichki* (chicken eggs) and *kulichi* (tall, cylindrical yeast cakes made with raisins and walnuts), which women wrap in white napkins and carry to the church. After mass, people return home with family and friends to a feast that begins with vodka and abundant *zakuski* (appetizers) and ends with kulich and *paskha*, a molded cake made with *tvarog* (milk curd), flavored with sugar, raisin, and almond (the term *paskha* also denotes Easter). In between the appetizers and sweets, many dishes are served, including these traditional signatures of Russian cuisines: *holupky*, meat- and rice-stuffed cabbage leaves; *kuritsa*, chicken; *buzhenina*, pork loin; and *kasha*, buckwheat (Davidson 1999; Yoder 2003).

The Buddhist precept *gongyang* connotes providing valued foods or goods to Buddha and priests, for veneration of the deceased and other religious customs. The offering ceremony is followed by *balugongyang*, meals for the nuns and monks. *Balu* is a nested set of four wooden bowls. The largest is for *bab*, boiled rice; the second largest holds *guk*, soup; the third is for water; and the smallest is for side dishes. Typical temple foods include *muguk*, white radish (daikon) soup; *neulgeun-hobak guk*, pumpkin soup; *twigin dubu jorim*, fried soybean curd; *gaji jim*, steamed eggplant; *gochu bugak*, unripe chile pepper fried with glutinous rice; *yachae bokkeum*, fried mixed vegetables; *okjamhwa twigim*, fried hosta flower (fragrant plantain lily, *Hosta plantaginea* Asch., Liliaceae); and *u-eong*, burdock kimchi (*Arctium lappa* L., Asteraceae). Five pungents—asafetida (*Ferula asafoetida* L., Apiaceae), onion, leek (*Allium ampeloprasum* L., Liliaceae), garlic, and chive (*A. schoenoprasum* L.)—are avoided because they diminish serenity.

One of the temple dishes of southern India that is sacralized for the god Vishnu is *ven pongol*, a casserole made of rice and mung bean (*Vigna radiata* Wilczek, Fabaceae) flavored with cumin, ginger, black pepper, and cashew nut (*Anacardium occidentale* L., Anacardiaceae). In northern India, pilgrims eat a souplike version, *kichdee* (Lee 2002; Banerji 2007).

Calendrical Occasions

In India, the many deities of the Hindu pantheon are celebrated with feast days that intercalate with thirteen harvest celebrations. During the monsoon season, the festival of Rathajatra celebrates a journey undertaken by Jagannath (a compassionate iteration of Krishna) to recover from monsoon fever (e.g., malaria, dengue). A suitable festival food for the rainy season is eggplant fritter accompanied by *khichuri*, a dish of rice cooked with *dahl* (pulses, commonly lentil, chickpea, and mung bean). At the end of the monsoon season, when most of India's rice has been harvested, temples mark the Kanu festival with pilaf (rice browned in oil and cooked in a seasoned broth) prepared with tamarind and nuts, the constituents signaling four aspects of the deity: soft, bland, sharp, and strong. Eager to attract worshipers, whose presence pleases the deities, Hindu temples offer pilgrims beverages and foods that are both nourishing and appetizing. One of the most common Hindu temple offerings is coconut, a fruit of the gods. The ingredients and preparation of *prasad*, "temple food," vary seasonally. They are further adjusted to coordinate with the *dosha*, "life forces," following Ayurvedic principles that balance three food categories (fortifying, stimulating, and calming), six qualities (cold, hot, heavy, light, oily, and dry), and six tastes (pungent, bitter, astringent, salty, sour, and sweet). At the end of fall when all the pulses have been harvested, temple cooks offer *shondal*, a dish of chickpea seasoned with lemon, sesame, chile, asafetida, coconut, and coriander (Luard 2001; Flood 1996).

In Oaxaca, Mexico, before a field was planted, the farmer buried in its center a plate of tortillas, tamales, and other foods glazed with turkey blood. Afterward, women combined chocolate, tomato, and chile into a *mole* sauce for a stew that was shared by the community. Fiesta de los Elotes (the term *elotes* denotes green maize) was celebrated in October, when hundreds of ears were harvested and relatives and friends were given two cooked ears each to eat with chile and salt. Other customary fiesta foods include *chiles en nogada*, meat- and fruit-stuffed mild chile peppers topped with walnut sauce; *bacalao*, codfish stew; tamales and tacos in all their guises (see chapter 3); and various *mole* dishes. The first appearance of the Virgen de Guadalupe, Mexico's patron saint, is marked on December 12, when pilgrims visit her shrine, La Basilica de Guadalupe, outside Mexico City. In the shrine's atrium, women cook gorditas, maize snacks two inches in diameter, and sell them wrapped in colorful paper (Luard 2001; Long-Solís and Vargas 2005).

Mediterranean calendrical traditions include villagewide sharing of fresh milk products after lambing season in November. In communities of southern Greece, *galopita* (milk custard) is baked for Christmas and the new year, and milk is distributed by shepherds to friends and relatives who do not have their own flocks. Rice festivals in Japan are timed to coincide with planting or harvest and typically feature *kagami mochi* (sweet cakes made with pounded glutinous rice) and *sake* (rice wine).

Celebratory foods for the new year include *zoni* (rice soup) and kagami mochi topped with *dai fdai* (mandarin orange, *Citrus reticulata* Blanco, Rutaceae), which connotes long life. Mochi also is made at Shinto temples, where it is offered to the deities and distributed among worshipers (Richie 1985; Kochilas 2001; Long-Solís and Vargas 2005).

In the Champagne region of France, the grape harvesters' feast centers on *choucroute de vignerons*, nominally sauerkraut but literally larded with many cuts and kinds of pork. One recipe that calls for four cups of sauerkraut further specifies four slices of pork fat, one knuckle, eight slices of ham, eight large frankfurters, a large garlic sausage, and eight tablespoons of lard (Luard 2001), inviting speculation about the historical significance of pigs in this region, the symbolism of the denominator four, and cardiovascular health.

In Norway, feasts that signal the first catch of codfish center on the signature dish *skrei-molje*, a stew of cod in seawater fortified with cream and potatoes. Similarly, Russian ports on the Black Sea celebrate first-catch with—for those who can afford it—*ikra s blini*, or salmon roe (caviar) served with yeast-flour crepes and garnished with *smetana* (sour cream). In Amsterdam, the feast centers on raw *groene harıng*, "green herring," seasoned with onion. China's dragon-boat festival ensures fishermen's safety through consumption of meat, lotus seed (*Nelumbo* spp., Nelumbonaceae), date, water chestnut (*Trapa* spp., Trapaceae), and *zongzi*, which are glutinous-rice dumplings wrapped in bamboo or reed leaves (Poaceae) and filled with red bean (Luard 2001).

Naw Ruz, "new day," starts the Iranian year at the spring equinox (the third week of March). The festival table is set with *haft sin*, seven dishes that contain the seven sacred essences symbolizing the seven spirits who watch over humans: birth, health, life, happiness, light, beauty, and prosperity. All the dish names begin with the Persian letter *sin* ("s") (*haft sin* means "the seven s's"): *sabze*, a mixture of aromatic sprouted herbs that represent the world returning to life; *samanu*, a sprouted wheat confection that symbolizes regeneration; *seeb*, "apple," a symbol of life on earth; *seer*, "garlic," which protects against evil; *senjed*, which denotes either "jujube" (*Ziziphus jujuba* Miller., Rhamnaceae) or the flower of *sonbol*, a wild, strongly fragrant hyacinth (*Hyacinthus* spp., Asparagaceae), the first flower that blooms in the spring; *somagh*, the sour and astringent fruit of sumac (*Rhus coriaria* L., Anacardiaceae), whose red color evokes sunrise and new beginnings; and *serke*, "vinegar," symbolizing age and patience. Other festival dishes signal birth and new growth; these include sprouted grain; hard cooked eggs; and a goldfish in a bowl of water or its metaphor, an orange. Young people receive *aajil*, which consists of nuts mixed with raisins and other confections that will sweeten children's experiences during the rest of the year (Luard 2001).

At nightfall, another table is set with the first meal of the year. The centerpiece is *sabzi polo*, which is pilaf prepared with sunflower oil, saffron, garlic, cilantro (*Coriandrum sativum* L., Apiaceae), parsley, dill (*Anethum graveolens* L., Apiaceae), chive, and fenugreek (*Trigonella foenum-graecum* L., Fabaceae). In households that are more affluent, fresh fried fish and *kuku sabzi* (an herbed egg cake) are served. The following day, celebratory meals are fashioned around *reshteh polo*, a noodle and rice dish whose substantiality helps one prosper in life. The haft sin remain on their own table for at least thirteen days, until the festival Sinzdah Behdar, the name of which means "out the door with thirteen" (Luard 2001).[1]

Kashmiri celebrations of lunar cycles are marked by spiced meat dishes, rice, seasonal vegetables such as lotus, and green tea (Luard 2001). The Korean lunar new year (Gujeong) occurs in January to mid-February and is marked by a three-to-five-day celebration (*seol*). This festival features *teokguk*, or rice cake soup, which is the signature of the celebration; its consumption is encouraged by parents to ensure that their children will pass another year of life. The key ingredient is *garaeteok*, round sticks of rice cake that are sliced and cooked. Also served are *yakwa*, small round cakes made of wheat flour, honey, and oil. Daeboreum celebrates the first full moon. *Yakshik* is a sweet rice dish made with glutinous rice and chestnut, pine nut, soy sauce, honey, and sesame oil. (The affix *yak* in *yakwa* and *yakshik* denotes medicine.) *Bureom*, "nuts," are eaten early in the morning to protect against boils. *Ogokbab* is rice boiled with four other grains (*gok*), including staples such as millet and wheat. As with the Chinese tradition (see chapter 3), the Korean five (o) is a key principle that imparts healthfulness to this food (Lee 2005; Kim 2007).

In the past, Koreans observed the Jungyangjeol autumn festival on the ninth day of September by the lunar calendar. The celebration featured *gukhwajeon* (*gukhwa*, "chrysanthemum," *Chrysanthemum coronarium* L., Asteraceae; *jeon*, "pancake"), made with glutinous rice powder, along with *gukhwaju*, alcohol; *gukhwateok*, rice cake; *eoran*, fish roe; *yujacha*, citron-honey tea (*Citirus medica* L., Rutaceae); and *yujajeongwa*, honey-preserved citron. Singjeong, the solar new year, is less important to Koreans and is celebrated for one day, with many of the same foods (Kim 2007).[2]

In South America, the traditions of Mardi Gras (known as Carnaval, from the Latin *carne levare*, "leave the flesh") were introduced by the Spanish and subsequently became largely secularized, syncretized, and reinterpreted in the context of indigenous South American and African customs. Carnaval meals highlight meats and are typically calorie- and fat-dense. For example, in Colombia, families and friends share *arepas*, maize pancakes; *bandeja paisa*, ground beef with chorizo (a garlic-and-chile-spiced pork sausage), cassava, red beans, fried egg, rice, and fried plantains (*Plantago* spp., Plantaginaceae); *ajiaco*, chicken stewed with potatoes and capers (*Capparis spinosa* L., Capparidaceae); maize on the cob with cream; and *canelazo*, a rum-based beverage (Lovera 2005).

Worldwide, the traditional selection and combination of festival foods varied by region and demographics. There is more homogeneity in the modern era, which has been influenced by the expansion of market economies and other processes related to globalization. Many foods and traditions have been reinvented, reflecting both the erosion of traditional knowledge and a propensity for contemporaneity that includes exploring new commodities, including foods and beverages. Thanksgiving dinners in the southwestern United States are a confluence of foodways that were originally from Mesoamerica but have been adopted in the Southwest, with those that had been established in the colonial Northeast and incorrectly, but iconically, attributed to the collective feasting of early Pilgrims and Native Americans. Southwestern-style Thanksgiving includes pumpkin soup, achiote-basted turkey with chile gravy, cornbread stuffing, zucchini with chayote (*Sechium edule* Sw., Cucurbitaceae) and yellow squash (*Cucurbita* spp., Cucurbitaceae), cumin-spiced wheat rolls, cranberry-orange and cilantro salsa, pears (*Pyrus* spp., Rosaceae) poached in tequila with raspberry (*Rubus idaeus* L., Rosaceae) and prickly pear sauce, and lemon *bizochitos* (Baker and Baker 2003; Lovera 2005). This blended feast is not a passive artifact of proximity but, as in other times and places, an outcome of deliberate processes of reciprocity, transposition, and transformation across national and cultural boundaries.

On Tonga, all ceremonial occasions include kava circles (see below), religious observances, and the exchange of foods and traditional wealth items such as pandanus fruit (*Pandanus tectorius* Sol. ex Park., Pandanaceae), baskets, and tapa (bark cloth) made from the paper mulberry tree (*Broussonetia papyrifera* Vent., Moraceae). Ceremonies center on civic events featuring royalty, nobility, or government; church activities; and individuals, marking marriage, first and twenty-first birthdays, and death. The exchanges forge association by accentuating social ties to a particular individual or social group. The gift of first fruit (*polopolo*) is given to the nobility and to landowners or caretakers and other high-ranking individuals who are connected to the harvesters, for example, elder sisters, called *fahu* (Evans 1996; Fifita 2007). Similarly, on Pohnpei and Fiji, respectively, first fruit ceremonies (*i sevu* and *nohpwoai*) are celebrated with *kap* (yam), *mar* (breadfruit, *Artocarpus altilis* Fosb., Moraceae), and other staples. As with all elaborate feasts throughout Polynesia, these include pig and *sakau* (another term for kava). Variations on this pattern are observed throughout Polynesia (Pollock 1992).

The beverage kava has been strongly associated with ceremonies of all kinds throughout Polynesia and the diaspora. The drink is infused in cold water from the roots of the shrub *Piper methysticum* Forster (Piperaceae), which may have been first consumed three thousand years ago in northern Vanuatu and subsequently transported among canoe plants (chapter 3) as Polynesians colonized other island groups. Although kava played an important role in medicine and in cosmogonies and other religious inspirations, its greatest salience for Pacific Islanders is that it fosters sociability and identity by contributing to circumstances that are devoted to relaxation and well-being. In the past, kava marked significant social occasions such as embarkations and voyages' end, contract and treaty signatures, the induction of chiefs, and life-course transitions such as marriage, birth, circumcision, and death. The level of formality associated with kava drinking varied with context and ranged from informal sessions at day's end to rigidly structured ceremonies superintended by dignitaries. As occurred in other colonial contexts, European authorities were intimidated by the political and social cohesion that kava forged and discouraged its use (see chapter 5, section on sweat lodges). Kava is something of a national beverage in contemporary Vanuatu and Fiji; in Hawaiian and

Tahitian cultural and political revitalizations, it is a powerful symbol of community and mediates negotiations and conflict resolutions. Kava bars have emerged in urban areas throughout the Pacific and the diaspora and offer largely deracinated experiences that have few or no ritual components. During the past decade, kava has entered the global market, as both a recreational beverage and a dietary supplement advertised for insomnia and anxiety. It is still used today in traditional Pacific Island medicines for bronchitis, sinus disorders, and earache (Merlin and Raynor 2004).

The six kavalactones that are the active constituents of this plant occur in distinct ratios in different cultivars; they vary in potency and with different growth conditions and are synergistic. The effects of kava increase when the active and resinous constituents are separated; this explains, at least in part, the traditional preparation of kava, which begins with grinding, chewing, or pounding the root. Research has not clearly established that potency is enhanced by the salivary enzyme amylase, but if that is the case, this empowers the biocultural lens by suggesting another level of human agency in influencing how kava affects physiology. Drinking kava effects muscle relaxation; analgesia, local anesthesia, and sedation; pupil dilation and other visual effects, antifungal action, and diuresis (Singh 2004). The literature is equivocal about whether kava is associated with hepatotoxicty, which may be caused by contaminants and other constituents in commercial kava preparations or may occur indirectly, through kavalactone inhibition of cyclooxygenase, which protects hepatic function (Clouatre 2004; Baker 2008).

Foods and Beverages Associated with Death and Funerals

Funeralization embodies culturally constructed sequences of actions that begin in anticipation of death, through disposition of the body, and extensions beyond that. Foods for mourning and funerals affirm the conviction and expectation of death, bridging the gap between living and dead. Like other routinized customs, funeral practices represent stability, impart meaning, and enhance the acceptability of death. Some celebrations of the deceased overlap religious customs; in many, elements of resurrection or return shape people's actions and provide continuing bonds with the dead.

Funerary customs may attend to the soul, shadow, or other entities that leave the individual after death. Other practices—such as preparing, transporting, situating for some period of visiting or viewing, and disposing of the body—center on the dead person. In some cultures, the dead are buried as soon as possible; in others, intervals between death and disposition mark a liminal phase of variable and valuable duration. Related, but discrete, funeral customs serve the still-living, including family and others who were emotionally connected to the dead, as well as other social groups of which the individual was a member, in work, worship, and community. These survivors also experience a transition as they "enter through rites of separation and emerge . . . through rites of reintegration into society" (van Gennep 1960:147). As grief consumes the bereaved, they fill their metaphorical void with foods and beverages that trace a patterned chain of continuity.

Feeding the Deceased

In some cultures, food and other resources assure the deceased sustenance in the afterworld. The Jivaro of the eastern Andes provide the dead with plantain, chicken eggs and meat, cassava, and *chicha* (an alcoholic beverage made from maize). Traditional customs of wealthy Ba Venda of South Africa include butchering an ox and a goat, so that the deceased will own livestock in the afterlife: the cooked flesh is eaten, and the stomach contents mark the grave. Panamanian mourning practices include, for nine days after death, placing lighted candles and the statues of saints on a white-draped table, beneath which is placed a glass of water with a stem of basil to quench the thirst of the returning spirit of the dead. Nine also signifies in Jamaican customs; fried fish and cake are set out for the deceased for nine nights after burial, allowing time for the soul to leave. In addition, maize-meal johnnycakes, originally called "journey cakes," are placed in the casket for long-term nourishment. Wild rice (*Zizania aquatica* L., Poaceae) has been a sacred food for many Native American groups, including the Ojibway, for whom *manoomin* is a key component of origin narratives and religious celebrations. It is regularly offered to the dead, being supplied for many years through a window of the *jiibegamig*, "grave house" (Habenstein and Lamers 1963; Rogak 2004).

Appeasing the Suprahuman

Funerary customs also center on the deities who will receive the dead, on their spirits, and on the ancestors whom they will join. In Ecuador, the deceased is laid out with potato-maize cakes, utensils, and a sprig of rosemary, a powerful weapon for confronting difficult circumstances in the afterworld. Traditional customs in Mirzapur, India, include offering to the ghosts of the dead two black chickens, cakes, and burned molasses with butter. To ensure that the dead had enough food, ancient Etruscans who had the means depicted funeral feasts on the walls of burial vaults and regularly visited these vaults with fruit, wine, and meat for both the deceased and the deities. Occasionally, small animals would be sacrificed inside the vault; the blood that soaked the floor was a sign that the essence of the deceased continued to exist. Archaeological evidence from sites around the world reveals funerary food offerings for the dead and for the family's ancestors, among both royalty and commoners: the remains of beer, wine, cakes, and meats are common. Chinese *qingming* (literally, "clean" and "brightness") is the customary cleaning of graves that takes place in April, to appease the spirits of the dead. It is accompanied by burning incense and paper money, and setting out food. Customary offerings are hard-cooked eggs, steamed whole chicken, cha shao, and dim sum (see chapter 3). Similarly, Japanese ancestor rituals provide a strong sense of social membership, in which the most common gifts offered are food and drink (Habenstein and Lamers 1963; Rogak 2004; CHCP 2007).

Reciprocity and Funerary Redistributions

Funerary customs may be expressly or implicitly reciprocal (see chapter 1, section on food sharing). A traditional Iranian mourning food is *halva*, a confection made from sesame, honey, saffron, sugar, and rose water (*Rosa* spp., Rosaceae). At the funeral of an elderly person, children should eat half of all the halva served, so that it imparts the dead person's longevity to the young people's continued lives. After burial, the place where the deceased had lain is marked with halva, syrup, and a lamp, items that are removed to the grave the following day. Another example of mutual exchanges occurs among the Chukchee of Siberia when relatives and neighbors who gather for the funeral offer meat, marrow, and tobacco leaves and reserve a portion for the dead. The remainder is spread on stones near the body and is consumed as a tribute that connotes meat offered by the deceased. In another example, during his or her waning days, a Thai person might compile a small book of recipes that is copied and distributed at the funeral, a metaphoric meal of the deceased's favorite foods (Bendann 1930; Habenstein and Lamers 1963; Rogak 2004).

Funerals and related practices include foods and beverages consumed in memory of the deceased, occasions that, explicitly or not, have the effect of redistributing resources. After traditional Iranian burials, halva, figs (*Ficus carica* L., Moraceae), and dates are offered to neighbors and passersby; the poor are the recipients of the piece of meat that substituted for the deceased when his body was removed from the home. The water and cake or large bowl of food that the Ainu traditionally place next to the head of the deceased are later distributed to close relatives; everyone who attends the funeral receives additional millet cakes. Similarly, at Celtic wakes, a bowl of food is set on the chest of the deceased while mourners transition from keening to a dancing and feasting phase. An appropriate dish is *colcannon*, mashed potatoes seasoned with butter, cabbage, and leek. Sweets and coins are distributed at Chinese funerals to mitigate sorrow. Romanian customs include the family providing the entire village with *colaci* (ring-shaped breads), *coliva* (bulgur wheat cooked with honey and studded with candy), and the fruit and candy with which a *pom* (a tree branch) has been decorated. At traditional Greek funerals, the family of the deceased presents the priests with *bobota* (maize cakes) or with cooked maize. This represents the resurrection of the soul and is mixed with sugar, which symbolizes a contented afterlife. Others attending the funeral are offered *kolliva*, a version of bobota prepared with bulgur wheat. Worldwide, Muslim funeral customs include distributing food to the local community, being mindful of those who have least access to resources (Bendann 1930; Habenstein and Lamers 1963; Luard 2001; Rogak 2004).

The motif of Belgian funeral foods is black or colorless and is exemplified in slices of crisp black bread (soul bread), white wine, and chocolate funeral cakes. *Jai* (called "monk's food" or "Buddha's delight") is traditionally served during Chinese new year celebrations and before funerals, signaling that death is a new beginning for the deceased and his family. Constituents of this complex vegetarian dish vary regionally and commonly include mushrooms, snow peas (*Pisum sativum* L., Fabaceae), bamboo shoots, tofu, water chestnuts, carrots, groundnuts, and long rice (rice noodle). Estonians serve food in the home of the deceased after the burial; common centerpieces are roast pork, beef- and rice-stuffed cabbage rolls, pasta, and chicken soup (Luard 2001).

The foods that attend funerals commonly are richly spiced, marking funeralization with strong culinary statements. An Ethiopian funeral food is *niter kebbeh*, which is butter spiced with onion, garlic, ginger, turmeric, cardamom, clove, and nutmeg. Dutch *doed kakes*, "funeral cakes," are thick biscuits made with wheat, molasses, and caraway seed (*Carum carvi* L., Apiaceae) and are imprinted with the initials of the deceased. They are given to funeral attendees, who may save rather than eat them, reinforcing their purpose to sustain the memory of the dead. Similarly, in Mexico, Día de los Muertos ("Day of the Dead," falling on November 1 and 2, for children and adults, respectively) is marked by fruit and sweets that are saved as mementos of the deceased. This fiesta strongly communicates the fundamentals of both national cuisine and popular Catholicism. It welcomes the return of the souls of the dead to provide them with the beverages and foods they enjoyed during life. Tamales are always included, as is *pan de muerto*, "bread of the dead," flavored with orange and anise (*Pimpinella anisum* L., Apiaceae). Other Mexican funeral foods are life-size, skull-shaped cakes with the name of the deceased inscribed on the forehead; maize; and the beverage *atole*, made with *masa* (maize meal), water, cinnamon, vanilla, *piloncillo* (unrefined solid sugarcane), and optional fruit and chocolate. Analogs of Día de los Muertos occur in other cultures, when food is taken to the burial site at fixed calendrical intervals. Customs similar to Chinese qingming occur at the same time in Korea and Japan. At Mongolian funerals, mourners eat rice pudding with raisins; South African *begrafnisrys*, "funeral rice," also contains raisins and is flavored with sugar, cinnamon, and lemon (Bendann 1930; Habenstein and Lamers 1963; Rogak 2004; Long-Solís and Vargas 2005).

Festivals, Funerals, and Pharmacology

The foregoing selective review of funeral customs reveals a common underlying theme of foods and beverages that are both sacralized offerings and secular items for community consumption. Motifs of nurturing and emotional and physical connections link the recently dead, the living, and the long-dead ancestors and spirits. Iterative themes are represented in food types, modes of preparation, presentations, and circulation. These foods and beverages embody great diversity in meanings and in their chemistries.

Perhaps most pharmacologically striking are the spices that mark these celebratory foods. A sizeable literature addresses the pharmacologic potential of spices, although only a small proportion of that work has been contextualized to particular circumstances of consumption, such as discussed in chapter 2 (see also Etkin 2006a:ch. 3). From the preceding discussion, I abstracted a few spices to suggest the spectrum of pharmacologic potential. Fenugreek has cholesterol- and glucose-lowering effects and is antioxidant and antiviral (Kwon et al. 2002; Madar and Stark 2002; Hinneburg and Neubert 2005). The aromatic costmary (*Balsamita major* Desf., Asteraceae), one of the plants of sabze, has a long medicinal history that is consistent with its antimicrobial, antioxidant, and anti-inflammatory actions (Pieroni et al. 2004; Venskutonis et al. 2005). Asafetida is anticarcinogenic, antioxidant, and hypotensive (Saleem et al. 2001; Fatehi et al. 2004). Hosta flowers have anticancer activity (Plants for a Future 2004), hyacinth species are antibacterial (Asano et al. 1998), lotus is antioxidant (Lavid et al. 2001), and saffron has antitumor activity (Abdullaev 2002). Caper contains antioxidant phenols as well as isothiocyanates that are cancer-preventive (Germanò et al. 2002).

Some of the foundational, rather than flavoring, foods also are pharmacologically noteworthy. For example, breadfruit is antiatherosclerotic and antibacterial (Shimizu et al. 2000; Wang et al. 2006). Burdock is antimicrobial, antithrombic, and antioxidant (Pereira et al. 2005). Buckwheat lowers cholesterol (Kayashita et al. 1995). Mung bean and lentil are antidiabetic and antioxidant (Madar and Stark 2002; Fernandez-Orozco et al. 2003), chickpea has anticancer effects (Giron-Calle et al. 2004), and pandanus fruit is high in vitamins A and C and calcium (Engleberger et al. 2003).

To the extent that these pharmacologic findings can be evaluated in the contexts of the feasts and other occasions described above, we can speculate about how the consumption and circulation of these foods and beverages may impact physiology on both individual and community levels. For example, we might consider how simultaneous or closely sequential consumption of pharmacologically dynamic meal elements may contribute to circumstances of synergy or antagonism with other foods and drugs (Thompson and Ward 2005; Schooling et al. 2006). Further, we can consider how people's interpretations of those physiologic actions influence whether and how they embrace some foods and beverages (but not others) as items of association. An even richer contextualized consideration of the pharmacologic potential of foods and beverages of occasion is possible where there is more ethnographic depth. The discussion that follows draws on my Hausa research, first describing general and specific foods, then highlighting several life-course transitions during which association underscores both the role of commensality and the reciprocal and other relations that eventuate in the circulation of nutrient and symbolic resources.

"Abincin Alada," Hausa Foods of Custom

In Hurumi, *abinci dan abin sha* (referring to foods and beverages) that are identified for ceremony and occasion do not deviate so much from daily fare as they are embellished by more-dramatic expressions that feature a dish's most valued or signatory ingredients, for example, more meat and spice. Enhancement also includes culturally marked presentations such as in *kwarya* (made of *duma*, or traditional calabashes, *Lagenaria siceraria* Standley, Cucurbitaceae); *kwano*, enamelware; and *kasko*, earthenware bowls. Beyond signaling, dressing up a food heightens expectations and taste, enriches nutrient composition and pharmacologic potential, and expands the dimensions of sociability.

Hausa foods and beverages of association are, generally, kayan kwadayi (see chapter 3), which Hurumi residents describe as flavorful, rich, and special; these are contrasted with foods that are *gahoho*, that is, ordinary and less flavorful. Some kayan kwadayi overlap the category of *zafi*, "hot," referring to foods and beverages that are nutritious and promote satiety and healing. Examples of kayan kwadayi include *kayan zaki*, "sweet foods," notably those that contain or to which is added *sukari* (sugar) and *zuma* (honey); *kayan maiko* or *makwalashi*, foods that have high oil or fat content; *nama*, "meat," including flesh and organs of *kaza* (chicken), *zabo* (guinea fowl), *awaki* (goat), *tunkiya* (sheep), and *saniya* (cow); *kwai* (guinea fowl or chicken eggs); madara and the more commonly consumed nono (fresh and fermented cow's milk). *Kayan marmari* are a class of kayan kwadayi that are not regularly available, including locally seasonal fruit and vegetables as well as exotics that are irregularly accessible through *masu yawo* (regionally itinerant vendors) and *kasuwa* (markets). Kayan kwadayi include once-exotic items that today are produced in Nigeria's commercial sector and by some cottage industries: *burodi*, bread; *taliya*, pasta; *lemo*, soft drinks; and *minti*, candy.

Goro, "Kola Nut"

For Hausa, *goro* (kola nut, *Cola acuminata* Schott & Endl., *C. nitida* Schott & Endl., *C.* spp., Sterculiaceae) is a ubiquitous and powerful icon of sociability, the centerpiece of classed, gendered, and otherwise demographically marked exchanges around which Hausa society coheres. Relative to other foods of association, goro is expensive, an observation that is cast into bolder relief by the everyday nature of its exchange in circumstances that grade from the most mundane (for example, passing someone on a village pathway) to the most sacred (such as Ramadan celebrations). The most formalized and visible exchanges occur during marriage transactions, gifting at naming ceremonies, greeting political and religious leaders, and marking deaths and Muslim holy days. If goro is not available, coins can be substituted and are in that case lexically tagged "goro."

During any occasion, more than one individual might be distributing goro; many exchanges are conscious horizontal and vertical reciprocities. Although translated as "nut," goro is the seed of the *Cola* tree (see chapter 3, note 7); seeds are split into their cotyledons and further subdivided if the number of people present warrants breaking these into smaller pieces. Individuals of higher rank are privileged with the first and better pieces (better because they are larger and not oxidized). The red color that kola chewing imparts to teeth and lips is valued cosmetically. This is sociability written on the body, a metaphor that is extended through *kunshi*, wrapping the body with cloth that has been soaked in infusions of *lalle* (henna, *Lawsonia inermis* L., Lythraceae) to impart red color to the feet, lower leg, forearm, and hand. Proverbs further reveal how goro expresses Hausa values related to sociability: "Karamin *goro* yafi babban dutse" (A small kola is better than a large stone) and "Wanda ya ba ka barin *goro*, in ya san guda, ya ba ka" (Even a small gift shows good will).

The stimulant properties of kola are attributed to caffeine, theobromine, and theophylline (see chapter 2). The seeds also contain antioxidant proanthocyanidins, catechins, and other phenolics. Anti-inflammatory, astringent, and diuretic activities have been reported; in addition, the seeds have a high fiber content and significant amounts of magnesium, phosphorus, and potassium (Daels-Rakotoarison et al. 2003; Abulude 2004).

The astringent, bitter, and aromatic qualities of goro are signs for Hausa medicinal applications that parallel the social functions of kola nut. Goro is included in complex mixtures of plants that bind social relations and ensure the success of business alliances. Cotyledon color, shape, size, and perishability all signify the utility of a particular kola nut: *farin* (white) goro is preferred over *jar* (red) and *farin jar* (pink) for medicines that promote prosperity and good marriage relations. Larger and more deeply colored goro are more powerful. *Kurman* (deaf) goro, which has a barely discernible seam between the cotyledons, is a constituent of medicines that silence creditors. Goro also imparts strength and protects against sorcery.

Kayan Zafi, "Spices"

Hausa spices contribute to the overall flavor and color profile of individual dishes, beverages, and meals. Because virtually all are used in combinations, their synergies generate further complexities and reflect their botanical, phytochemical, and functional diversity. Some are signatures, that is, flavor prints that mark particular foods and sign social asymmetries through varied applications, combinations, and frequency and volume of consumption. *Kayan zafi*, "hot things," is the Hausa gloss for spices generally and embodies flavor metaphors as well as preventive and therapeutic idioms of healing and fortification through heat.

Barkono, "Chile"

Although native to South America, *barkono* is the iconic spice of Hausa cuisine. Its global circulation from place of origin resonates the themes of European expansion, globalization, and the commodification of peoples and their foods (see chapter 2). In Hurumi, barkono cultivars are distinguished by taste, form, size, and suitability for food and medicine. *Tsiduhu*, the most pungent and smallest, and the slightly larger barkono (the term denotes a particular cultivar) are regarded to be the most powerful and are preferred for medicines and to dress up ordinary dishes. The less pungent chiles include *bunsurun barkono*, "goat's chile," the next largest; the lobed and round *ataruhu*; a larger, long and thin variety, *dan kadana*; and the largest local chile, *tattasai*, which is drupe-shaped. These milder chiles are indicated for children's medicines.

As outlined in chapter 2, phytoconstituents in barkono contribute to a broad pharmacodynamic profile, including these activities: antimicrobial, carminative, antioxidant, counterirritant, anti-inflammatory, and triglyceride-lowering. Hausa use barkono to treat fevers, gastrointestinal disorders, and wounds; barkono also mediates in sorcery (*sammu*), witchcraft (*maita*), and communicating with spirits (*iskoki*). Its prominent role in food and medicine finds structural parallels in cultural constructions that span parables, allegories, and other narratives; epithets; and compositional elements of Bori, a folk religion that predates conversion to Islam and centers on a pantheon of malevolent and benign iskoki (Etkin 2006a:ch. 3, note 3).

Yaji (Aromatics and Pungents)

As barkono is the singlet signature flavor of Hausa cuisine, *yaji* is its composite counterpart, offering shades of complex taste and texture. Yaji generally implies hot, pungent, and sharp flavorings. Regionally, it refers to the specific combination of the eight spices mentioned in the previous chapter: chile, ginger, melegueta pepper, flower pepper, clove, guinea pepper, kulla, and Benin pepper. Of these, only chile is cultivated locally. Hurumi residents purchase prepared yaji or individual constituents at markets. Several women prepare yaji in volume, powdering the ingredients together using a mortar and pestle in anticipation of their own needs as well as to sell to other compounds.

The plants that constitute yaji all are pharmacologically dynamic. Singly and in combination they represent significant antimicrobial, anti-inflammatory, antioxidant, and carminative potential and are vitamin-rich (Etkin 2006a:ch. 3, appendix). Yaji is commonly used for all conditions that emanate from *sanyi* (physical and metaphoric cold), including *zazzabi*, fevers; *sanyin jiki*, joint pain; and *ragwan jini*, a general lethargy that emerges from weak jini.

Daddawa (Soup Base and Condiment)

In Hurumi, the foundation of the eight common miya (soups) and a widely used condiment is *daddawa*, a pungent fat- and protein-dense fermented product made from the dry seeds (*kalwa*) of *dorawa*, the African locust bean tree (*Parkia filicoidea* Welw., Fabaceae). Other seeds can stretch or substitute for kalwa. *Daddawar gurji*, prepared with melon seeds (*Cucumis melo* L., Cucurbitaceae), is favored for *daci*, "bitter," and *danke*, "sticky," qualities. Seeds of *yakuwa*, red sorrel (*Hibiscus sabdariffa* L., Malvaceae), are used for *daddawar batso*, which is markedly pungent. An artifact of shifting ecological circumstances, kalwa substitutes that no longer exist in the region include seeds of *loli* (*Psorospermum guineense* Hochr., Clusiaceae); *kirya*, African mesquite (*Prosopis africana* Taub., Fabaceae); and *taura*, tallow tree (*Detarium senegalense* Gmelin, Fabaceae). Hurumi residents no longer recall the unique culinary characteristics of loli, kirya, and taura daddawas, but they do remember medicinal uses. This reflects that the Hausa sensory lexicon for foods is significantly less developed and precise than that for medicines.[3] For example, the healthful potential of a food is described as "strengthening" or "promoting digestion," while medicines are understood to encourage the egress of disease agents through the skin or mouth, dislodge majina, counteract internal sanyi, or dissolve accretions of gishiri or jini (Etkin and Ross 1982).

In the past, several Hurumi women generated income by preparing daddawa for sale. Although there is high and steady demand for this foundational food, its production is labor-intensive and hardly remunerative. Today, virtually all compounds rely on market sources, including commercial products. Daddawa production begins with several kilos of kalwa. Invoking gender correspondence and reproductive metaphors in Hausa alimentation (see below, *ci*, under *Suna*), a small volume of yakuwa seeds is added to the kalwa as *namijin daddawa*, "male daddawa," that drives fermentation (*ruba*). After the seeds are boiled for twenty-four hours and the testa are discarded, the softened, separated cotyledons are rinsed, boiled for another two hours, drained, and spread to a depth of five to six inches on mats made from *kijinjiri* fronds (*Phoenix reclinata* Jacq., Arecaceae). In another reproductive metaphor, a handful of *ayawu*, unfinished daddawa from an earlier batch, is added to seed the process. Fermentation proceeds over the next thirty-six hours, driven by proteolytic spore-forming bacilli; this generates a viscid, ammonia-redolent mass that is sun dried and formed into *labu* (one-inch spheres). The labu are smoothed and shined by application of the infused root and whole plant, respectively, of *gwandar jeji* ("wild papaya"/wild custard apple, *Annona senegalensis* Pers., Annonaceae) and malaiduwa. This sealing and strengthening of labu finds a structural parallel in the common use of these plants in *maganin karfi*, which is a medicine against knives, gunshot, and other weapon injuries.

Daddawa is the most important food base in Nigeria and, depending on household resources, can be the primary regular source of protein. It is a flavorful, preservable product made from unpalatable and inedible seeds. Kalwa have high protein and fat content. During the first twenty-four hours of fermentation, levels of indigestible oligosaccharides (primarily raffinose and stachyose) are significantly reduced by galactosidase hydrolysis. Protein quality is improved: *Bacillus* species produce glutamic acid and extracellular proteinases, and protein hydrolysis increases digestibility. The nutrient value of daddawa is higher than that of unprocessed seeds, containing 18–47 percent protein and 31–43 percent fat. The fermented product is also rich in calcium, iron, and phosphorus; the level of potassium doubles. Vitamin B (thiamine, riboflavin) content is higher. Antinutritive and toxic constituents such as phytic and hydrocyanic acids and oxalates are removed, and some lactic acid bacteria and *Bacillus* species are active against pathogenic microorganisms (Iwuoha and Eke 1996; Odunfa and Oyewole 1998; Omafuvbe et al. 2000; Beaumont 2002; Ouoba et al. 2007).

Kalwa substitutes and other ingredients also are pharmacologically and nutritionally dynamic. Compared to full-kalwa daddawa, the variations prepared with seeds that stretch or substitute for locust seeds have similar mineral, protein, and fat contents. Gurji is antioxidant and anti-inflammatory; gwandar jeji is antibacterial, antiparasitic against *Leishmania* and *Trypanosoma* species, and anthelmintic; and malaiduwa extracts are antimicrobial and antiprotozoan and protect red blood cells from sickling. One can only speculate about the physiologic implications of the discontinued use of some pharmacologically active seeds. For example, loli is active against pathogenic protozoa and infectious dermatitis, while taura has antidiabetic and cholesterol-lowering actions (Sahpaz et al. 1994; Rayment et al. 1996; Barminas et al. 1998; Alawa et al. 2003; Menvielle-Bourg 2005; Lino and Deogracious 2006; Ahua et al. 2007; Ojekale et al. 2007).

Nama da Madara, "Meat and Milk"

Hurumi livestock management strategies include not sacrificing young animals, favoring their more lucrative sale as adults. This applies primarily to cattle, goats, and sheep; some chickens and guinea fowl are raised for egg production and other household use, but these too are more commonly for sale. Animals that become too sick or old to be transported to market are killed and dressed in the village in a manner conforming to Islamic customs. As there is no means to preserve the meat, the animal's owner wants to distribute it right away. Some is sold, but other portions are gifted, typically privileging the imam and the *sarki* (the village chief). Other recipients include relatives, friends, and people in special circumstances such as the sick, elderly, or pregnant. This gifting cements relationships, expresses deference, and redistributes resources among a larger segment of the population than would otherwise receive this nutritional and social benefit.

As part of regular meals, meat is most often added to the soups that accompany *tuwo*, a dense porridge made from guineacorn (*Sorghum* spp., Poaceae) or millet, or less commonly from rice or maize. *Tuwo da miya*, the mainstay of Hausa daily cuisine, is the centerpiece of at least one of three daily meals, but the frequency and volume of meat additions are low, in some households only for the weekly Jumma'a *salla*, "Friday sabbath." For salla, as well as the Hausa occasions described below, ordinary fare is dressed up with (more) meat and other animal products and embellished with snack foods (see chapter 3).

In the context of celebration and association, nono and the full-fat milk kindirmo are consumed alone or as special dressings for porridges and other grain-based foods. The production of nono, discussed in chapter 3, results in a two- to threefold increase in the content of free amino acids. Lactic acid modification of the protein casein improves digestibility and stimulates peristalsis and salivary, stomach, and pancreatic enzymes. Fermented milks improve immune function, prevent cancers, and lower cholesterol and blood pressure. Individuals who are lactose intolerant (see chapter 1) derive more nutrition from fermented milk products, in which much of the lactose has been metabolized by lactic acid bacteria (species of *Lactobacillus, Lactococcus,* and other genera). Consumption of low-lactose fermented milk improves general nutrition by allowing absorption of milk nutrients as well as preventing nutrient loss from other foods secondary to the rapid intestinal transit that ensues when lactose-intolerant individuals consume fresh-milk products (Nagao et al. 2000; Ishikawa et al. 2003; Seppo et al. 2003; Etkin 2006a:ch. 4).

Gari/Kwaki, "Cassava"

Coarse fermented *rogo* (cassava) meal, known as *gari,* is ubiquitous in the cuisines of sub-Saharan Africa, where it was introduced more than 150 years ago by freed slaves from Brazil, who learned the production of *farinha de mandioca* as one of their adaptations to forced plantation labor (see chapter 2). Women prepare gari from fresh, peeled cassava tubers that are grated, mashed, and set into porous containers such as cloth bags and baskets (*kwando*). The weight of stones placed on top of the container forces liquid from the soft mass, which is fermented by lactic acid bacteria (*Lactobacillus* and *Cornebacterium* spp.) that hydrolyze the carbohydrates and produce organic acids. These acids promote growth of the yeast *Geotrichum candidum,* which gives rise to the aldehydes and esters that impart the characteristic *gardi,* "nutlike," taste and smell of gari. After one to three days, the fermented pulp is roasted for about thirty minutes, alternating drying and cooking. The dry, granular gari expands three-hundred-fold when boiled in water (Odunfa and Oyewole 1998).

In western and central Africa, gari is a staple food for more than 100 million people; for a large percentage of southern Nigeria's residents, it makes up as much as half of the daily caloric intake (Odunfa and Oyewole 1998). *Fufu* is another common term for gari, and the local name in Hurumi is *kwaki.* Rogo production is common throughout the region, where it is usually consumed in boiled or roasted preparation. Hurumi residents do not prepare kwaki, however; instead, they purchase it at local markets where most is sourced from southern Nigeria. Consequently, compared to other cassava products and to other carbohydrates, kwaki is expensive and, thus, reserved for special occasions.

Hurumi women boil kwaki to make the food *teba*, which has a porridgelike consistency; it is eaten with miya or is flavored with spice). There is some irony in the fact that, for Hurumi residents, a food whose history intersects their antecedents' enslavement is also a valued food of occasion. Such is the manner by which cultural (re)constructions of foods transform products over time and space to adapt to local histories and circumstances.

Like kalwa, rogo is an item that is inedible when raw and more nutritious after fermentation. During solid substrate fermentation, low-pH-enzyme hydrolysis of the glycosides lotaustralin and linamarin releases toxic hydrocyanic acid, making cassava a safe food. Also participating in this hydrolysis are lactic acid bacteria, which produce acids that force out the weakly ionized hydrogen cyanide and sustain a suitable pH for the enzyme linamarase (which occurs in both these bacteria and cassava). Compared to the unfermented tuber, kwaki has greater nutrient value: higher fiber content, increased protein availability, and substantially reduced phytate and toxin levels (Odunfa and Oyewole 1998; Lei et al. 1999; Cardoso et al. 2005).

Hausa Celebrations and Occasions

Islam is so pervasive in Hausa lifeways that Allah is invoked on all occasions, ranging from mundane speculations about the weather to major holy days. Many occasions are marked by formal prayer, commonly under the guidance of the imam. *Biki* means, literally, "feast" and is a gloss for the celebration of life-course transitions. Several Hausa occasions are celebrated with the foods and beverages of association described above.

Suna, "Naming Ceremony"

The naming ceremony (*suna*) occurs seven days after a child's birth, typically early in the day after the morning tuwo has been prepared and consumed in individual households. As with all Hausa customs, this brief ceremony and accompanying activities are gendered. Men arrive first and assemble outside the *zaure*, a roofed structure at the compound entrance.

The head of a Hausa household offers *goro*, "kola nut," to guests at a *suna*, "naming ceremony." Goro is a ubiquitous and potent icon of sociability throughout Hausaland. Although the most visible and ritualized exchanges occur during civil and religious ceremonies and in the presence of dignitaries, goro also is transacted during virtually all encounters, even common meetings while people travel from home to farm.

Here, goro are distributed by male household members or by *maroki*, praise singers who engage in a traditional Hausa oratory (*roko*) that proclaims another's name to honor him or her—in this case, the parents, their families and guests, and high-ranking religious or secular functionaries who are in attendance. Men sit on *tabarma* (mats made of woven grass, Poaceae), while small groups of women move through the zaure to segregate themselves inside with the mother and baby, a mirror for the men's grouping outside. The process unfolds when the imam arrives, in some cases accompanied by a small retinue. He and other principals enter the zaure, and all men in attendance repeat three times the opening sura of the Koran, the Fatiha. As the imam states the baby's name, the maroki calls it out publicly; gender symmetry is reinforced when women call in response, from inside.

In a subsequent phase of the suna, the *wanzami*, "barber-surgeon," shaves the baby's head and surgically cuts (but does not excise) the *beli*, "uvula," and, for girls, also the *angurya*, which are vaguely characterized features of the vaginal wall (and probably not the *tantani*, "hymen"). The *ungozoma*, "midwife," returns the infant to its mother. The closest friends and family remain and are served by the host with fresh tuwo, roasted ram (or other meat, depending on economic circumstances), and goro and other kayan kwadayi. Included in this social group are the ungozoma; wanzami; maroki; *mahauci*, butcher; *kaka*, maternal and paternal grandparents; and sarki. Also present is the *boka*, a specialist of indigenous medicines who is distinguished from other traditional healers by *gani* (future-telling) and the knowledge and mediation of iskoki. Again, the domains of men and women are mirror images in which groups of four or five share bowls of food.

The responsibilities of the wanzami indicate a web of symbolic representations that link human reproduction and alimentation. The rationale for cutting the beli and angurya is that these block consumption, denoting both eating food and having sex. *Ci*, "to eat," is a root metaphor for other tropes, particularly those in which ingesting food corresponds with intercourse, both of which are expressed in the homonym *ci*. Elaborations of the metaphor include referring to the vagina and penis as mortar and pestle, the vagina as the locus of consumption, and the penis and testicles as the *murhu*, "hearth" (see *ciki*, below). The homonym *sanwa* refers to both cooking water and semen. As evidenced in the following sections, idioms of conception, reproduction, sexuality, and development are transformed by the fire that is alimentation, which converts the raw to the cooked.

Aure, "Marriage"

During the months preceding a formal marriage ceremony, there is substantial exchange of *gara* (*kayan aure*), "gifts," between the families of the *amarya* (bride) and *ango* (groom). The suitor's presentation of *kayan dandane* (literally, "tasty goods") elicits the acknowledgment of the amarya's family. In the next phase, the prospective groom offers *kayan zance* (goods of conversation) to demonstrate his sincerity. Later, much of the *kayan sa rana* (goods of the day), which fix the date of the wedding, are distributed to relatives of the amarya. Closer to the wedding day, reciprocal exchanges are transacted by the two families, and the frequency and volume intensify, all the while contoured by the relative and particular economic standing of the households. Friends and relatives of the bride and groom make dramatic shows of traveling in groups through the village to deliver kaya, which include many foods, money, textiles, henna, perfume, clothing, mats, and other household items.

Abincin aure include goro, raw grains, groundnuts, and other staples that fill large calabashes; whole pumpkins and other fruit; livestock; tsire and other cooked meats; dressed-up tuwo da miya; and sugar cubes, *finkaso* (fried wheat cakes), and other kayan kwadayi. Additional reciprocal exchanges, as well as community redistributions, are part of the *bikin aure*, the day-of-the-ceremony feast that features a great variety of foods. This public, reticulated series of exchanges that secure Hausa marriages is a key strategy for the coherence of domestic well-being and is vital for forging interfamily bonds and community associations. One of the series of exchanges is *kayan cuko* (literally, "goods that fill up"), a metaphor for both intrafamily and intracommunity redistributions of foods and other resources. Today, these traditional transactions are being increasingly transformed by circumstances of contemporary economy and commodity. As in most aspects of Hausa daily life, the bikin aure is a gendered celebration with conspicuous structural symmetries. Women converge inside the groom's father's compound, drumming on calabashes and mor-

Hausa girls simulate the celebration of *aure*, "marriage." The girl seated and hidden under cloth is the shy bride. The covered enamelware dishes, here empty, represent the many foods that are exchanged by the bride's and groom's families during sequential phases of the engagement, as well as the foods exchanged and served to guests on the day of the ceremony.

tars, dancing, and singing humorously bawdy songs that link eating with sex. In a parallel celebration, men congregate outside the compound, consuming the same foods and offering commentary on the goings-on in the compound interior. In both domains, foods and beverages of celebration are abundant and are the subject of muted praise from the guests and of the dramatic, stylized exaltations of the maroki.

Ciki da Haihuwa, "Pregnancy and Childbirth"

In Hurumi, pregnancy (ciki) is a life phase that traditionally has not been a time of association; that is, pregnant women do not constitute communities. Most live in noncontiguous compounds and have little opportunity to communicate regularly (see chapter 3, section on *kulle*/purdah). Sisters-in-law in the same compound who are synchronously pregnant might be an exception, but they would most likely be pairs or triples, not larger associations in the sense used in this book. Co-wives (*kishiya*, from *kishi*, "jealousy") who may otherwise enjoy congenial relations commonly become competitive—that is, *dis*associative—when one or both are pregnant. Ungozoma circulate among *gida*, attending to individuals rather than promoting community. During my last field research, the four ungozoma in Hurumi divided their responsibilities geographically by village sector, attending women regularly but infrequently during the pregnancy. The same ungozoma generally assists all women in the same compound. *Haihuwa*, the terminus of pregnancy, also is not a nucleus for community. A woman gives birth in her own sleeping daki and, for all but the first birth, typically is alone. The ungozoma is cognizant of an imminent birth but, barring difficulties, is called to the compound only after the baby and placenta are delivered (she cuts the *cibiya*, "umbilicus"). Like most traditional peoples, Hausa regard pregnancy as a predominantly healthful phase, for the duration of which concerns center on eating nutritious foods, hygiene, and avoiding overexertion. During pregnancy, a woman's diet generally improves through increased diversity and the inclusion of more kayan kwadayi, but she eats alone or with her usual compound mates, not with other pregnant women.

In contrast to the experiences of pregnant women in the West, and like their counterparts in other traditional cultures, Hausa do not pathologize pregnancy. Although protections against sorcery and witchcraft increase during pregnancy, it is not managed by medicines intended to affect the woman's and fetus's physiologies. Bitter medicines can harm the fetus by dislodging him from where he sits in the *mahaifa*, "womb," balanced on three *gammo*, the circular head pads that cushion heavy head loads such as *tulu*, the earthenware vessels in which water is transported (see chapter 5). The three gammo are a structural parallel of the arrangement of three stones for the *murhu*, "cooking hearth." Dislodgement from the gammo during the first six gestational months results in fetal loss, invoking the culinary idiom of insufficient cooking. A baby born in the seventh or ninth month will survive, but one born during the eighth will not (and rains during the eighth lunar month portend drought). The principles of *heat restoration* and *seven and nine, but not eight* also occur in circumcision customs (see section on *kaciya*, below).

Cin Kasa, "Geophagia"

The consumption of soil, geophagia (geophagy), occurs in societies of diverse ecologies and customs. It is a culturally constructed practice that coheres around very specific soils that are sourced and prepared in prescribed ways. Where it occurs, geophagia usually is associated with women, commonly during pregnancy. Among Hausa, geophagia not only is unique to pregnancy but also is a vehicle for the association of women who otherwise do not connect as a community. For *cin kasa* (*ci*, "to eat"; *kasa*, "earth"), Hurumi women specify a white soil, *farar kasa*, that has a high *tabo* (clay) content. Cin kasa unites pregnant women around a pattern of consumption that requires sourcing a product that is not harvested locally and must be purchased through market networks. Community emerges as pregnant women consult one another, usually via their children, about where to purchase farar kasa and how to pool resources to purchase in volume sufficient to reduce cost. For Hurumi residents, the absence of local or even regional sources of edible earth contributes to its meaning and enriches the experience of its consumption. Secondarily, cin kasa also forges community among not-yet-married women who, anticipating their own childbearing, learn the broader culture of pregnancy through interactions with pregnant sisters, compound mates, and neighbors. The objectives of cin kasa are to prevent and treat nausea, protect the mother and fetus from harmful substances that might contaminate foods and beverages, and treat gastrointestinal symptoms. The shared knowledge of pregnant women and their associates specifies volume and consumption schedules for kasa; inappropriate consumption and overconsumption are regarded as abnormal.

A common Western perspective on geophagia misunderstands the practice by lumping it together with *dysphagia* or *pica*. Pica derives etymologically from *magpie*, referring to a bird whose diet is characterized by broad omnivory. The term denotes aberrant feeding practices that extend beyond ordinary environmental explorations such as those of children who experiment by tasting or ingesting items they encounter. Clinically remarkable pica is idiosyncratic and pathologic and includes the consumption of a variety of nonfoods, including charcoal, ice, and hair. In some cases, pica results from the erosion of traditional knowledge or other cultural discontinuities, for example, when residence and environment change and the meaning underlying the consumption of soils is transferred to substitutes such as laundry starch, with harmful physiologic consequences. When such cases draw clinical attention, out of context, we can understand how biomedical care providers might conflate geophagia and pica. Conversely, customary geophagia is systematic, with the intention of influencing physiology. Underscoring the nonpathologic nature of this custom are key characteristics of geophagia: the widespread prevalence of geophagia throughout history, its similar features in diverse cultures and ecologies, and, significantly, the lack of evidence of adverse effects in traditional contexts of use.

Several hypotheses converge to suggest the physiologic implications of geophagia, which is part of the routine behavioral repertoires of many reptile, bird, and mammalian taxa, including nonhuman primates. The soil types most commonly consumed are clays, which share several dynamic properties. Colloidal structure permits the adsorption (concentration of constituents at colloidal surfaces) of organic compounds, a process of surface assimilation that is similar to the chemical binding of impurities and toxins by activated carbon (charcoal), a material with a large surface area and high degree of microporosity. In clay, oxygen-silica tetrahedra are reticulated into hexagons, resulting in a large surface-to-volume ratio that binds water. At the same time, platelike stacking properties of clay particles make the soil relatively impermeable to water. The dense structure of oxygen and hydroxyl ions in the tetrahedra affords the binding and exchange of minerals such as aluminum, calcium, iron, and magnesium (Bohn et al. 2001).

Substantial scientific evidence supports the hypothesis that healthful aspects of consuming clay soil include the adsorption of microorganism and plant toxins or other unpalatable allelochemicals such as tannins, alkaloids, and oxalates; regulation of gut pH and motility, which mediates nausea; antidiarrheal action; and the elimination of endoparasites. Ethnographic data from populations worldwide mark the use of clays in the preparation of food and medicines. For example, wild potato (*Solanum* spp., Solanaceae) contains glycoalkaloids that protect the plant against microorganisms and herbivores but make this potential food unpalatable and toxic for human (and most other animal) consumption; the Aymara of Bolivia traditionally used clay soils to detoxify this important food resource. Similarly, villagers in Sardinia and Native American Pomo in California used clay to detoxify and render palatable acorns (*Quercus* spp., Fagaceae), which have a high tannin content. Australian Aborigines treated bloodroot rhizomes (*Haemodorum coccineum* Hook, Haemodoraceae) with clay, presumably to eliminate the toxin phenalenone, and the Ainu boiled clay with the roots of corydalis (*Corydalis ambigua* Cham. & Schltdl., Papaveraceae) to reduce alkaloid content (Mahaney et al. 1999; Johns 2000; Krishnamani and Mahaney 2000).

A popular lay hypothesis about human geophagia is that it compensates for nutrient deficiencies. While some edible soils have a significant supplementary potential for iron, zinc, and other minerals, there is no evidence that geophagia involves an appetite for particular nutrients, and no one nutrient explains geophagia in a comprehensive sense. More significantly, even in cases in which geophagia might contribute nutrients, traditional uses of soil are explicitly to increase the palatability and safety of certain foods and for the treatment of nausea and other gastrointestinal complaints.

Mai Jego, "Nursing (New) Mother"

Kwana arbain, the first forty days postpartum, are considered a period of risk for both *mai jego*, "new mother," and *jinjiri*, "infant." Mai jego may develop complications of childbirth, primarily infection and bleeding, and may not produce sufficient breast milk. Concerns for jinjiri center on a suite of intersecting symptom complexes that are prevented and managed by mediating mai jego's diet. The symptoms of *fara* center on anemia, noted as a lightening of the skin and weakness; this can progress to *shawara*, a complex that intersects with hepatitis, signaled by yellow conjunctiva, liver sensitivity, and fatigue. It can lead to *bayamma*, failure to thrive. *Mayankwaniya*, which can incorporate or eventuate from fara, overlaps with protein-calorie malnutrition, marked by weight loss, hair depigmentation, abdominal distension, and failure to thrive.

These health concerns are mediated by magani and customs that focus on warming mai jego and jinjiri. In the aftermath of haihuwa, mai jego's body is *danye* (raw) and vulnerable. This is remedied by *dahu*, "cooking," with foods and medicines that restore the body's heat, importantly, to the reproductive organs. Jinjiri, recently delivered from the cooked, ripe womb (*nunannan ciki*), also is raw, exposed generally—and in particular, exposed to sanyi. Kwana arbain also is called *wankan* (wash) *jego*, referring to the twice-daily stylized bathing of mai jego and jinjiri. On a special murhu in a less traveled part of the gida near mai jego's daki, water is boiled in a multi-gallon drum (traditionally metal) and is infused with medicinal plants. Special branches are dipped into the drum and are used to spray the body: *darbejiya*, or *neem* (*Azadirachta indica* A. Juss., Meliaceae); *sandal*, eucalyptus (*Eucalyptus saligna* Smith, Myrtaceae); and *tsamiya*, tamarind. Mai jego also sits twice a day in a *kwatarniya*, a shallow earthenware basin of warm water in which medicinal plants have been infused. The theme of warming links discontiguous parts of the gida: embers from the bath fire are placed in a *kasko*, a small earthenware bowl, in the center of the sleeping daki, or directly under the *gadon kasa*, a raised earthenware bed. The infused plants, which drive away spirits and repel sorcery, include aromatics such as daddawa, yaji, and *tafannuwa* (garlic). The medicines also repel *dauda*, "pollution," both in the literal sense of protecting against dirt and infection and as an allegory of spiritual cleanliness, which extends to not having sexual relations for the duration of kwana arbain.

Depending on economic circumstances, parity, the health of mai jego and jinjiri, and the presence of other adult women in the compound, the ungozoma may participate in postpartum activities, for example, assisting with the hot water baths. Otherwise, the rhythms of *dahun jiki*, "cooking the body," are circumstances of seclusion that restore the bodies of, and cement relations between, mai jego and jinjiri. They connect as well to *uban jinjiri*, "father," who does not participate directly but, for the duration of kwana arbain, collects the water for bathing, provides firewood and kayan kwadayi, and otherwise has a higher than usual physical profile inside the compound.

Apart from the twice-daily wanka, kwana arbain are marked by customs of association whose core principles are gifting, reciprocity, and redistribution. The volume, frequency, and elaboration of mai jego's dietary enhancements and exchanges depend on the resources of uban jinjiri, the visitors, and mai jego herself. More so than occurs during ordinary visiting, kwana arbain are marked by a steady procession of women and children to mai jego's compound to celebrate jinjiri and to deliver and receive gifts. Common exchanges include yaji, daddawa, nama, and other kayan kwadayi. Male relatives and friends are received by uban jinjiri in the zaure, where, minimally, goro and money are exchanged; tsire, kosai, and other kayan kwadayi customarily are shared as well.

All mai jego's foods are flavored with yaji. *Yajin haihuwa*, the portion designated for visitors, may be stretched by adding roasted gero or *maiwa* flour. This is acceptable and anticipated; the primary goal is to have enough to share among the community of visitors. Mai jego's tuwo, the iconic super food, should always be fresh, signaling renewal and restoration, whereas ordinarily, tuwo can be remaindered from the previous meal or even meals from the previous day. All of mai jego's midday meals include *kunun kanwa*, which is an everyday gruel (*kunu*) that is marked with an abundance of *kanwa*, "natron," a sodium carbonate salt that has more medicinal than culinary uses. Visitors share this kanwa, as well as another food that marks the postpartum, *kanwa* (this term is a homonym of the salt), a rich dish prepared with the boiled legs and head of sheep, goat, and chicken. Otherwise, the nama that mai jego consumes during kwana arbain should be roasted, which is a signal that ordinary fare is now in the public arena and conveys a message that forges community (see above, the discussion of sited and gendered cooking).

The physical and metaphoric convergence of yaji and daddawa are represented in *yajin daddawa*. Yaji composed primarily of daddawa is an emergency substitute that is prepared right after birth if no yaji was purchased in advance. The principal ingredient is daddawa, the most likely condiment to be available in quantity. Barkono and cittar aho also are likely to be among household food stores and typically make up more of the yajin daddawa relative to other spices. So important is the complex yaji, with all its nuances of taste and function, that within a day uban jinjiri replaces yajin daddawa with the conventional version.

Kaciya, "Circumcision"

In a structural analog to childbirth, the wanzami circumcises boys aged seven or nine, but not eight years old. The principles that guide kwana arbain also are embodied in the kaciya customs that govern cold, food, and pollution. Customarily, several boys constituting an age cohort (*dan kaciya*) are circumcised at the same time, each held by the wanzami's assistants in a sitting position on the ground. The ceremony takes place

When Hausa women prepare large quantities of grain- and groundnut-based foods (for example, for ceremonial foods or gifts), husbands bear the expense of taking advantage of Hurumi's grinding mill. Here, children wait in line with their mothers' grains in calabash and enamelware bowls.

A Hausa woman uses a pestle to pound millet in a mortar, the first stage of flour production, in anticipation of preparing porridge for her family's evening meal. The full process of alternate pounding and winnowing to produce even coarse flour consumes an average of two hours per meal preparation.

outside the compound of a prominent individual and is public, attended primarily by adult men and teenage boys, who cohere temporarily in this gendered association. The cutting phase lasts about one minute, with blood and foreskins directed into individual holes that later are sealed with the excavated soil, to which magani have been added. During a prolonged rinsing phase, water infused with astringent and antimicrobial plants is poured over the cuts and runs into the holes. Among these botanicals, the most prominent are *gabaruwa* (thorn mimosa, *Acacia nilotica* Del., Fabaceae) and gwandar jeji. Finally, the medicinal plants are applied directly to the cut. A structural parallel to the customs of kwana arbain, these actions signal concern with dauda in both literal and figurative terms. Dan kaciya are the focus of the ceremony and ministrations of the wanzami, while also constituting a compressed nucleus of their own association around which the members of the larger group engage in *hira*, "conversation." Rather than being festive, this occasion is suffused with a gravity that signals a transition to more-responsible (notably, more-religious) lifeways. Goro are exchanged; the wanzami are given money and perfume; and the maroki praise the boys, the wanzami, and attendees. After about two hours, the ceremony concludes with the consumption of kunun kanwa, the same gruel that marks mai jego's diet. First dan kaciya share one bowl, then more bowls for shared consumption are distributed among the larger group.

The circle of community shrinks over the next fifteen days, as the dan kaciya remain in their respective gida, centers of parallel associations in the company of their nuclear families. Dan kaciya receive friends and relatives, but on a significantly smaller scale than does mai jego. Visitors gift money, chickens, and kayan kwadayi, all of it redistributed among dan kaciya's family and visitors. The application of medicines continues to promote healing and deflect dauda, which includes avoiding the contamination of menstruating women; the boy's parents do not have sexual relations during the recovery phase. Care is taken so that sanyi does not penetrate the vulnerable body of the boy: fires warm the sleeping hut for the recovery period, and the foods consumed are literally and symbolically heating. The boys of the dan kaciya and their families eat the same foods that mai jego shares during kwana arbain: nama, nono, kayan kwadayi, kunun kanwa, fresh tuwo, kanwa, and liberal use of daddawa and yaji. A successful healing is marked by a special bath, new clothes, and, from households that can afford to do so, distributing kayan kwadayi or money to families of more modest circumstances.

Symbolic symmetries that link Hausa circumcision recovery and the postpartum include the principle of seven and nine, but not eight; repelling dauda; and heat restoration and avoiding sanyi through warm foods and magani, including yaji and daddawa. Bodies are cooked literally at murhu, including the special one created for wanka during kwana arbain. In another link, the three-stone hearth metaphor invokes both male external reproductive organs and the positioning of the developing fetus in the womb. These liminal phases are marked in much the same way as other occasions that have high social salience. They also are phases of heightened health risk that share concerns about infection, inflammation, edema, and loss of blood and heat. The aromatic constituents and pungent tastes of yaji and daddawa impart a physical sensation of heat; as discussed above, the individual constituents also embody significant pharmacologic potential.

Hausa Foods of Occasion: Where Meanings Intersect Health

Foods and beverages of association influence health generally by providing a greater array of consumables and a more diverse nutrient content. Meats and other animal products increase dietary protein. Beyond that, the pharmacologic and nutrient potentials of particular foods and beverages have been outlined in the preceding discussion. Among kayan kwadayi, I draw additional attention to fermented foods and honey and bee products.

Nono, Kwaki, and Daddawa

The healthful qualities of nono, discussed above, extend as well to kwaki and daddawa. Fermentations improve palatability, nutrient solubility, and bioavailability. Protein metabolism, for example, releases a more diverse pool of amino acids, some of which are generated by the fermenting microorganisms. During fermentation, protein hydrolysis yields granules of smaller size, with relatively larger surface area, that are more accessible to enzymatic degradation in the gastrointestinal tract. Fats also are more digestible after enzymatic metabolism. Bacterial fermentations yield B vitamins. Fermented foods enhance immune function; reduce blood pressure and serum cholesterol; and are antimicrobial, antioxidant, cancer-preventive, and antiatherogenic. The mechanisms of action have not been characterized but are likely to include altering gut pH; mediating immunomodulatory sites; competing with pathogens for nutrients, growth factors, and receptor and binding sites; and producing antimicrobial metabolites and lactase (Nagao et al. 2000; Ishikawa et al. 2003; Kim et al. 2003; Seppo et al. 2003; Etkin 2006a:ch. 4; Parvez et al. 2006). Finally, customs of redistribution both cement community and ensure the circulation of nutrient and social benefits among a larger segment of the population.

Zuma (Honey) and Bee Products

The Hausa encourage bee (*kudan zuma,* "fly of honey") colonization of *kwangi,* which are beehives made from hollowed tree sections, or braided branches and grasses, that are placed in trees. Rounded calabash pieces seal both ends, with holes drilled to allow the bees to pass in and out. At least thirty-five plant species, representing eighteen families, are used to fabricate kwangi. These include *shafin zuma,* species that are used to line the beehive, which are identified by both their physical attributes (appearance, physiologic effects) and the metaphors they project (plants that call and welcome). The most commonly used trees are palms. Zuma and the emptied honeycomb (*totuwa*) are consumed as kayan kwadayi and also as medicines. Some individuals specify *autan zuma* (*auta,* "youngest"), a light-colored zuma that is the last out of the kwangi. To some extent, the kwangi foundation, especially the liner species, influences the chemistry of the honey produced, which has already been affected by the diverse phytochemistries of pollens and nectars from the plants on which kudan zuma forage, as well as by ecological and seasonal parameters. On this knowledge, Hausa selection of medicinal honeys is informed fully or in part by selecting for the particular construction elements of different kwangi. These species present considerable phytochemical diversity. For example, aduwa has cytostatic activity (Pettit et al. 1991), danya is antioxidant and antidiarrheal (Braca et al. 2003), and malaiduwa is antiprotozoan and antimicrobial and protects red blood cells from sickling (Moody et al. 2003).

Pollen and nectar are collected by foraging bees, which express this food into comb cells, where the tongue and wing action of worker bees evaporates the water content of nectar to 15–20 percent; secretion of a salivary enzyme metabolizes sucrose to the simple sugars fructose and glucose. Honey is cached in capped comb cells and fed to adult bees. The primary carbohydrate source for honeybees, it contains small amounts of minerals, vitamins, colloids, and enzymes. Pollen contains lipids and high levels of calcium, iron, and vitamins, notably riboflavin. It is the primary protein source in kudan zuma diets, representing as much as 30 percent of the dry weight (Linskens and Jorde 1997).

Beyond the honey itself, comb constituents also offer phytochemical and nutritional potential. Beeswax is produced by the metabolism of honey in fat cells that are associated with wax glands located on the ventral side of the worker bee's abdomen. Wax is used in the construction of honey and brood combs, networks of hexagonal compartments that house pupae and food. Propolis (from the Greek *pro*, "in defense," and *polis*, "the colony"), known as "bee glue," is a necessary constituent of hive integrity, serving as a lining for insulation, for hive repair, and to reduce entry size in cold weather. A composite of bee activity and plant parts, propolis is both physiochemically and metaphorically complex. It contains beeswax, bioactive bee secretions, and pollen that is transformed by bees during its transport and manipulation by worker bees for hive construction, defense, and repair. Also present are botanical exudates that are conveyed from mandibles to corbiculae (pollen baskets) on the back legs of foraging bees, from which they are unloaded by the specialized middle legs of workers and are incorporated into hive construction and defense. A complex of more than 150 compounds makes up the aromatic fraction of propolis. Resins and balsams that bees collect from buds and bark lesions constitute 55–70 percent of the plant material. In addition, 25–30 percent is contributed by beeswax and 5–10 percent by volatile and essential oils (Seeley 1995).

Larvae and adult bees are fed beebread, a composite food confected with honey (about 12 percent), pollen, and worker bee secretions and cached in comb cells (see chapter 1, section on provisioning). An example of a composite being more than the sum of its constituents, those of beebread are biochemically transformed into a food with fermentation-enriched increased protein, vitamin K, and lactic acid levels. Royal jelly, fed to the worker egg selected to be the next queen, is a dressed-up beebread that contains 34 percent honey, ten times more biopterin and pantothenic acid, and more mandibular and hypopharyngeal gland secretions (Moritz and Southwick 1992). These stored foods and the hive itself offer humans the same benefits they provide for bees.

Hausa use zuma and all parts of the hive for food and medicine. They understand that propolis has both metaphoric and physical ambiguity because its specific makeup varies by hive, season, and ecology. As mentioned above, honey and other bee products offer substantial nutrient advantage. All bee products are antimicrobial. Honey is specifically anti-leishmanial in cutaneous infection and has long-standing and culturally diffuse applications in healing wounds and burns. The osmolarity of honey accelerates healing by encouraging dehydration. Dilute honey solutions have stronger antimicrobial activity because the hypopharyngeal gland enzyme glucose oxidase catalyzes an oxygen-glucose reaction that produces the potent antimicrobial hydrogen peroxide and gluconic acid. Honey also is antioxidant and protects against gingivitis and periodontal disease. Royal jelly reduces serum lipids, is hypotensive, protects against ulcers, and contains hormones that enhance fertility in some animals. Bee venom is anti-inflammatory, hypotensive, and antioxidant. Immunotherapy by envenomation diminishes the risk of systemic allergic responses to bee sting. Flavonoids, the primary active constituents of propolis, are strongly antioxidant and relieve some of the side effects of cancer chemotherapies. Immunostimulatory, antitumor, anti-inflammatory, and antimicrobial effects also have been reported (Ito et al. 2001; Husein and Kridli 2002; van der Weyden 2003; Oršolić et al. 2003; English et al. 2004; Cimolai 2007; Sforcin 2007).

Conclusion

Foods and beverages of occasion, like those highlighted in earlier chapters, embody enormous diversity. This applies to sourcing, exchanging, presentation, nutrient content, pharmacologic potential, and meaning. A biocultural perspective nuanced by political economy is relevant to foods and beverages of occasion, as are the themes discussed elsewhere in the book: cultural constructions of commodities, globalization, identity, and agency in health promotion.

CHAPTER 5

Aspects of Health, Hype, and Identity in Bottled Water

THE FOCUS OF this chapter is on bottled drinking water—more specifically, the individual-sized, branded products that accompany many people through their daily personal and public routines. Carrying drinking water is practical for some activities, such as exercising, but other situations, particularly where tap water is close by, do not seem to warrant it: attending lectures, visits to physicians' offices, job interviews. These latter cases are emblematic of a widespread social phenomenon, the larger context of which is health and consumer culture. A sense of community issues from people's shared impressions that regular hydration is healthy, that the sources and supplementing of drinking waters are significant, that branded waters advertise and label accurately, and that the purported healthful qualities of different brands can be distinguished. Bottles for individual consumption are props that help forge association through the messages they convey: bottled water (and its consumption, if only presumed) is a tangible entity that projects health, authenticity, and, early in its popularization, some degree of sophistication. A biocultural perspective is the primary analytic lens for what follows, locating people and their waters in particular ecologies and exploring health implications.[1]

Mineral Waters and Spas

One cannot underestimate the importance of water for all organisms. Throughout human history, advances in the means of locating, collecting, storing, carrying, and distributing water have been vital elements in the evolution of our technologies. As but a single example, for thousands of years, various modes of dowsing, or water witching, have been used to locate water sources. This sort of divination, often with ritual components, assumes a psychological control over the physical environment, using a forked stick, pendulum, or **L**- or **Y**-shaped divining rod made of wood or metal. Most commonly, the vibration or other movement of the device is taken as evidence of the location of underground water. Today's practices may have originated in fifteenth-century Germany, where dowsing was used to find metals. While dowsers assert that they possess inherited, paranormal abilities to detect energy fields, the bioscientific community notes a lack of evidence or reproducibility and dismisses these claims (Jansson 1999). If nothing else, however, dowsing is a metaphor that expresses the significance of water and people's motivation to have agency in its location and collection.

Rain "dances" and other water-encouraging customs also are widespread and are commonly coordinated with lunar cycles. The Cherokee of the U.S. Southeast performed ceremonies to stimulate rain and to wash away disaffected spirits. For Zuni rain customs, dancers wore turquoise and feathers, which represent rain and wind, respectively. Many native peoples in South and North America used rainsticks, hollow tubes made from plants, commonly saguaro (*Carnegiea gigantea* Britton & Rose, Cactaceae) and other cacti, whose spines were reversed to line the inner surface. A rainlike percussion was created when small beads or stones placed inside the stick moved from one end to the other as it was upended. In other regions, bamboo is a good source material for rainsticks.

The earliest hominids would have carried and stored water in natural vessels such as calabashes and, later, fashioned water containers out of wood, clay-lined earthenware and wicker baskets, and animal horns, hides, and other organs. More-advanced technologies for domesticating water include ceramics, metals, and glass. The most recent developments in beverage containers are plastics, commonly the thermoplastic polymers polyvinyl chloride (PVC) and polyethylene terephthalate (PET). Humans and other animals also exploit rain, including its adventitious collection from rock depressions and tree boles; large-volume water harvest exploits snow and glacier melt and natural bodies such as springs, rivers, and oceans.

Beyond its tangible qualities, water also captures the imaginations of people who speculate where bodies of water might take them on river quests and sea voyages (see chapter 2) and who, questioning its genesis, weave it into their cosmogonies. Water is one of the five elements in

Chinese cosmology (see chapter 3, section on manapua). For the Ibibio of Nigeria, moon/water and sun/fire engaged in a dynamic tension to create the universe and its inhabitants. The origin narratives of the Hindu goddesses Sarasvati and Laskshmi and the gods Brahma and Vishnu center on the sacred lotus, a water plant (Croutier 1992). Fresh water, ocean navigation skills, and the sea are part of the fabric of Marshallese origin narratives. "Bwil im Kartak" is an account of a "living seamark," a navigation sign in the form of a bird that guides people who are lost at sea back to land. "Litarmelu kab Lainjin" describes how visitors from distant places imparted navigation knowledge to a woman who established the foundations of pan-Marshalls navigation (Genz 2008). In languages that are grammatically gendered, the sea is commonly feminine, marking its association with emerging life: the Sumerian *mar* denotes both "sea" and "womb"; the Japanese *umi*, "ocean," is homophonous with the term for "birth" (Croutier 1992).

Pima, Blackfoot, and Apache Native Americans describe an old man riding a raft who conjured the earth out of water. Other Native North Americans invoke a deity who sent an animal to the bottom of the sea to retrieve mud from which to fashion the earth. In the U.S. Southwest, Navajo apprehend natural and spiritual worlds comprising both male and female aspects, underscoring the balance and duality that is fundamental to the Navajo way of knowing. This extends to ceremonial images, including rainbows, lightning, and rain, which are integral to Navajo origin narratives and are key symbols in weaving and other patterns. For each of six geographic directions (the four compass points, and below and above), Zuni religion designates rain spiritual leaders who live in clouds and are accompanied by six advocates, which are rain-carrying birds. Other design themes throughout North America include water serpents, turtles, frogs, and fish (Baxter and Bird-Romero 2000; Heard Museum 2008).

Throughout the arid U.S. Southwest, native peoples invoke rain through a variety of customs, many of which center on the connection between rain/water and life and growth. Some of these expressions, such as depictions on ceremonial garb, are durable; others, such as sand and body paintings, are transient. For Hopi, water is sacred and undergirds many other symbols in ritual and secular customs. It is a theme in cosmogonies, ritual attire, persons' names, kiva (ceremonial chamber) iconography, and songs that summon the cloud chiefs to rejoin the cycle of life that joins people with other animal and botanical forms. Rain, clouds, and other waters are the essence of the dead; the clouds that return are the ancestors, and "their rain [is] both communion with and [a] blessing of the living . . . [the earth's waters are] transubstantiated human life" (Whitely and Masayesva 1999:404). In a related motif, Hopi communicate with their deities through intermediaries, *katsina*[2] spirits that embody the essence of everything in the natural world and cosmos and come to the Hopi in the form of rain-laden clouds. The spirits are represented by katsina "dolls," three-dimensional figures traditionally made by men from the root of the cottonwood (*Populus* spp., Salicaceae), which is associated with water; these figures are dressed in materials that evoke water-related themes. People also dress as katsina spirits to perform ceremonial dances (Teiwes 1991).

The imagery and customs of many peoples in the U.S. Southwest include dragonflies (Aeshnidae), insects that are intimately associated with water and serve as harbingers of the summer rains.[3] Whereas flies (Muscidae) have two wings, the dragonfly has four, arranged in two pairs. Its elongated body was a common theme in traditional religions and played a prominent role in origin narratives. It still is depicted as a vertical line with one or two horizontal beams in pottery, basketry, prayer sticks, masks, textiles, and other items of utilitarian and ceremonial material culture. The Christian patriarchal (or archiepiscopal) cross also has two horizontal beams and was carried in Roman Catholic liturgical processions in front of, or by, archbishops. When the Spanish tried to impose Christianity and its universal symbol, the images fused in a powerful way that, for some, imparted ambiguity to both the iconic cross and the dragonfly, as well as to their combined identities. Forcing the cross finds symmetry in other colonial aggressions: for example, in the Hopi village Awatovi, a mission house was superpositioned over a kiva, symbolizing the succession of the new religion. Among some native peoples, as an extension of the image and symmetry, saints' images were destroyed, crosses and rosaries were broken, and the remains were covered with ashes, feathers, and animal skins. Although in the end the Spanish largely prevailed, the dragonfly endures in contemporary expressions, being depicted in rock art, jewelry, pottery, and textiles (Bird 1992; Baxter and Bird-Romero 2000).

Classical European mythology associated water with creation and destruction: Aphrodite was a goddess of beauty and love who protected sailors (her central imagery was "born of foam"); water nymphs were divine spirits associated with mountain springs and rivers; mermaids and sirens captured the imagination as "irresistible women without souls" and represented both the dangerous and the life-affirming aspects of water. A multiheaded sea-dwelling dragon or snake that requires human sacrifices occurs in the oral traditions of disparate cultures such as Vietnam, Senegal, and Scandinavia. Scotland's Loch Ness monster finds analogs in many of the world's oceans and lakes (Croutier 1992:26). Leonardo da Vinci extolled the paradoxical qualities of water, describing it as sharp and strong, acidic and bitter, healthful and poisonous, fast and slow. "It suffers change into as many natures as are the different places through which it flows. And as the mirror changes . . . so it alters with the nature of the place" (da Vinci quoted in Croutier 1992:13). Water enlivens language, which itself "has a *liquid quality*, a flow in its overall effect, water in its consonants" (Bachelard, quoted in Farber 1994:43). Farber (1994:42–43) invokes the images conveyed by the idioms "two ships passing in the night," "blood is thicker than water," "still waters run deep," "in over your head," "feel drained," "an outpouring of emotion," and "a free flow of ideas." A timely addition is "surfing the Internet."

The bioscientific perspective on the origin of life also centers on water, explaining a primordial "soup" that contained organic materials, which evolved into complex molecules whose coordination mediated metabolic processes. The first cells that evolved, heterotrophs, fed on the organic matter; later, autotrophic cells produced their own food; and over the course of billions of years, the great diversity of life-forms evolved.

Healthful Spaces

"Therapeutic landscape" is a compelling metaphor that captures the broad-based potential that the physical environment and its emotional and aesthetic extensions have to affect health. Theoretical perspectives that offer cogent insights into such sites include anthropological approaches (biocultural, ethnoecology) and the idioms of cultural (human) geography that explore spatial variations among cultures and the contributions of place to the social fabric (e.g., Nazarea 1999; Ellen et al. 2000; Norton 2005). Therapeutic landscapes are settings where healthful circumstances (however characterized by a particular culture) promote physiologic, emotional, and social health. They can be natural, such as mountains and forests. Others have been naturalized through interior and exterior design of constructed places: such therapeutic landscapes include gardens, parks, natural features that are factored into architectural design, planted interior spaces such as courtyards, and the placement of potted plants, aquaria, and fountains. Nature is pictorialized and commonly standardized in constructed landscapes. One goal of developing gardens and related landscapes is to establish sites in which the serenity and other aesthetics of place are transposed to the inner self. Today, these landscapes also provide opportunities to manage the sites in ways that conserve biological and cultural diversity.

Worldview and Therapeutic Landscapes

The concept of therapeutic landscapes is central to the worldviews of many cultures whose members apprehend a universe in which the physical environment is contiguous with society and who view people as a life-form that participates in a broader community whose diverse inhabitants are governed by a single set of rules of conduct. These views are consistent with classical anthropological understandings of totemism and animism. Totemism denotes the structuring of human social units on the patterns of other species. In Marovo, Solomon Islands, all organisms and nonorganic entities constitute a contiguous land-sea environment in which human groups are structured by ancestral totems, such as the shark and crocodile, through which identity is forged; interspecific relations are mutually protective (Hviding 1996). A symmetrical inversion is found in animistic models, in which nature is patterned on human society and in which natural entities (plants, animals, minerals) have souls, temperaments, and social relations. The Makuna of northwestern Amazonia also attribute to these entities " 'culture'—habits, rituals, songs, and dances of their own" (Århem 1996:185). Water and forest clans are juxtaposed to distinguish "natural and cosmic domains: river and forest, water and land, edible fish and game" (Århem 1996:190).

Seaman's (1992) account of geomancy in a rural Taiwan community likens it to acupuncture and to Chinese medicine generally, structured by a microcosm-macrocosm philosophy in which anatomical features and rhythms of the bodies of humans and other animals, as well as the physical earth, have counterparts in society. They have analogs as well in the topography and cycles of the physical environment. A shift in any domain generates repercussions in the others, so that the whole is dynamic and experiences cycles of disequilibrium and rebalance.

In the current literature that specifies or implies therapeutic landscapes, most attention is paid to the positive effects of people-place proxemics via passive-visual activities and the participatory decorating, altering, and grooming of landscapes (Etkin 1994c). These activities include managing gardens for and by children, the elderly, and immigrant communities. Various modes of interacting with plants are included in activities for individuals who are physically or mentally impaired. Animal/pet therapy factors in other landscape inhabitants. Some researchers in gender studies have traced through history what they regard to be special and empowering relationships that women share with plants and animals, although some of these accounts seem sentimental and forced. Plants, especially flowers, are featured in paintings and other reproductions of nature, as well as in marriage, funerary, and religious customs. Commercial enterprises ranging from small employers to large corporations soften their internal and external environments with plants, pools, and aquaria to improve employee morale and, presumably, maintain or improve productivity. (Re)connections and identity are forged through restoration of natural landscapes and the development of cultural-heritage gardens, home (commonly front-yard) gardens and ponds, and interiorscapes that project messages of ethnic affiliation, wealth, and other demographics (Flagler and Poincelot 1994; Shoemaker 2002; Cooper Marcus 2003).

Water in Therapeutic Landscapes

Constructed and natural water sources are prominent in therapeutic landscapes. "Water, and especially the play of water in fountains [has been] . . . a measure of the vitality of the . . . world" (Comito 1978, in Relf 1992:34) and reflects a "correspondence between the tranquility of the [place] . . . and [that] of the inner self" (Cool 1981, in Relf 1992:43). At least since 2700 BCE in China, India, and other Asian cultures, the lotus, water lily (*Nymphaea* spp., Nymphaeaceae), and related water plants were valued for aesthetic, religious, and medicinal uses. Egyptian tomb wall frescos from 1225 BCE feature canals, ponds, and water plants. Waters and flowers also decorated pillars and other architectural elements, and the dry flowers and seeds of lotus were included in sarcophagi (Slocum and Robinson 1996). In Nepal, Khumbu Sherpa cite water sources, rocks, and trees as the residences of *lu*, female spirits who are worshiped primarily by women and who convey both good luck and misfortune (Spoon 2008).

Since earliest times, Chinese and Japanese imperial gardens were structured by pools, canals, and other water features. The shoreline was linked by bridges to islands and teahouses and dressed by willow trees (*Salix* spp., Salicaceae) to provide reflection and shade. Gardens are depicted in seventh- to ninth-century wall frescoes painted by Buddhist monks in cave temples along the Silk Road. Public gardens imitated the patterns created for royalty and wealthy landowners, but on a smaller scale. Southern Europe had been exposed to many designs by the Middle Ages, during which time gardens, prominently in Italy, were constructed around extravagant marble fountains from which issued channels that connected to other water features. The Villa d'Este gardens in Tivoli are exemplary of sixteenth-century Roman design that "embraced all the inventions of the new art of water gardening . . . an overall picture of cascades, waterfalls, fountains, water jets, fish ponds, grottoes, and terraces, each dependent on its neighbor, and all linking up to the villa itself" (Slocum and Robinson 1996:19). In these examples, water is a medium of association.

Water-centered gardens later were imitated throughout Europe, prominently in Spain, France, and later England. Adopting Italian design, the splendid garden at Versailles was begun by André le Nôtre in 1662 and literally blossomed into a place where a central cruciform canal connected smaller waterways, hundreds of fountains, hydraulic engineering, and classical statues. In England, this opulence was translated into canals and other long, rectangular expanses of water. Over time, the architectural plans included less statuary and featured still waters, rather than fountains and other moving waters. The first gardens in the United States also imitated those of Europe, particularly English gardens, and later diversified into many styles. Today, water and water plants are the centerpiece of most large U.S. gardens, such as the New York, Chicago, and Denver Botanical Gardens; Florida's Cypress Garden; and the Kenilworth Aquatic Gardens in Washington, D.C. (Slocum and Robinson 1996).

Moving waters, fountains, and waterfalls can be tranquil or vocal or intermittently both. Since ancient times, wells and springs have been sites where people appease spirits and deities through supplication and gifts. Archaeologists have established that since at least 6000 BCE, coins and other valued items (e.g., polished stone arrowheads) have served as votive offerings at natural, and later constructed, wells and fountains. Well worship was common in parts of India and other Eastern countries with dry climates, which follows a logic of valuing scarce resources, but analogous practices also occur in temperate and tropical regions. In England, the centuries-old custom of well-dressing combines public thanksgiving with religious practices: wells, springs, and other sources are decorated with botanicals, both simply and with elaborate garlands and flower arrangements. These customs originated as expiations of Celtic water deities and later were appropriated as Christian practices, including designating the wells with saints' names (Slocum and Robinson 1996; Chapelle 2005). That water from a site can propitiate its resident spirits compounds its meaning and potency. Logical associations transfer the spirituality of geolocation to waters that issue from those places. Some villages transposed the dressing custom to taps when water was first piped to those locations.

Chapelle (2005) describes traditional water culture in Thailand from an implicitly biocultural perspective. Households store water outside the home in *maaw nahm*, large earthenware vessels that are cooled by condensation, so that passersby can quench their thirst. From a physiologic perspective, this custom has practical implications in a hot environment. Maaw nahm also illustrate the Thai ethos that emphasizes *nahm jai*, literally "water heart," which evokes "hospitality, warmheartedness, and benevolence" (Chapelle 2005:8). Community is expressed through stocking and renewing with clean well or rain water and by inscribing and otherwise decorating maaw nahm, some of which are housed in roofed niches or located within discrete structures.

The histories of many religious and political leaders and prominent healers include accounts of fantastic transactions and transitions at wells and springs. Sites of pilgrimage and miraculous healing occur all over the world. The waters of the Grotto of Massabielle in Lourdes, in southern

France, have been famous since the mid-nineteenth century. Also called the Cave of Apparitions or Miraculous Cave, the grotto is the site where, in 1858, Bernadette Soubirous (later Saint Bernadette) purportedly was instructed by the Virgin Mary to drink from a previously unknown spring. To this day, Lourdes remains an extremely popular pilgrimage destination where Lourdes Eau Naturelle is dispensed from the spring for on-site cures and is sold and shipped internationally. Similarly, the saint Paraskeva Pyatnitsa presides over healing springs in Russia, while in Georgia, the sick have been beckoned since the fifth millennium CE by the sulfur springs of Tbilisi, which means "warm." In county Louth, Ireland, wells are enshrined for Saint Brigit, who accepts torn bits of supplicants' clothing as a metaphor for their shed ailments. Throughout Scotland and England, many of the healing springs are disease-specific (Croutier 1992; Burnett 1999).

Hydrotherapy

Preventive and therapeutic traditions from many parts of the world promote health through hydrotherapy (drinking and bathing) in on-site mineral, thermal, and oceanic waters. Still today, some waters are reputed elixirs of life, while others have more specific therapeutic targets. Chinese documents record a long history of knowledge of mineral waters, notably hot springs, which were used primarily medicinally but also for cold-weather agriculture and cooking. So fundamental was this resource that emperors were judged by how well they maintained and grew their waterworks. For the most part, Japanese hot springs were used for bathing, but they also served as sites for fermenting miso from soybeans, rice, or other grains; cooking; and heating rooms. Babylonian physicians were water experts whose therapeutics included ablutions in rivers and medicinal baths. Ancient Egyptians deified the Nile River: priests bathed in it to purify themselves before entering temples, and its water was bottled as medicine and shipped considerable distances. Early Hindu texts describe religious cum medicinal bathing in rivers and natural springs and in public waterworks in places remote from the sources. Water also has been a significant aspect of the history of Christianity, reflected in baptismal customs and christenings that are traced to the rituals of Osiris and Isis, the moon divinities of ancient Egypt. In Christian iconography, the Fountain of Living Waters, later named the Fountain of Life, has been associated with baptism since the fifth century CE (Slocum and Robinson 1996). Upon entering a church, Eastern Orthodox and Catholic Christians dip their fingers into holy water and make the sign of the cross. In other religions, too, water is cleansing and purifying and a metaphor for spiritual verities (Croutier 1992; Routh et al. 1996; LaMoreaux and Tanner 2001) (see section on Hausa, below, and *wankan jego* and *kaciya* sections in chapter 4).

Ottoman Empire public baths had both popular and religious origins, deriving from Turkish and Mongol steam rooms and Islamic ablution customs. In early Greek and Roman times, public baths (*thermae*) were sites of healing and entertainment during which bathing assumed extravagant and ritualized dimensions. The great technologic accomplishment that is the aqueduct system of Rome was constructed originally to provide bathwater and, later, drinking water as well. This elaborate long-distance channeling network eclipsed earlier ones in Egypt, Assyria, Greece, Babylonia, and Persia. During five centuries, from 300 BCE to 226 CE, eleven aqueducts served Rome's citizens, carrying water as far as fifty-seven miles from its source. Parts remain in use or are standing testimonies to the technical and managerial skills that designed Rome's waterways. Customs were maintained on a less elaborate scale in medieval European bathhouses, which offered therapeutic waters and served as settings for confederation where people socialized and conducted business. Spirituality (as well as sociability) was embraced in Scandinavian and Benelux saunas, where, like other leisure activities, this mode of association was the purview of the wealthy (Routh et al. 1996).

Bathing did not benefit from the advances of the industrial revolution and declined in Europe during the sixteenth to eighteenth centuries. Accelerated urbanization compromised water supplies, which contributed to epidemics of infectious diseases. This encouraged the English to innovate plumbing and sewer systems; one outcome was that the bathtub was moved from public sites into residences. Giving the bathtub "a location of permanence was one of the major social and architectural" advances in the history of bathing (Croutier 1992:94)—prior to that time, only the very wealthy had the resources to afford private facilities and staff to attend them.

In eighteenth- and nineteenth-century Europe, as healing centers developed around sources of spring waters, retiring to inland watering sites became a signature of the commercialization of leisure. These cities of water catered to a spa society composed of the aristocracy, the otherwise wealthy, and the creative—artists, composers, and authors. "Spa literature and spa music virtually oozed out of the fountains" (Croutier 1992:114). Exclusive hotels housed theaters, casinos, and ornate water bars. Evening entertainment forged romantic, political, and business confederations; "spa towns were transformed into a dreamland for snobs and fortune hunters" (Croutier 1992:115), where community was defined by the exclusion of people who had fewer resources. These fashionable and flamboyant places of affluent sociability appealed to Europe's royal families and nobility. The most memorable spas had existed in less ornate forms since early historic, perhaps prehistoric, times: these include Bath (England), Vichy and Evian-les-Bains (France), Wiesbaden and Baden-Baden (Germany), Montecatini Terme and Salsomaggiore (Italy), Bad Ragaz (Switzerland), and Marienbad (Czechoslovakia).

Colonists transposed the spa tradition in a more muted form to North America, where customs were blended with what Europeans learned from Native Americans about locating healthful waters and creating sweat lodges. In various permutations, sweat baths were customary in societies whose geography ranged from Alaska to the Yucatán, across the Great Plains, and throughout New England. These sites of association were rejuvenating and therapeutic communities of shared identity that served religious as well as social functions; compared to the demographically structured European spas, they were largely inclusive. Later Europeans (notably, Christian missionaries and government entities) were threatened by the sense of community, cum potential social and political agency, forged by these sites of association (see chapter 4, section on kava). They discouraged, and in many places brutally obstructed, use of these sacred places. Still, the connection between health and water remained a common generic idiom for both Native Americans and Europeans.

In the 1760s, a man allegedly was cured of a skin infection in Stafford Springs, Connecticut, a site that became "famous overnight for its reputation of curing the gout, sterility, pulmonary [disorders, and] hysterics.... It soon became the New England *Bath*, where the sick and rich resort to prolong life and acquire polite accomplishments" (Chapelle 2005:107).

During the next century, a U.S. hydropathic movement promoted pure water for illnesses of all kinds and zealously advanced its purifying powers for transgressions and impiety. While conventional medicine relied on bloodletting and regarded women's physiology as abnormal, hydrotherapy welcomed female practitioners and recommended mild remedies such as changes in diet and exercise. These circumstances offered, for those who could afford it, a "retreat for the nineteenth century woman searching for an alternative philosophy that [emphasized] her . . . strengths" (Farber 1994:92–93). In time, U.S. spas—Poland Spring (Maine), Saratoga Springs (New York), Calistoga (California), and Hot Springs (Arkansas)—came to emulate the splendor of their European counterparts. These opulent places of association offered billiards, cards, dancing, horse racing, and gambling. Worldwide, the popularity of spas declined after the 1930s but was revived during the 1960s (Routh et al. 1996; Burnett 1999). In the United States today, spas more resemble resorts than sites for taking the waters. Most are associated with leisure, recreation, and preventive health care. Some offer foods prepared with spa waters. Claims for specific cures have been consolidated into the generic healthfulness of hydrotherapies. A testimony to the continued faith in the healthful attributes of water is embodied in the superfluity of personal, hotel, club, and municipal swimming pools, spas, saunas, and whirlpools.

In addition to the traditional modes of water therapy, since the early 1980s, the aquatic continuum of care employed by formally credentialed physical and associated therapists has included Watsu, a portmanteau of water and shiatsu. Programs and therapy teams vary, but the centerpiece of Watsu is body massage performed while the client is floated in water and is stretched and moved to "dance." In contemporary biomedicine, balneotherapy involves immersion of patients in mineral water baths or pools for the treatment of back pain, fibromyalgia, arthritis, and dermatologic disorders, most commonly atopic dermatitis and psoriasis. The mechanism of action by which this broad spectrum of disorders improves is not known but is suggested to include immunomodulatory and mechanical effects (Matz et al. 2003; Faull 2005). The veracity of the popular wisdom that baths are relaxing (and the corollary, that such relaxation is healthful) is difficult to gauge, although approximations are possible. Measures of the sensitive salivary stress indicators cortisol and chromogranin A in healthy Japanese men suggest that a benefit of spas and other waters is moderate stress relief, with the most pronounced effects occurring in individuals with higher levels of stress (Toda et al. 2006).

The dark side of spas and other waters is the risk of waterborne infections. Guidelines exist, of course, for cleaning and other maintenance of spas and other facilities, but the growth of microorganisms is encouraged by warm waters; chlorine, bromine, and other disinfectants evaporate at temperatures above 84ƒaF, reducing antimicrobial activity and encouraging increased titers of microorganisms such as *Staphylococcus*, *Mycobacterium*, and *Pseudomonas*. "Hot tub lung," dermatologic disorders (folliculitis, carbuncles, abscesses), and gastrointestinal and other infections have been linked to personal, public, club, and hotel swimming pools, spas, hot tubs, saunas, and whirlpools (Embil et al. 1997; Hartman et al. 2007; Merck 2007).

Drinking Water

Like that of spas, the history of drinking water followed a classed trajectory. In postmedieval Europe, especially in towns and cities, drinking waters were not clean and, with some regularity, were responsible for epidemics of typhoid, dysentery, and cholera. Those who could afford to do so drank wines, ales, and beers, all of which included heating in the process of preparation—in combination with alcohol fermentation, this discouraged the growth of microorganisms. As municipal waters became more polluted, the primary beverage for the lower classes was a "small beer" with low alcohol content (0.5–1.0 percent), which was sufficient to check the growth of microorganisms and not threaten dehydration. Before the eighteenth century, only titled aristocrats had the options of time and resources to travel to healthful springs. During the 1700s, the growth of commerce and industry produced a nouveaux riche class that emulated the gentry in all ways, including seeking recreation at spas. Even if these destinations were not as therapeutic as claimed, they afforded some small percentage of people a few days of drinking significantly cleaner water than that at home. This would have had a generally salubrious effect in readjusting populations of intestinal flora and reducing what was then widespread chronic gastrointestinal upset (Routh et al. 1996; Chapelle 2005).

Traditionally, waters were consumed or otherwise used at the source, at spas and baths where people "took the waters" or "took the cure," and at seaside locations that offered thalassotherapy (from the Greek *thalassos*, "sea"). There were hundreds, perhaps thousands, of spa towns worldwide, some having a considerable reputation beyond their regions. Many of these still exist today, building on the cachet of former celebrity. Other spas are more recent designs as tourist destinations that offer hydropathic hotels, referred to in short as "hydros" by the cognoscenti. They offer mineral waters, hot springs, sauna, hydrotherapy, thermae, curortology (mud-water-climate therapy), and combinations thereof. During the past few decades, spa tourism has again become a popular phenomenon worldwide; in many cases, the source and composition of the water are not as significant as are the sociability and reputed healthfulness of the experience.

For several hundred years in Europe, waters also have been bottled at the source and transported to urban centers, where they were merchandised by grocers, spicers, and apothecaries. During the 1700s, bottled waters from 9 of the 65 spas in England were transported to most parts of the country. Entrepreneurs in London also imported Continental waters from Bad Pyrmont and Seltzer in Germany and from Spa in Belgium. Low-mineral content, mild-tasting waters were favored for drinking and were measured into individual-sized bottles, or "doses," that were more affordable. Bottle trade diffused medicinal waters through a larger segment of society beyond the spa set, although access to such waters, like other resources, was still asymmetrical. During an era of overindulgence among the wealthy, eighteenth- and nineteenth-century European physicians prescribed chalybeate (iron-containing) waters for restorative purposes, saline waters for purgative action, sulfur waters to improve the complexion, and others for gout and rheumatism. "All were projections of health and beauty to a society greatly concerned with appearance and bodily functions" (Burnett 1999:10).

Fountains of youth are an interesting notion in the human experience of healing and restorative waters. Ancient Chinese writings extol the virtues of rejuvenating waters, such as the fountain of Pon Lai and the springs of Mount Lao Shan, to which emperors of the Chin and Han dynasties made pilgrimages. The Aztec water god Quetzalcoatl drank from the fountain of immortality, and Alexander the Great is reputed to have searched for a rejuvenating river in India in the fourth century BCE.

Slavonic traditions invoke *zhivaya voda*, "living water," to return life to the dead. Ponce de León's search for a fountain of youth in today's Florida is a piece of the fabric of European expansions (see chapter 2). Purportedly he was drawn to Bimini, a place that Caribbean natives described as prosperous and full of clear, bubbling springs flecked with gold and silver and reputed to extend longevity and reverse aging. He named the land La Florida, evoking its floral bounty. Whether he was in fact looking for one, de León's "discovery" of a fountain of youth is apocryphal: his name was attached to the legend only after his death (in 1521), in the 1575 *Memoir* of Hernando d'Escalante Fontaneda, on which Antonio Herrera y Tordesillas (1601–1625) based his history of the Spanish in the New World (*Historia general de los hechos de los castellanos*). As is common in legends, the central theme is a metaphor, distilled into a monolithic icon. The Floridan Aquifer (an underground geologic formation that conducts groundwater) is one of the largest in the world, underlying an area of about 100,000 miles and discharging into hundreds of springs, no one of which would have been *the* fountain. Many of these springs today are the heart of the state's tourist industry, as well as sources for commercial bottled waters (Croutier 1992; Chapelle 2005; Keyshistory 2006).

The United States

In the United States, civic authorities' concern about water intensified during the eighteenth century when growing population density both escalated demand for water and compromised its cleanliness. At least in part as a result of poor water quality, New York City assumed a leadership role as early as the 1670s, when it began to order construction of public wells with costs shared by the city and residents adjacent to the water sources. At the end of the colonial period, visitors observed that people and horses alike were reluctant to drink the city's water, and those who could afford to purchase natural spring waters from water carriers (who by 1761 were licensed by the city) would do so. Drinking clean(er) water might have been a primary concern, but another important factor in the development of a citywide water supply was the risk of fire from ubiquitous candles and open fires.

By the mid-eighteenth century, all responsibility for wells and pumps had come to rest in the city's hands. Increasingly, in the larger urban centers, water regulations were established with more responsibility assigned to municipal authorities; by contrast, in many U.S. colonial towns and rural areas, residents were responsible for well construction and maintenance. Although the Revolutionary War disrupted services of all kinds, postwar recovery to standards of the colonial era (most remarkably in port cities) was relatively fast (Duffy 1990).

For the decade that began in the early 1790s, a series of yellow fever epidemics accelerated efforts to promote sanitary reform, including establishing health boards and improving water supplies and quality. In 1799, Philadelphia became the first city in the United States to establish a public water system that pumped water from a surface source through pipes to residences. The establishment of waterworks drove the corollary problem of drainage. Substantial progress was made in the first decades of the 1800s when increased water pressure was facilitated by engineering improvements such as the refinement of cast-iron piping and steam power. At the turn of the twentieth century, the number of public water systems reached 3,000; early in the twenty-first century, an estimated 170,000 public and private water systems exist in the United States (Duffy 1990; Roberts 2003).

By the early nineteenth century, drinking water had shed its aura of impoverishment and was linked to discernment and affluence. The consumption of bottled water began in the 1820s with the commercialization of the naturally effervescent Saratoga Springs in Upstate New York. First marketed as "Doctor Clark," the water was intended primarily to treat gastrointestinal disorders. In 1844, Poland Spring in Maine began marketing its bottled water for kidney disorders. As in Europe, these and other sources were gradually embellished by hotels and advertised as sites of elaborate entertainments that forged identity and sociability for the wealthy (Chapelle 2005).

By midcentury, affordable glass bottles had become more readily available, and spring waters came to be regarded as relatively clean sources of potable water. During the second half of the 1800s, as comprehension of microbial sources of illness expanded, commercial ventures began bottling clean waters from rural areas for consumption by urban populations whose water supplies were commonly contaminated. The distribution of drinking water in five-gallon vessels, a practice already established in Europe, helped to control waterborne infections. Although only the wealthy could afford bottled drinking water at first, it had come to be regarded as a "desirable amenity rather than a luxury" (Chapelle 2005:4) by the turn of the twentieth century.

The advent of chlorinated municipal water supplies early in the twentieth century eclipsed bottled waters. Again, Philadelphia pioneered in efforts to improve the quality of drinking water. Like many other nineteenth-century U.S. urban centers, the city suffered epidemics of cholera and typhoid and other fevers. During the same time, advances in microbiology identified pathogenic microorganisms, their sources, and how to control them. Experimentation began in 1909 to add solid hypochlorites to drinking water, and by 1913 the process had been perfected to using liquid chlorine. That same year, Philadelphia inaugurated the first permanent water treatment facility in the United States and witnessed diminished rates of waterborne infections. Other cities rapidly imitated this success, and by 1941 chlorination had come to be used by 85 percent of the 5,372 U.S. water treatment facilities (Chapelle 2005:15). Not only was safe tap water more convenient, it also carried the cachet of novelty and technology at a time of advancing knowledge in the control of disease, which contributed to the perception that specific medicines, not waters, were efficacious (see chapter 3, sections on water safety and street foods).

Also coincident with growth in the industrial sector is the shift in consumption of bottled water from the home to manufacturing plants and retail establishments that could not afford, or did not want, to pay for adequate plumbing and bought five-gallon jugs instead. Thus, the prestige and profitability of bottled water were further diminished as its consumption became a classed phenomenon, associated with blue-collar labor. Industry leaders such as Poland Spring, Mountain Valley, and Saratoga reduced their scales of production and redirected product focus; most local bottlers closed their operations (Duffy 1990).

By the 1960s, growing concern was being expressed with the dark side of science and technology. The panache of chlorination and reverence for the technology of water delivery certainly had worn thin. The vulnerability of nature to anthropogenic impacts was revealed through the popularization of works such as Rachel Carson's *Silent Spring* (1964). Although Carson's intent was to document the hazards and long-range, pantrophic effects of pesticides (primarily DDT), *Silent Spring* was an intentional metaphor for environmental issues writ large. It and other pioneering expositions were foundational to the substantiation of public environmental movements, academic ecology, and government entities such as the U.S. Environmental Protection Agency, established in 1970. Over the next decades, environmental (ecological) subjects were critically examined in public, academic, and governmental forums. Foremost among the issues discussed were the far-reaching effects of water contamination and its potential impact on public water supplies. This, in the larger context of a growing health-consciousness, helped to repopularize bottled water in the United States. Increasingly, individual-sized, branded bottled waters have become available in most retail establishments, hotels, restaurants, and vending machines. They now are delivered to places of work and again, as in decades past, to homes (Chapelle 2005).

In response, the status of the workplace cooler has risen from that of a classed, low-prestige necessity that offered potable water in places with poor infrastructure; in contemporary offices and factories, it is a beacon of informal social networking, typically on themes that have little professional content, such as sporting events and, in caricature, office gossip. It worked its way into lexical tags: "around the watercooler" is a metaphor for gathering during the workday, a site of downtime; "watercooler shows" refers to television programs that have a large following, for example, those with elements of surprise in plot, no plot (the "reality" genre), and sports. We find analogs in all societies, not only in workplace break protocols but also in other custom domains. Freestanding five-gallon water bottles are the health-conscious replacements of the water fountains connected to municipal water supplies. Most recently, those multigallon sources are being replaced by machines that vend individual-sized bottled water.

French Perrier water was officially launched in the United States in 1977, when its distributor linked bottled water to exclusivity and celebrity, flying dozens of journalists to *Source Perrier* in Vergeze, France, and producing advertisements that featured famous personages such as Orson Welles with the tagline "There is a spring, and its name is Perrier," driving U.S. sales up more than 3,000 percent between 1976 and 1979. The health image was reinforced in 1979 when Perrier America sponsored the New York City Marathon: six thousand runners sporting Perrier T-shirts and gripping branded water bottles crossed Central Park, just as long-distance running was emerging as a popular exercise phenomenon. Soon, other high-end companies such as Evian and Poland Spring began campaigns to advertise drinking water in small, individual-sized bottles, with dramatic results. Restaurants and bars that had previously served water in glasses began serving bottled water, as was the custom in Europe. Some upscale restaurants offered the services of "water sommeliers." Even in New York City, which many regard to have one of the world's best municipal water supplies, gauged by cleanliness and taste, the popularity of bottled water escalated, a phenomenon that cynics regarded, at least in its early phase, to be a projection of "elegance, sophistication, and conspicuous consumption" (Chapelle 2005:6). Water clubs and water-tasting events became popular vehicles for sociability. By the early twenty-first century, the image of bottled water had been remarkably transformed as tap water and fountains increasingly were viewed with distrust and contempt. Today, issues of image and identity are at least as compelling as are legitimate and imagined concerns about the risks of chlorination, fluoridation, and contamination. Whereas taking the waters in earlier centuries was regarded to be healthy because of the reputed characteristics of specific waters, by the late 1900s bottled waters were no longer thought to be therapeutic for particular illnesses. Today, despite (re)marketing campaigns, much of the hype has been condensed into a single abstract theme, generic lifestyle "healthfulness."

In the imagination of some, bottled water derives from protected sources, about 75 percent from springs and aquifers, while most tap water originates in lakes and rivers. Whereas the U.S. Environmental Protection Agency governs municipal tap waters as commodities, the Food and Drug Administration (FDA) regulates bottled waters as food products under the Federal Food, Drug, and Cosmetic Act. This means that tap waters are more strictly regulated and disinfected than are bottled waters. More specifically, FDA supervision applies to water sold across state lines, suggesting that as much as 60–70 percent of the bottled water marketed in the United States may be exempt from FDA oversight (NRDC 2006).

The FDA Standard of Identity distinguishes *processed* from *natural* waters. In the first category, waters usually are drawn from municipal supplies and chemically altered so that they are cleaner, more palatable, or fortified—for example, removing dissolved solids, adding flavors, or adding minerals such as fluoride. *Purified* water is collected from the surface or underground sites and is treated to be safe for human consumption through processes such as deionization, distillation, and reverse osmosis. It differs from *tap* water only in how it is distributed to consumers. Produced in the same way, *enhanced* water has added flavors or minerals. *Natural* waters are drawn from natural sites and remain chemically essentially the same after bottling. Lakes, streams, and rivers yield *surface* water. *Spring* water from natural underground flows should be collected only at the spring or by tapping the source below the surface through a bore hole (a shaft drilled vertically or horizontally into the ground). *Mineral* water is sourced from underground sites and is not treated; it must have a constant mineral content, which can be accomplished by artificially supplying minerals or gases. *Well* water is collected through a bore hole that connects to an aquifer. *Artesian* refers to water confined by hydrostatic pressure in an aquifer. After treatment, naturally effervescent *sparkling* water must contain the same amount of carbon dioxide as at the source. Fifty-nine percent of bottled water consumed globally is purified, while the rest is mineral or spring water (FDA 2002; Wateryear 2005).

The FDA exempts from contamination and water-testing standards several types of what would generally be considered to be bottled water. Both federal and state regulations do not define products that are labeled "disinfected," "carbonated," "soda," "seltzer," "filtered," and simply "water." For these, the FDA requires that they not be "adulterated," a term that has not been defined. Significantly, this regulation has never been enforced. Science-based public-interest groups that advocate stricter supervision of bottled water quality characterize FDA regulation and enforcement as "trivial . . . and in many cases weaker than international standards" and deem state government oversight to be "ill equipped and understaffed" (NRDC 2006).

Water Chic

Today, bottled water is a global cultural phenomenon and one of the most dynamic sectors of the food and beverage industry, with annual consumption increasing by about 12 percent. Italians consume the most bottled water per person, about 49 gallons per year. The United States is the largest consumer of bottled water: 8.2 billion gallons annually, second only to carbonated soft drinks. The most rapid growth in sales of bottled water occurs in some developing countries, such as Mexico and Indonesia, while the fastest growth in the world is in China (Gleick 2004; Arnold and Larsen 2006; International Bottled Water Association 2006).

In the developed world, where water supply infrastructures guarantee safe water that is as healthy as most bottled waters, the latter can cost 10,000 times more than tap water—as much as $10.00 per gallon (Chapelle 2005; Arnold and Larsen 2006), a figure considerably higher than what many people pay for gasoline, about which they complain. A significant, but not determined, proportion of this consumption is from the individual-sized bottles that are the focus of this chapter. While labor, marketing, and distribution are costly, high profit margins—25 percent or more—offer strong incentive for the beverage industry to proliferate brands. Bottling enterprises number in the thousands, at the same time that there is a strong trend toward consolidation as multinational industry leaders endeavor to secure their command of major markets. Brands that sold in the greatest quantity in the United States in recent years include Dasani and Aquafina, products of Coca-Cola and Pepsi-Cola, respectively. The water division of the world's largest food company, Nestlé, sells some seventy brands, including the popular Perrier, Poland Spring, and Arrowhead. This multibrand corporate consolidation resembles the carbonated beverage industry, in which more than 90 percent of sales are controlled by three multinationals (Pepsi-Cola, Cadbury/Schweppes, and Coca-Cola), but in the bottled water industry, only about 50 percent of global sales are controlled by the top four bottled waters: Aquafina; Poland Spring and Arrowhead, both in the Perrier Group; and Sparkletts, by Groupe Danone (Gleick 2004).

The aggregate of bottled waters presents a baffling array of brands and imaginative assertions about healthful qualities. Gauging the relative merits of these products is confounded by inconsistent labeling, including references to quality conveyed by terms such as *pure, alpine, geyser,* and *natural.* The apprehension of such designations varies among bottlers, regulatory entities, and consumers. Regardless, the exact source is less relevant than are the circumstances of the catchment area from which the water is collected, and it is contradictory to claim purity when the impurities that mineral waters contain were the original incentive for consuming them. Understanding whether and how bottled waters might be healthful is further obscured by labels that depict glacial expanses, pristine streams, and other sites that have no bearing on the water's source. For example, Yosemite and Everest bottled waters are drawn from suburban Los Angeles and southern Texas, respectively. When the FDA discovered that Alaska Premium Glacier Drinking Water "from the last unpolluted frontier" was actually sourced from a public water system in Juneau, the bottler was required to include this information on the label. Recently, Coca-Cola and Pepsi-Cola have been forced to label their minimally dressed up Dasani ("pure, fresh taste") and Aquafina ("pure water, perfect taste") "comes from a public water source." Further, for all brands, ingredient labeling is not uniform: only some constituents might be recorded, and contents are reported on scales that span parts per million, milligrams per liter, and micrograms per liter. Water chemists note that their own research yields constituent values that show discrepancies from those recorded by bottlers and are inconsistent over time and between one batch and another. Advocacy, government, and research groups find that a significant number of brands exceed permissible limits for one or more regulated biological or chemical contaminants (Pip 2000; NRDC 2006). Because the bottled water industry is for the most part self-regulated, "it is a wonder—and a tribute to the safety of the tap water that is the basis of most bottled products—that problems do not occur more often" (Nestle 2006:410).

Hausaland

Everything and everybody in Hausaland are strongly influenced by the marked seasonality of rainfall, including, of course, food production but also religious training, the timing of marriage property exchanges (see chapter 4), and disease epidemiology. In this part of the Sahel, *ruwan sama* (i.e., rain, literally "sky water") falls between late May and September, yielding less than about thirty inches annually. Crops are seeded in early June, and harvests begin in late September; granary stores are gradually and unevenly depleted until the next harvests. The great majority of Hurumi residents attend to this rain cyclicity, but year-round production is possible for a small proportion of the population who own land in the *fadama* area adjacent to the river along one boundary of the village. Those residents manage *lambu*, which are irrigated gardens planted primarily with nonstaples such as tomato, leafy greens, and medicines (see chapter 3).

During most of my field research in Hurumi, households depended for water generally (*ruwa*), including drinking water (*ruwan sha*), on several in-village *rigoji* (wells) and eventually on traveling to the nearest roadside village when it received piped water. There, water delivery still was centralized to two or three locations rather than being linked to individual compounds. Roof runoff and any other rainwater collected during the rainy season satisfies only a small proportion of needs.

In view of the proscriptions of purdah (see chapter 3), which constrain married women's movements outside their own compounds, water is collected by men and older children to provide sufficient resources for drinking, food preparation and cooking, cleaning utensils, personal hygiene, and domestic animals. Well water is collected into locally made *tulu* and other earthenware vessels (and increasingly into plastic containers) that are carried on the head and, in the case of households that are more affluent, by bicycle (*keke*) and donkey (*jaki*). In many respects, that gendered division of labor among Hausa resembles traditional patterns in the West, with most domestic chores being the purview of women. For laundry, however, in the light of significant labor and time demands, water collectors do their households' laundry close to the source, at several in-village wells and a seasonal *bingi*, a shallow pond that fills during *damina*, the rainy season.

These sources of ruwa become beacons of association. As each wellgoer takes his turn to collect, the group engages in hira about the task at hand and other matters. Even in this small village, and though water is collected daily by every compound, the individuals involved and times of collection vary so that this association is a shifting social collective. During damina, groups are smaller and individuals encounter one another less frequently. During *rani*, the dry months, when the water table is low, the group coheres around the difficulty of reaching the source, unpalatable water, and the arduous trek back to the gida.

Like many other traditional peoples, Hausa employ several methods to clean drinking water. Some are for the collective, such as dropping into a well leaves of gwandar jeji, which, as mentioned in the preceding chap-

Water collectors congregate at a well during the dry season. The flowering *mangwaro* (mango tree) signals that it is January, when the water table is especially low. Water is transferred from a rope-suspended half calabash to earthenware *tulu*. Households with more resources use *jaki* to transport the tulu; other Hurumi residents carry the tulu themselves, supported on the head and cushioned by *gammo* (circular head pads that balance heavy loads).

ter, is antibacterial, antiparasitic against *Leishmania* and *Trypanosoma* species, and anthelmintic (Sahpaz et al. 1994; Alawa et al. 2003).

However, most water-cleaning activities are conducted within individual domestic units. Turbid water is filtered into storage vessels through *barki* (cloth) or *faifai* (which are circular mats made with *ciyawa*; grass, Poaceae) covered with dried leaves of the young *goruba* (doum palm, *Hyphaene thebaica* Mart., Arecaceae). Faifai also serve as winnowing mats and covers for food and water vessels. Seeds of *zogale* (horseradish [or drumstick] tree, *Moringa oleifera* Lam., Moringaceae) and leaves of *kokiya* (monkey orange, *Strychnos spinosa* Lam., Loganiaceae) and gwandar jeji are tossed into or rubbed inside water vessels, where they "coagulate," that is, precipitate or adsorb, soil and other impurities (Göttsch 1992). The flocculating principles in zogale are dimeric cationic proteins

(Ndabigengesere et al. 1995). The plant also has antibacterial, antiviral, anti-inflammatory, hypotensive, hypocholesterolemic, and antitumor activities (Guevara et al. 1999; Ghasi et al. 2000), which are consistent with Hausa use of this food and medicine for gastrointestinal complaints, sore teeth and gums, wounds, and fevers. Kokiya is active against trypanosomes and bacteria (Moshi and Mbwambo 2002; Hoet et al. 2004) and is commonly used by Hausa for sores and gastrointestinal disorders.

Inside the compound, collected water is partitioned by domestic units (see chapter 4) and by use. Each married woman in a compound stores her own *ruwan sha*, "drinking water," which is a derived and more intimate nucleus of association. Storage vessels such as *tulu, randa,* and *kwatarniya* vary in size and form but share the attribute of water seeping through the porous fabric of the earthenware vessel and evaporating from the surface, thereby cooling the water. Depending on the vagaries of social dynamics, co-wives and other women in the compound may congregate near one of those drinking water stores. Through the evening, the groups diminish as they cohere around individual women and their children. Later in the evening, if the woman shares intimacies with her husband, the group shrinks to two; if it is the turn of a co-wife, the woman is alone and the pattern dissolves.

In addition to being important for hydration in Hausaland's hot and dry environment, and a core of association, ruwa is a vehicle for medicines. Magani (principally plants) are infused or concocted individually; for composite medicines, the ingredients may be bundled. *Tsime* and *jiko* refer to water infusions prepared over long and short durations, respectively. *Sha da shafe* refers to drinking and rubbing or rinsing the body with the same solution, or drinking the solution and rubbing the undissolved residue on the body. Some medicines are delivered as Islamic verses that the imam writes with *rine* (vegetable dye) on an *allo* (wooden Koranic writing board), which is rinsed with water that is collected for the patient to drink. In this way, the medicine is internalized to combine metaphoric, religious, and physical therapeutics. The importance of water for Hausa healing customs in the postpartum period is described in the preceding chapter.

Alwala, "ablutions," are performed before each of the five daily prayers that are a pillar of Islam. While women pray within the compound, men attend the village mosque or wherever is expedient, such as on the

The author and her associate, Ibrahim Muazzamu, interview Sali manu (holding his son), who is especially knowledgeable about Hausa therapeutics.

farm while at work or in a specially designated area at a market. They carry water for ablutions in *buta* (small earthenware vessels that traditionally were substituted by gourd vessels) or, more recently (particularly in urban centers), by bottled water. Thus, the buta that in the past projected Islamic identity may today be a symbol that conflates faith and modernity, nuanced by health concerns. Similarly, in-compound water (and food) vessels gradually give way to plastic counterparts.

Water and Health

The primary constituent of plant and animal bodies is water, which accounts for about 70 percent of human body weight, with large volumes in lung, brain, blood, digestive, and muscle tissues. The body's intra- and extracellular compartments are separated by semipermeable membranes through which water passes freely, transported by eleven types of aquaporins, proteins that are distinctly and variably distributed throughout the body. Intra- and extracellular spaces hold 60–70 percent of the body's water; sustaining homeostatic balance within those fluid compartments is accomplished through complex coordination of organ functions and the endocrine system (Lutz and Przytulski 2006).

Water is the body's primary solvent and medium for enzymatic and other chemical reactions and transports key metabolites such as hormones, nutrients, and antibodies through the lymphatic and blood systems. It is a solvent for many small molecules and a structural component of many large ones, such as glycogen and protein; it serves as a lubricant in joint fluids, mucus, and other secretions; and it gives shape to cells (Lutz and Przytulski 2006).

Maintaining hydration is fundamental to health: lack of water leads to death significantly faster than does insufficient food or lack of food. Insensible (not noticeable) water loss occurs through the skin (evaporative) and lungs (expiratory), averaging 800 milliliters to 1 liter daily and is almost electrolyte-free. The amount and rate of loss are influenced by body and environmental temperatures, air humidity, altitude, and activity levels. Sensible water loss includes significant loss of sodium and chloride through the kidney as urine, the skin as perspiration, and the intestines in feces. The AI (Adequate Intake), which prevents the adverse effects of water loss, is 3.7 liters for 19- to 30-year-old adults.[4] Foods should provide 20 percent of that, beverages 80 percent. Foods that have a high water content include chicken meat (52 percent), drained canned tuna (61 percent), apples (84 percent), lettuce (96 percent), and celery (95 percent) (Lutz and Przytulski 2006). Individuals should regulate water consumption to adjust to environmental variables (e.g., heat, altitude) and activity. The Institute of Medicine explains that "the vast majority of healthy people adequately meet their daily hydration needs by letting thirst be their guide," but the International Bottled Water Association asserts that individuals should drink "eight 8-ounce glasses of water a day." The water association "proves" this with a hydration calculator into which one types only weight and exercise minutes per day, which typically results in exaggerated estimates of water needs (Nestle 2006:402).

Expressing aesthetic and health concerns, many consumers cite better taste and fewer contaminants to rationalize drinking bottled instead of tap water. Taste surveys administered to ordinary consumers as well as sommeliers and other professional tasters, however, reveal that the ranking of brand versus tap water is inconsistent among and within individuals, commonly is influenced by context, and is not patterned. Advertising and public perceptions aside, these products are not necessarily more healthy than tap water. In the United States and Europe, public water supplies are more strictly regulated than are bottled waters. As much as 25–40 percent of bottled water is tap water to which are added minerals whose health benefits have not been established: "[B]ottlers tout arcane methods of distillation and filtration and add minerals to get a better, more 'watery' taste" (Moskin 2006). These packaged tap waters include the number one and two best-selling brands, Aquafina and Dasani, the "creations" of Pepsico and the Coca-Cola Company, respectively. The French government has advised regular switching of brands of bottled water on the theory that the micronutrients may be harmful in accumulated doses. Commercial bottled waters range widely in mineral content; few contain optimum levels of minerals such as calcium, magnesium, and sodium, which, because they occur commonly in the earth's crust, are found in many mineral waters (Chauret 2004; Jamal and Eisenberg 2004; Arnold and Larsen 2006; NRDC 2006).

Bottled-water regulations in North America and Europe are quite different. The U.S. FDA specifies that *mineral waters* must contain 500–1,500 milligrams per liter of dissolved solids, the total mineral content. For a water to be advertised as a "good" source of, or "rich" in, a particular solid, it must contain at least 25 percent of the Dietary Reference Intake for that nutrient. In Europe, water with any measurable mineral content can be marketed as a mineral water, and its original characteristics cannot be altered. *Spring waters* can be modified. Investigation of 30 U.S. bottled waters revealed these ranges: calcium, 0–546 mg/L (milligrams/liter); magnesium, 0–126 mg/L; sodium, 0–1,200 mg/L. Median values for European bottled waters are, respectively, 115 mg/L, 24 mg/L, and 20 mg/L (Jamal and Eisenberg 2004:326). Advocates of bottled products recommend high calcium and magnesium content in view of the protective role of these minerals against cardiovascular disease, diabetes, some cancers, osteoporosis, arthritis, and dental caries. These are not recommended for individuals with renal and other diseases (Pip 2000).

Conversely, other common groundwater solutes found in some bottled products pose health risks. High sodium consumption has been linked to hypertension. Nitrates, sulfates, lead, and cadmium present diverse toxicologies, including cancers and gastrointestinal and neurologic effects. Good-quality water at the source may become contaminated during processing, transport, and storage. Contaminants include microorganisms, asbestos from filters, and organic compounds such as toluene and phthalates leached from bottle plastic. One concern is that many bottled waters contain no fluoride, a micronutrient provided by many municipal water systems; the anticariogenic action of fluoride is well established (Pip 2000; Silva et al. 2004; NRDC 2006).

One of the latest iterations in the evolution of bottled drinking water is *enhanced water*, a category once dominated by Gatorade. Playing on the bad tap-water-taste and health themes, today's enhanced waters are (further) embellished with such components as vitamins, minerals, oxygen, caffeine, sugar, soy, carbohydrates, and flavors. Recent marketing trends reveal efforts to bolster the healthful image of bottled products. One company promotes its sugar-, calorie-, and carbohydrate-free and vitamin-enriched water by announcing its new partnership with the University of Miami Diabetes Research Institute Foundation, stating that "a portion of the proceeds [of product sales] . . . will benefit the Foundation [by] supporting cure-focused research" (Bevnet 2006). Compared to other marketing ploys, this effort to convince consumers that the bottler is concerned about diabetes, and health generally, is particularly transparent.

As outlined in the foregoing discussion, the emergent nature of the individual-sized bottled water market, including the refashioning of products, makes general or definitive statements about the healthfulness of these waters difficult. Other global concerns about bottled water, including the portable single-serve products, include pressure on the environment generated by used, "one-way" bottles; depletion of aquifers that provide local drinking water and agricultural irrigation; and the amount of energy consumed in the production and distribution of bottled water, notably in countries such as the United States, where municipal water supplies are inexpensive and high quality. In the developing world, where a substantial proportion of the disease burden could be prevented by improved water management, health infrastructures have been moving away from water and sanitation issues for the past four decades (Bartram 2008). In these countries, the high cost of bottled water contributes to asymmetrical access to basic resources, including health, and reduces pressures on governments and other providers to deliver sufficient and safe water.

The Future of Bottled Waters

Will the expansion of the individual-sized bottled water market simply continue into the future? There is evidence both that new niche markets will be created and courted and that in some sectors the trend will at least slow, if not reverse.

Bottled Water for Everyone

The ever-expanding product lines that are marketed to pet owners now include bottled waters for companion animals. If consumers claim to discern among waters by taste, they can be persuaded that their pets have the same palate. Pawier, Inc., took the initiative in 1990 with a vitamin-enriched bottled water for dogs, other companies followed with K9 Quencher, PetRefresh, and Aqua Dog. Dogade builds on the cachet of the first enhanced bottled water for people. DogWater is packaged in bottles that serve as throw toys when empty. Today's pet products serve a variety of animals (cats, horses, raccoons) and, like human products, are variably flavored and dressed up with meat, fish, and parsley-chlorophyll. Paradoxically, Gutter Water and Toilet Water identify preferred drinking sources for pets that apparently do not need *bottled* water after all. One woman's testimonial for PetRefresh recounted that her cats preferred to drink from the tap rather than their water bowl, but they *will* drink bottled water from the bowl. Here, the bowl—not the water—appears to be the issue. In another irony, Pawier's bottled water has been supplanted by the company's water-soluble vitamin supplement, which can be given orally or mixed into food or tap water (Carlton 2005), in which case the bottled feature has been phased out. Pet products, like their human counterparts, morph into whatever forms consumers can be persuaded to buy. In these examples, the health rationale has been dropped when it is no longer profitable for the industry and is forgotten by consumers.

New Sources for Bottled Waters: Desalination

Technologies for ocean desalination have existed for a long time and continue to be of interest in discussions of resource depletion. Environmental, government regulatory, and other entities consider whether processing ocean into drinking water is practical on a large scale. Concerns have been raised that desalination is expensive; there is risk that low-income communities near desalination facilities will be most impacted by costs and pollution; privatization may contribute further to social asymmetries; the integrity of coastal and estuary environments will be threatened to a greater extent than now; and public health experts question the quality of desalinated water, especially in the light of how contaminants are concentrated during the process. Finally, there are many alternatives (Public Citizen 2007).

Water sourced from deep in the ocean is colder and has a higher salt content than that collected closer to the surface. Desalinated deep ocean water has become the principal foreign export of Hawai'i: for the past several years, five commercial entities have been shipping more than 37 million dollars' worth of bottled seawater, primarily to Japan (International Herald Tribune 2007). On the Big Island, a state commercial venture associated with the National Energy Laboratory of Hawai'i Authority (NELHA) pumps deep ocean water through a three-thousand-foot pipeline and transports it to four of the companies that desalinate, filter, and bottle the water. The state encourages this industry to diversify Hawaii's tourism-dependent economy; in addition, benefits accrue to the state from royalties, rent, and a charge to use the NELHA logo.

Although Japanese desalinated bottled ocean drinking water has been retailed since the mid-1990s, that product is not sourced at a comparable depth; more significant is that it does not share the strong brand recognition of Hawaiian commodities, which evoke nature, purity, and high quality. In Japan, some of the products are promoted as supplements that encourage weight loss, decrease stress, and improve digestion and skin tone. In late 2005, Koyo USA opened their MaHaLo brand showroom and water bar in Waikiki, featuring the Hawai'i-sourced deep ocean water. Shortly thereafter, Koyo secured State Health Department approval to sell the bottled ocean water in Hawai'i and began sales in high-end shops, restaurants, and hotels. Koyo and other companies anticipate extending into U.S. mainland retail markets, where the cost will be substantially less than in Japan (four to six U.S. dollars for a 1.5 liter bottle).

The purported attributes of deep ocean water are that it is "thousands of years old [and] protected from modern impurities such as pollution, agricultural and industrial run-off, hormones, and pathogens . . .

the cleanest and healthiest source of drinking water on our planet." Also, it carries the exotic and remote cachet of the islands and the constructed image that it is an "unlimited resource" (DOH 2007), which seems counterintuitive.

Think Outside the Bottle

Despite aggressive promotions to drink more, and more varieties of, bottled water, the popularity of this beverage of association is diminishing in some sectors. In the summer of 2007, the city council of Ann Arbor, Michigan, passed legislation that disallows selling or otherwise providing branded bottled waters at municipal events. During the same months, demonstrations against bottled water took place in municipalities large and small across the United States. Increasing numbers of activist and advocacy groups encourage local governments to prioritize municipal water systems to diminish the environmental degradation and social impacts of bottled water; these groups pressure the bottled water industry and the FDA to desist in making false claims for water sourcing and content. Campaigns such as that waged by the watchdog group Corporate Accountability International instruct that the sourcing, production, and distribution of plastic bottles and bottled waters are environmentally and socially costly. In January 2008, Chicago became the first major U.S. city to impose a five-cent surcharge on bottled water, generating hyperbole that invokes black markets, a suburban flight of shoppers, and predictions that, once lured to other purchase sites, Chicago residents will transfer all their shopping outside the city (Owen 2008). Because the surcharge does not apply to enhanced or carbonated waters, only those that compete directly with tap water, it is premature to speculate how Chicago's consumption of branded waters will be affected. Early in 2008, the Hawai'i State Legislature (and likely others) contemplated a similar law, one element of which may be to apply the surcharge also to bottled water produced in the state (Bevnet 2008).

Other evidence of the decline in popularity of individual branded bottled waters is people resuming, or for the first time committing to, refilling bottles (branded or not) from the tap. Although all intact bottles are refillable, the bottled water industry encourages consumers to renew with fresh, cap-sealed bottles. The clear, thin-skinned bottles only appear to be less substantial than thick-walled counterparts such as those originally produced for recreational exertion. In fact, those clear bottles are quite durable, which makes litter an even more significant problem.

Refilling any old bottle embodies statements of identity that project agency—even resistance. Recently, some restaurants have taken very public steps to shun bottled waters, serving instead (and at no cost to patrons) regular and on-site-carbonated tap water. Although cynics have called this "reverse snob appeal" and anticipate the next "water fad," the "drink local" shift is an expression of environmental concern and an extension of the "eat local" and Slow Food movements (see chapter 1) (Burros 2007; Wolf 2007).

To capitalize on, and only perhaps to assist, what might be a trend toward decreased consumption of branded, bottled waters, home water treatment technologies are expanding, refining design through integration, and filling more niche needs. Water softeners are point-of-entry systems that use cation exchange resins to reduce the amount of minerals such as magnesium and calcium. The most common point-of-use systems deliver to a single faucet (the kitchen sink being most customary) or to a supplemental tap situated next to the sink. Other technologies are charcoal filters integrated into the faucet, gravity-based (pour-through) pitchers that are stored in the refrigerator, and the caps of portable, refillable water bottles. For other consumers whose preference for bottled waters bears on carbonation, manufacturers have begun to promote affordable, in-home seltzer makers that produce volumes ranging from one-liter bottles to limitless supplies that issue from plumber-installed at-sink units.

One twist on improving the quality of home tap water is the promotion of ionizers, most popularly those that generate "alkaline water." The subtext is that pH adjustment promotes health. Individuals who have a basic knowledge of bioscience refute manufacturers' claims by pointing out that most drinking water is too nonconductive to respond to significant electrolysis; once water encounters the very acidic gastric fluid, whatever level of alkalinity might exist will be overwhelmed; the body easily regulates pH; and different body parts, even individual cells, present different pH environments. Beyond false claims is that these ionizers are very expensive, ranging from one to several thousand dollars, before installation.

We can only speculate what impact will emerge from the collective efforts of environmentalists, restaurateurs, and isolated local governments. It is possible that redoubled marketing efforts will offset the reverse trends that encourage bottling tap water (indeed, cynics would say that this is the most likely outcome).

Conclusion

As the historical treatment of mineral waters and their extension into the contemporary bottled water phenomenon suggests, individual-sized bottled water is a site of identity and community, as were the water gardens, spas, and baths from which bottled waters metaphorically and literally emerged. The use of bottled water is not specific to the developed nations, however; traditional water customs in rural Nigeria have also facilitated the consumption of bottled waters, which has recently increased exponentially. In addition, the culture and biology of water extend to several health implications, including those of bottled waters—for people, other species, and the environment.

Overview

THE OVERARCHING THEORETICAL foundation of this book draws on *biocultural perspectives* as they help us to understand human cultures and ecologies through time and space. This integrative approach reflects an understanding that the tangible characteristics and physiologic effects of all aspects of foods and beverages (production/collection, transformation, circulation, and consumption) both undergird and are influenced by their cultural constructions and social transactions. This is evident, for example, in the physiologic consequences of adoptions of new foods and the unhealthful consequences of appropriating foods, labor, and land from places of contact. A recurrent theme is that food and beverage diversity is generically good because it ensures the availability of a range of macro- and micronutrients and other constituents that serve a wide spectrum of preventive and therapeutic purposes.

I address a variety of issues through the lens of *political economy*. Some contemporary theorists in behavioral ecology advance rigid models of human behavior that can work to the disadvantage of ethnic, gender, and other demographic categories. For example, the services of a wet nurse characterize both ends of a resources continuum: the affluent can afford to employ such individuals, while other women provide the services to earn income. However, such distinctions of political economy are not peculiar to humans: the social and physical dynamics of beehives offer an interesting case of classed, aged, and gendered food-related behaviors. In a highly salient example of political economy, the appropriation of spices is emblematic of the asymmetries of European expansions. Similarly, the appropriations of coffee, cacao, and tea mirrored those of other Europe-driven cash crops whose production included forced labor and the transformation of local food-producing landscapes. As in their places of origin, the beverage uses of coffee, cacao, and tea were gendered and classed, while their medicinal uses were not marked by demographics. The flavoring of these beverages with sugar created a tangible and metaphoric fusion that also was iconic of European expansions.

Other issues of political economy include the phenomenon of spas, which still are structured by demographic asymmetries, in contrast with the democratic ideologies of Native American sweat lodges, traditions that remain important today to promote health and serve as the symbols and substance of revitalization movements. Similarly, the consumption of bottled waters is classed, gendered, and marked by other demographics; this is in contrast with the relative absence of such distinctions from most street foods, which do not signal prestige or demographics and have no social function beyond providing a loose nexus of association.

Other themes that emerge from these chapters include *food transfer and redistribution*, as manifested in sharing and provisioning, asymmetrical exchanges, prioritizing of foods and beverages, blending and symmetrical exchanges, and reciprocal transfers. In particular, the redistribution of foods and beverages during rituals and celebrations has the effect of making nutrients and pharmacodynamic constituents (and at least temporary agency) available to a wider population.

The *cultural significance* of some foods and beverages is signaled by their role in origin narratives. In addition to having symbolic importance, these consumables are substantiated by a wide array of nutrients and pharmacodynamic constituents that contribute to their meaning and directly shape their use.

Foods for Another Day

In planning this book, I considered other foods and beverages of association but did not find sufficient scholarly literature on physiologic actions, phytoconstituents, and historical and ethnographic aspects. Foods included among items of remittance that are sent back to places of origin sustain communities in the diaspora and link them to home. Movie foods and beverages are consumed in company—but in the dark and with limited sociability. In the films themselves, foods are both tangible consumables and metaphors: these include the shared theme of *Chocolat, Como agua para chocolate,* and *Bread and Chocolate*; the splendor of *Babette's Feast*; Sweeney Todd's meat pies as tropes; Nancy Drew's disarming lemon bars; and Juno's enormous bottle of Sunny Delight and hamburger telephone, and her characterization of Paulie as "the cheese to [her] macaroni."

"Gastroanomalies" evoke identity and nostalgia for U.S. family meals of the mid-1900s. These "questionable culinary creations of the good old days," which are viewed through the lens of "retrospective condescension" (Lileks 2007:9), lend themselves better to cultural studies than to biocultural perspectives but are compelling nonetheless. The iconic TV dinner was introduced to U.S. consumers in 1954 and suited lifestyles in which the television in the living room was a magnet for children, who were drawn to dinnertime programs that featured cartoons and science fiction movies. Parents rounded out the family unit, which encouraged household sociability and perhaps extended the duration of time that members of a family spent in one another's company. But in later decades, the TV dinner eroded into singles' meals and, like movie foods, simply something to eat in front of the screen (often, multiple and individual screens). As another example of family food, foods served for school lunch programs in the United States evoke the country's democratic ethos through homogenization of the meal across class, age, ethnicity, and gender.

I also was drawn to foods of *dis*association: "comfort foods" that tend to be calorie- and fat-dense and are commonly eaten at home, by one person alone; other examples of such foods include the "no food" of anorexia and the "good food that turns bad" in bulimia. In principle, these and other, better-documented, contexts of eating and drinking lend themselves to a biocultural scrutiny that can offer insights into the physiologic implications of foodways in specific ethnographic and ecologic circumstances. There always will be more to research and more to say on the subject of foods and beverages of association and their nutritional and pharmacologic potential.

Notes

Chapter 1. Introduction

1. The first formal published treatment of gastronomy may be Jean Anthelme Brillat-Savarin's early-nineteenth-century *Physiologie du goût, ou méditations de gastronomie transcendante* (*The Physiology of Taste, or Meditations on Transcendent Gastronomy*). This book is a theoretical and historic account that focuses on enjoyment at the table by foregrounding the relationships between food and the sensory faculties. The more recent literature on food sociability treats historical continuities and divergences; food consumption and the reproduction of social relations; dramaturgical elements that accompany food events (dancing, oratory, and singing); how discourses of artisanship and technoscience influence food and beverage production, consumption, exchange, and diffusion; relations between commensality and power; and more-specific themes such as ritual feasting and cooking literature as a vehicle for political and social change. This literature is represented by Mennell et al. 1992; Lupton 1994; Mennell 1996; de Garine 1999; Probyn 2000, Dietler and Hayden 2001; Fernández-Armesto 2002; Petrini 2003; Bonnet 2004; Anderson 2005; Inness 2006; Heath and Meneley 2007; and Rubin 2007.

2. Even wax-eating species of Indicatoridae that do not recruit assistance are, by linguistic extrapolation, "honeyguides."

3. As a category of food, "meat" embraces much diversity, as do "plants." In the early Middle Ages, the term *meat* had an imprecise meaning, much like that of *food*. The same was the case for *viande*, the French counterpart for *food*. In England, the phrase *white meat* referred to cheese, milk, and other dairy products. The definition of *meat* narrowed over time and in contemporary English has come to denote the flesh of food animals (with exceptions, such as in the phrase *meat and drink*, meaning "food and drink," and *sweetmeats*, which are confections and contain no meat). In this book, the category of "meat" is conceived broadly to include fish and shellfish (molluscs such as snails and clams; crustaceans such as lobsters and shrimp).

4. This was the Associazone Ricreativa e Culturale Italiana (ARCI; the Italian Recreational and Cultural Association). The local Milanese movement that gave rise to the SF movement was named Arcigola, a fusion of *ARCI* and *gola*.

5. Ketosis is a metabolic process through which fat is converted by the liver into fatty acids and ketones, which the body can use for energy. This may be benign and should not be conflated with ketoacidosis.

6. This description of lactose intolerance is adequate for the present discussion, but it simplifies a more complex picture. Eleven polymorphisms of the regulatory gene cluster as

four common variants of the lactase haplotype (an alternative form of the genotype of a gene complex, not simply an allele). The most common in northern Europe decreases in frequency across southern Europe and India, where two other common variants occur; a fourth variant occurs in most other populations, except among Indo-European groups. Further, the age at which human lactase production diminishes is different among populations, ranging from two years for most to twenty years, and lactase persistence is of longer duration among intolerant individuals of predominantly lactose-tolerant groups (Enattah et al. 2002; Bersaglieri et al. 2004).

7. From a coevolutionary perspective, it is interesting to note that lactose tolerance is more common among European and American cat breeds compared to their Asian counterparts. That lactose tolerance did not evolve in the latter no doubt reflects the selective pressures of different feeding customs.

8. Metaphorically, this duration evokes the many twelve-step programs that are characterized by single and discrete objectives and symbolize human circumstances in spiritual, physiologic, and cognitive dimensions. That parallel strikes me as an effort by the ADA to co-opt powerful messages for self-improvement.

Chapter 2. The Imperial Roots of European Foodways

1. Except where otherwise indicated, the historical discussions draw on Sherry 1994; Fernándes-Armesto 1995; Lamb 1995; Watts 1995; Phillips 1998; Arnold 2002; and Fritze 2002.

2. The adjective *cordial* means "affable" and derives from the Latin *cord* or *cor*, "heart," which is suggestive of association. More narrowly, the noun *cordial* denotes a liqueur, a strongly flavored, sweet, high-alcohol-content beverage that in Europe historically was used as medicine and in contemporary societies is served before or after a meal. Etymologically, the term is linked to the Latin *liquifacere*, "to dissolve," referring to the flowers, spices, bark, and other plant parts that impart flavor. Some people distinguish liqueurs from cordials by noting that the former is typically flavored with herbs and the latter with fruit pulp or juice. Whereas coffee, cocoa, and tea fit the stand-alone definition of cordial in the past, these beverages are more pervasively consumed and are integrated into meals in today's cuisines.

3. My colleague Professor Yanhua Zhang of Clemson University generously reviewed the spelling of Mandarin words.

4. The most common adulterants were sloe (*Prunus spinosa* L., Rosaceae) for black tea and hawthorn (*Crataegus* spp., Rosaceae) for green. Ash (*Fraxinus* spp., Oleaceae), elder (*Sambucus nigra* L., Caprifoliaceae), and birch (*Betula* spp., Betulaceae) also were used. Pigment modifiers included *terra japonica* (tannins from *Acacia* species, Fabaceae), verdigris, ferrous sulphate, and sheep dung, the latter perhaps the least harmful (Moxham 2003).

Chapter 3. Street Foods and Beverages

1. Except where noted, this discussion of New York street foods draws from Taylor et al. 2000.

2. Its English common name is Japanese flowering apricot, designating where it was first observed in cultivation, although it is native to China. *Mume* is the Japanese representation of its Chinese name. In 1929 and again in 1964, it was designated China's national flower; the five petals connote the blessings health, virtue, wealth, old age, and natural death (Bernheim Arboretum and Research Forest 2007). (Five-kind domain lists vary through time, space, and literature; see Simoons 1991.) A debate continues to (re)name China's official flower (China Daily 2003).

3. Dim sum (the Cantonese term means literally "touch heart," an expression of good intentions or feelings; in Mandarin, *dian xin*) is a light meal comprising small portions of foods ranging widely in taste, texture, and composition. Steaming and deep frying are common methods of preparation. Service is typically from wheeled warming carts. Diners select individually, or collectively to share, among combinations of meat, fish, vegetables, seafood, and sweets. This style of eating grew out of teahouses and is linked closely to tea drinking. Today, Chinese hosts still offer their guests dim sum with tea (see chapter 2; see also Simoons 1991).

4. Hoisin is a pungent sauce that contains fermented yellow beans (*Phaseolus* sp., Fabaceae) seasoned with rice vinegar, sugar, salt, garlic, chile, and sesame oil.

5. In addition to these five, other spices that might be added vary regionally; these include *galangal* (*Alpinia officinarum* Hance, Zingiberaceae), ginger, and licorice (*Glycyrrhiza glabra* L., Fabaceae). The seemingly paradoxical addition of ingredients to *five*-spice is an example of how rules (that is, normative cuisine syntax) can break rules. Reference to the same mixture as "five-spice family" is a metaphor for both its composite structure and its symmetry in Chinese cosmology, a microcosm in the macrocosm.

6. According to Islamic custom, a man can have up to four wives, but the economic circumstances of Hurumi's men made this impractical; only three have more than two wives. Serial monogamy is a more common pattern in Hurumi. How strictly individuals follow purdah and other customs varies regionally and among and within extended-family compounds. This applies to modesty and other aspects of attire, as well as to how often and under what circumstances (visiting, seeking health care) a husband agrees that his wife can leave the compound. During my extended residences in Hurumi, I experienced the full range of kulle customs, from traveling to parents' homes once per month to visiting other compounds every day. The greatest flexibility was accorded to one of the principal medicine specialists, who consulted clients of both genders in a room with a discrete doorway added to the compound's exterior wall.

7. Aya, gyada, and gurjiya meet the culinary, but not botanical, definition of "nut": a single-seeded dry fruit that has a hard, thick pericarp (fruit wall). Aya is a small rhizome, an underground horizontal stem that superficially resembles a root. The two groundnuts are atypical legumes that develop nondehiscent fruit on their underground roots.

Chapter 4. Foods and Beverages of Occasion, Circumstance, and Ceremony

1. Transliterations of Farsi terms vary among sources. I used the spelling that appears in Luard 2001 (my primary source on foods of the Iranian new year), with corrections and ethnographic details generously offered by Jilla Piroozmandi.

2. The spelling of Korean terms and ethnographic details were reviewed by Soojin Kim, a graduate student in the Department of Anthropology, University of Hawai'i.

3. This imprecision is interesting in view of the central role of food, eating, and taste in the majority of Hausa parables and other narratives, in which food is not merely present, but its appearance coincides with a critical juncture of the narrative. In the story "Daddawar Batso," all the characters are tastes or foods: *daddawar batso* is a pungent soup base; *barkono*, chile; *gishiri*, salt; *albasa*, onion; *nari*, a groundnut-based food (Ritchie 1990; Etkin 2006a:31).

Chapter 5. Aspects of Health, Hype, and Identity in Bottled Water

1. A meaning-centered perspective is represented in Kaplan's biography of Fijian Water, in which she argues that "what happens to things has largely to do with the meanings given to them by people who use them" (Kaplan 2007:686, 701). Similarly, Wilk (2006b) considers how meanings are used in branding and marketing bottled waters. Neither author projects bottled water as a nucleus for association, however, or treats the biology and health implications of water.

2. This spelling/pronunciation is preferred by Hopi over the former gloss, *kachina*.

3. The Zuni narrative of origin of the dragonfly centers on a boy who created a grass toy that came to life, flew away, and returned with the Corn Maidens, who gave many plants and rain, which ensured that the plants would flourish (Bird 1992).

4. The AI is a value recommended by the U.S. Institute of Medicine's Food and Nutrition Board when a Dietary Reference Intake (DRI) cannot be determined. The DRI is the average daily intake of a nutrient for healthy individuals of a particular life stage, age, and gender.

References

Abdullaev, Fikrat I. 2002. Cancer chemopreventive and tumoricidal properties of saffron (*Crocus sativus* L.). *Experimental Biology and Medicine* 227:20–25.

Abraham, S. K., and H. Stopper. 2004. Anti-genotoxicity of coffee against N-methyl-N-nitrosoguanidine in mouse lymphoma cells. *Mutation Research* 561 (1–2): 23–33.

Abulude, F. O. 2004. Composition and properties of *Cola nitida* and *Cola acuminata* flour in Nigeria. *Global Journal of Pure and Applied Sciences* 10 (1): 11–16.

Addessi, Elsa, and Elisabetta Visalberghi. 2004. Social learning: Food. In *Encyclopedia of Animal Behavior*, ed. M. Beckoff, 593–99. Greenwood Press, Westport, Conn.

Adzu, B., S. Amos, M. B. Amizan, and K. Gamaniel. 2003. Evacuation of the antidiarrhoeal effects of *Ziziphus spina-christi* in rats. *Acta Tropica* 87:245–50.

Agizzio, A. P., A. O. Carvalho, S. F. Ribeiro, O. L. Machado, E. W. Alves, L. A. Okorokov, S. S. Samarao, C. Bloch, M. V. Prates, V. M. Gomes. 2003. A 2S albumin-homologous protein from passion fruit seeds inhibits the fungal growth and acidification of the medium by *Fusarium oxysporum*. *Archives of Biochemistry and Biophysics* 416:188–95.

Ahua, K. M., J. R. Ioset, K. N. Ioset, D. Diallo, J. Mauël, and K. Hostettmann. 2007. Antileishmanial activities associated with plants used in the Malian traditional medicine. *Journal of Ethnopharmacology* 110:99–104.

Alawa, C. B. I., A. M. Adamu, J. O. Gefu, O. J. Ajanusi, P. A. Abdu, N. P. Chiezey, J. N. Alawa, and D. D. Bowman. 2003. In vitro screening of two Nigerian medicinal plants (*Vernonia amygdaline* and *Annona senegalensis*) for anthelmintic activity. *Veterinary Parasitology* 113 (1): 73–81.

Almeida, Ana A. P., Adriana Farah, Daniela A. M. Silva, Elzíria A. Nunan, and M. Beatriz A. Glória. 2006. Antibacterial activity of coffee extracts and selected coffee chemical compounds against enterobacteria. *Journal of Agricultural and Food Chemistry* 54 (23): 8738–43.

Anderson, E. N. 1988. *The Food of China*. Yale University Press, New Haven, Conn.

———. 2005. *Everyone Eats: Understanding Food and Culture*. New York University Press, New York.

Anderson, R. A., and M. M. Polansky. 2002. Tea enhances insulin activity. *Journal of Agriculture and Food Chemistry* 50 (24): 7182–86.

André, Konan Brou, Datté-Jacques Yao, and Offoumou Atté Michel. 2006. Action of the aqueous extract of *Sesamum radiatum* Schum. & Thonn. (Pedaliaceae) on the cardiovascular system of mammalians: Hypotensive effect. *Current Bioactive Compounds* 2 (3): 263–67.

Andrews, Jean. 2003. Chili peppers. In *Encyclopedia of Food and Culture*, ed. S. H. Katz, 368–78. Charles Scribner, New York.

Aoude, Ibrahim, ed. 1994. Political Economy of Hawai'i. Special issue, *Social Process in Hawai'i* 35 [Department of Sociology, University of Hawai'i, Honolulu]:1–233.

Apgar, Joan L., and Stanley M. Tarka. 1999. Methylxanthines. In *Chocolate and Cocoa: Health and Nutrition*, ed. I. Knight, 153–73. Blackwell Science, Oxford.

Appleby, Paul N., Margaret Thorogood, Jim I. Mann, and Timothy J. A. Key. 1999. The Oxford vegetarian study: An overview. *American Journal of Clinical Nutrition* 70:525S–531S.

Arai, I., S. Amagaya, Y. Komatsu, M. Okada, T. Hayashi, M. Kasai, M. Arisawa, and Y. Momose. 1999. Improving effects of the extracts from *Eugenia uniflora* on hyperglycemia and hypertriglyceridemia in mice. *Journal of Ethnopharmacology* 68:307–14.

Århem, Kaj. 1996. The cosmic food web: Human-nature relatedness in the northwest Amazon. In *Nature and Society*, ed. P. Descola and G. Pálson, 185–204. Routledge, London.

Arnold, David. 2002. *The Age of Discovery, 1400–1600.* 2nd ed. Routledge, London.

Arnold, Emily, and Janet Larsen. 2006. Bottled water: Pouring resources down the drain. *Earth Policy Institute Eco-Economy Updates*, 2 February. http://www.earth-policy .org/Updates2006.

Asano, Naoki, Atsushi Kato, Miwa Miyauchi, Haruhisa Kizu, Yukihiko Kameda, Alison A. Watson, Robert J. Nash, and George W. J. Fleet. 1998. Nitrogen-containing furanose and pyranose analogues from *Hyacinthus orientalis*. *Journal of Natural Products* 61 (5): 625–28.

Astrup, A., T. M. Larsen, and A. Harper. 2004. Atkins and other low-carbohydrate diets: Hoax or an effective tool for weight loss? *Lancet* 364:897–99.

Baker, James W., and Peggy M. Baker. 2003. Thanksgiving. In *Encyclopedia of Food and Culture*, ed. S. H. Katz, 394–96. Scribner, New York.

Baker, Jesse. 2005. Best street food in New York is the "wurst." National Public Radio, November 11. http://npr.org.

Baker, Jonathan D. 2008. Kava Tradition and Toxicity: Local and Global Discourses about the Safety and Use of *Piper methysticum* G. Forst. (Piperaceae), an Indigenous Botanical Undergoing Pharmaceuticalization. Ph.D. diss., Department of Anthropology, University of Hawai'i.

Banerji, Chitrita. 2007. *Eating India: An Odyssey into the Food and Culture of the Land of the Spices.* Bloomsbury Press, New York.

Bankole, Mobolaji O., and Richard N. Okagbue. 1992. Properties of "nono," a Nigerian fermented milk food. *Ecology of Food and Nutrition* 27:145–49.

Barminas, J. T., H. M. Maina, and J. Ali. 1998. Nutrient content of *Prosopis africana* seeds. *Plant Foods for Human Nutrition* 52 (4): 325–28.

Barnard, C. J. 1983. *Animal Behaviour: Ecology and Evolution.* John Wiley, New York.

Bartram, Jamie. 2008. Flowing away: Water and health opportunities. *Bulletin of the World Health Organization* 86 (1): 2.

Baskes, Jeremy. 2000. *Indians, Merchants, and Markets: A Reinterpretation of the Reparti-*

miento and Spanish-Indian Economic Relations in Colonial Oaxaca, 1750–1821. Stanford University Press, Stanford, Calif.

Baxter, Paula A., and Allison Bird-Romero. 2000. *Encyclopaedia of Native American Jewelry: A Guide to History, People, and Terms.* Oryx Press, Phoenix, Ariz.

Beauchamp, Guy. 2004. Social foraging. In *Encyclopedia of Animal Behavior,* ed. M. Beckoff, 589–93. Greenwood Press, Westport, Conn.

Beaumont, M. 2002. Flavouring composition prepared by fermentation with *Bacillus. International Journal of Food Microbiology* 75 (3): 189–96.

Bendann, E. 1930. *Death Customs: An Analytical Study of Burial Rites.* Knopf, New York.

Bernheim Arboretum and Research Forest. 2007. *Prunus mume* "kobai" tree. http://www.bernheim.org.

Bersaglieri, T., P. C. Sabeti, N. Patterson, T. Vanderploeg, S. F. Schaffner, J. A. Drake, M. Rhodes, D. E. Reich, and J. N. Hirschhorn. 2004. Genetic signatures of strong recent positive selection at the lactase gene. *American Journal of Human Genetics* 74 (6): 1111–20.

Bevnet. 2006. Vitazest vitamin and fruit enriched water now available in New Jersey through Marz Beverage. http://www.bevnet.com.

———. 2008. Hawai'i considers bottled water tax. http://www.bevnet.com.

Biesele, Megan. 1993. *Women Like Meat: The Folklore and Foraging Ideology of the Kalahari Ju/'hoan.* Indiana University Press, Bloomington.

Bird, Allison. 1992. *Heart of the Dragonfly: The Historical Development of the Cross Necklaces of the Pueblo and Navajo Peoples.* Avanyu Publishers, Albuquerque, N.Mex.

Bixler, Ronald G., and Jeffrey N. Morgan. 1999. Cacao bean and chocolate processing. In *Chocolate and Cocoa: Health and Nutrition,* ed. I. Knight, 43–60. Blackwell Science, Oxford.

Blanco, Sebastian. 2005. Kanak attack. *Honolulu Weekly Newspaper,* 1 June. http://honoluluweekly.com.

Boehm, Christopher. 1999. *Hierarchy in the Forest: The Evolution of Egalitarian Behavior.* Harvard University Press, Cambridge, Mass.

Boesch, Christophe, and Hedwige Boesch. 1989. Hunting behavior of wild chimpanzees in the Tai National Park. *American Journal of Physical Anthropology* 78:547–73.

Bohn, Hinrich L., Brian L. McNeal, and George A. O'Connor. 2001. *Soil Chemistry.* 3rd ed. Wiley, New York.

Bonnet, Jean-Claude. 2004. La naissance de la gastronomie et l'écriture gourmande. In *Consuming Culture: The Arts of the French Table,* ed. J. West-Sooby, 2–10. Associated University Presses, Cranberry, N.J.

Braca, Alessandra, Matteo Politi, Rokia Sanogo, Haby Sanou, Ivano Morelli, Cosimo Pizza, and Nunziatina de Tommasi. 2003. Chemical composition and antioxidant activity of phenolic compounds from wild and cultivated *Scleroycrya birrea* (Anacardiaceae) leaves. *Journal of Agricultural and Food Chemistry* 51 (23): 6689–95.

Bryant, Carol, Kathleen M. DeWalt, Anita Courtney, and Jeffrey Schwartz. 2003. *The Cultural Feast: An Introduction to Food and Society.* 2nd ed. Thomson/Wadsworth, Belmont, Calif.

Bshary, Redouan, Andrea Hohner, Karim Ait-el-Djoudi, and Hans Fricke. 2006. *PloS Biology* 4(12). http://biology.plosjournals.com.

Burnett, John. 1999. *Liquid Pleasures*. Routledge, London.

Burri, Betty J. 2000. Antioxidant status in vegetarians versus omnivores: A mechanism for longer life? *Nutrition* 16 (2): 149–50.

Burros, Marian. 2007. Fighting the tide, a few restaurants tilt to tap water. *New York Times*, 30 May. http://www.nytimes.com.

Cann, Stephen A., Johannes P. Van Netten, and Christiaan van Netten. 2000. Hypothesis: Iodine, selenium and the development of breast cancer. *Cancer Causes and Control* 11:121–27.

Cardinale, E., J. D. Perrier Gros-Claude, F. Tall, E. F. Guèye, and G. Salvat. 2005. Risk factors for contamination of ready-to-eat street-vended poultry dishes in Dakar, Senegal. *International Journal of Food Microbiology* 103 (2): 157–65.

Cardoso, A. Paula, Estevao Mirione, Mario Ernesto, Fernando Massaza, Julie Cliff, M. Rezaul Haque, and J. Howard Bradbury. 2005. Processing of cassava roots to remove cyanogens. *Journal of Food Composition and Analysis* 18:451–60.

Carlton, Jim. 2005. For finicky drinkers, water from the tap isn't tasty enough. *Wall Street Journal*, 11 March, A1.

Carnesecchi, S., Y. Schneider, S. A. Lazarus, D. Coehlo, F. Gosse, and F. Raul. 2002. Flavonols and procyanidins of cocoa and chocolate inhibit growth and polyamine biosynthesis of human colonic cancer. *Cancer Letters* 175 (2): 147–55.

Carson, Rachel. 1964. *Silent Spring*. Houghton Mifflin, New York.

Chang, J.-C., M. C. Wu, I.-M. Liu, and J.-T. Teng. 2006. Plasma glucose-lowering action of *hon-chi* in streptozotocin-induced diabetic rats. *Hormone and Metabolic Research* 38:76–81.

Chapelle, Francis H. 2005. *Wellsprings: A Natural History of Bottled Spring Waters*. Rutgers University Press, New Brunswick, N.J.

Chauret, Christian. 2004. Tap water and the risk of microbial infection. In *Beverages in Nutrition and Health*, ed. T. Wilson and N. J. Temple, 335–48. Humana Press, Totowa, N.J.

CHCP (Chinese Historical and Cultural Project). 2007. Ching ming. http://www.chcp .org.

China Daily. 2003. National flower, tree, bird to be chosen. *China Daily*, 15 May. http:// www.china.org.cn.

Cimolai, Nevio. 2007. Sweet success? Honey as a topical dressing. *BC Medical Journal* 49 (2): 64–67.

Clarke, Joan. 1997. *Local Food: What to Eat in Hawai'i*. Namkoong Publishing, Honolulu.

Clouatre, D. L. 2004. Kava kava: Examining new reports of toxicity. *Toxicology Letters* 150:85–96.

Coe, Sophie D. 1997. Cacao: Gift of the New World. In *Chocolate: Food of the Gods*, ed. A. Szogyi, 147–53. Greenwood Press, Westport, Conn.

Coe, Sophie D., and Michael D. Coe. 1996. *The True History of Chocolate*. Thames and Hudson, London.

Consolini, A. E., O. A. Baldini, and A. G. Amat. 1999. Pharmacological basis for the empirical use of *Eugenia uniflora* L. (Myrtaceae) as antihypertensive. *Journal of Ethnopharmacology* 66:33–39.

Construction Worker. 2006. Conversation at Plate Lunch wagon near the site of hotel renovation in Waikiki, Honolulu.

Cooper Marcus, Clare. 2003. Healing havens. *Landscape Architecture* 93 (8): 85–91, 107–9.

Counihan, Carole M. 1999. *The Anthropology of Food and Body: Gender, Meaning, and Power*. Routledge, New York.

Croutier, Alev Lytle. 1992. *Taking the Waters: Spirit, Art, Sensuality*. Abbeville Press, New York.

CSPI (Center for Science in the Public Interest). 1997. Caffeine content of foods and drugs. http://www.cspinet.org/new/cafchart.htm.

Daels-Rakotoarison, D. A., G. Kouakou, B. Gressier, T. Dine, C. Brunet, M. Luyckx, F. Bailleul, and F. Trotin. 2003. Effects of a caffeine-free *Cola nitida* nut extract on elastase/alpha-1 proteinase inhibitor balance. *Journal of Ethnopharmacology* 89 (1): 143–50.

Dalby, Andrew. 2000. *Dangerous Tastes: The Story of Spices*. University of California Press, Berkeley.

Davidson, Alan. 1999. *The Oxford Companion to Food*. Oxford University Press, Oxford.

Dawkins, G., H. Hewitt, Y. Wint, P. C. Obiefuna, and B. Wint. 2003. Antibacterial effects of *Carica papaya* fruit on common wound organisms. *West Indian Medical Journal* 52:290–92.

DeFoliart, Gene R. 1997. An overview of the role of insects in preserving biodiversity. *Ecology of Food and Nutrition* 36 (2–4): 109–32.

de Garine, Igor. 1999. Gastronomie et diététique chez les Masa et les Muzey du Cameroun. In *Cultural Food*, ed. A. Guerci, 27–36. Erga Edizioni, Genoa.

den Hartog, Adel P. 2003. Taboos. In *Encyclopedia of Food and Culture*, ed. S. H. Katz, 384–86. Charles Scribner, New York.

De Souza, G. Coelho, A. P. S. Haas, G. L. von Poser, E. E. S. Schapoval, and E. Elisabetsky. 2004. Ethnopharmacological studies of antimicrobial remedies in the south of Brazil. *Journal of Ethnopharmacology* 90:135–43.

de Waal, Frans B. M. 2000. Attitudinal reciprocity in food sharing among brown capuchin monkeys. *Animal Behaviour* 60:253–61.

Dhawan, K., S. Kuman, and A. Sharma. 2001. Comparative biological activity study on *Passiflora incarnata* and *P. edulis*. *Fitoterapia* 72:698–702.

Di Bitetti, M. S. 2005. Food-associated calls and audience effects in tufted capuchin monkeys, *Cebus apella nigritus*. *Animal Behaviour* 69 (4): 911–19.

Dietler, Michael, and Brian Hayden, eds. 2001. *Feasts: Archaeological and Ethnographic Perspectives on Food, Politics, and Power*. Smithsonian Institution Press, Washington, D.C.

Dillinger, Teresa L., Patricia Barriga, Sylvia Escarcega, Martha Jimenez, Diana Salazar Lowe, and Louis E. Grivetti. 2000. Food of the gods: Cure for humanity? A cultural history of the medicinal and ritual use of chocolate. *Journal of Nutrition* 130:2057S–2072S.

DOH. 2007. Hawaiian Deep Ocean Water. http://www.deepoceanhawaii.com.

Donkin, R. A. 1977. Spanish red: Ethnogeographical study of cochineal and the *Opuntia* cactus. *Transactions of the American Philosophical Society* 67:1–84.

Duffy, John. 1990. *The Sanitarians: A History of American Public Health*. University of Illinois Press, Chicago.

Dugatkin, Lee A. 1997. *Cooperation among Animals: An Evolutionary Perspective*. Oxford University Press, New York.

DuPuis, E. Melanie. 2002. *Nature's Perfect Food*. New York University Press, New York.

Eisner, Thomas, Stephen Nowicki, Michael Goetz, and Jerrold Meinwald. 1980. Red cochineal dye (carminic acid). *Science* 208:1039–42.

Ellen, Roy, Peter Parkes, and Alan Bicker, eds. 2000. *Indigenous Environmental Knowledge and Its Transformations*. Harwood Academic Publishers, Amsterdam.

Elmadfa, Ibrahim, ed. 2005. *Diet Diversification and Health Promotion*. Karger, Basel.

Embil, John, Peter Warren, Mitchell Yakrus, Robert Stark, Stephen Corne, Donna Forrest, and Earl Hershfield. 1997. Pulmonary illness associated with exposure to *Mycobacterium avium* complex in hot tub water. *Chest* 111:813–16.

Enattah, N. S., T. Sahi, E. Savilahti, J. D. Terwillerger, L. Peltonen, and I. Jarvela. 2002. Identification of a variant associated with adult-type hypolactasia. *Nature Genetics* 30:233–37.

Engleberger, Lois, Maureen H. Firzgerald, and Geoff C. Marks. 2003. Pacific pandanus fruit: An ethnographic approach to understanding an overlooked source of provitamin A carotenoids. *Asia Pacific Journal of Clinical Nutrition* 12 (1): 38–44.

English, H. K., A. R. Pack, and P. C. Molan. 2004. The effects of manuka honey on plaque and gingivitis: A pilot study. *Journal of the International Academy of Periodontology* 6 (2): 63–67.

Eromosele, Ighodalo C., Catherine O. Eromosele, and Daniel M. Kuzhkuzha. 1991. Evaluation of mineral elements and ascorbic acid contents in fruits of some wild plants. *Plant Foods for Human Nutrition* 41 (2): 151–54.

Etkin, Nina L., ed. 1994a. *Eating on the Wild Side: The Pharmacologic, Ecologic, and Social Implications of Using Noncultigens*. University of Arizona Press, Tucson.

——. 1994b. The cull of the wild. In *Eating on the Wild Side*, ed. N. L. Etkin, 1–21. University of Arizona Press, Tucson.

——. 1994c. Consuming the therapeutic landscape: A multicontextual framework for assessing the health significance of human-plant interactions. *Journal of Home and Consumer Horticulture* 1 (2–3): 61–81.

——. 2002. Local knowledge of biotic diversity and its conservation in rural Hausaland, Northern Nigeria. *Economic Botany* 56 (1): 73–88.

——. 2003. Nutraceuticals, cosmeceuticals, and antiaging agents in U.S. popular culture. In *Proceedings of the International Symposium on Lycium and Antiaging Agents*, ed. Organizing Committee, 1–8. Ningxia Academy of Agriculture and Forestry Sciences and Shanghai Industrial Investment, Ningxia, China.

——. 2004. Polypharmacy, Complementary and Alternative Medicines (CAM), and Cancer. *Hawai'i Medical Journal* 63:349–50.

——. 2006a. *Edible Medicines: An Ethnopharmacology of Food*. University of Arizona Press, Tucson.

——. 2006b. Wild plant management in rural Hausaland: Local ecological knowledge contributes to the conservation of biodiversity. In *Proceedings of the International Congress of Ethnobotany*, ed. F. Ertug, 359–64. Zero Produksiyon, Istanbul, Turkey.

Etkin, Nina L., and Elaine Elisabetsky. 2005. Seeking a Transdisciplinary and Culturally Germane Science: The Future of Ethnopharmacology. *Journal of Ethnopharmacology* 100:23–26.

Etkin, Nina L., and Paul J. Ross. 1982. Food as medicine and medicine as food: An adaptive framework for the interpretation of plant utilization among the Hausa of northern Nigeria. *Social Science and Medicine* 16:1559–73.

——. 1994. Pharmacologic implications of "wild" plants in Hausa diet. In *Eating on the Wild Side: The Pharmacologic, Ecologic, and Social Implications of Using Non-cultigens*, ed. N. L. Etkin, 85–101. University of Arizona Press, Tucson.

——. 1997. Malaria, medicine and meals: A biobehavioral perspective. In *The Anthropology of Medicine*, ed. L. Romanucci-Ross, D. E. Moerman, and L. R. Tancredi, 169–209. 3rd ed. Praeger, New York.

Etkin, Nina L., Paul J. Ross, and I. Muazzamu. 1999. The rational basis of "irrational" drug use: Pharmaceuticals in the context of "development." In *Anthropology in Public Health*, ed. R. A. Hahn, 165–81. Oxford University Press, Oxford.

Evans, A. H., A. D. Lawrence, J. Potts, L. MacGregor, R. Katzenschlager, K. Shaw, J. Zijlmans, and A. J. Lees. 2006. Relationship between impulsive sensation seeking traits, smoking, alcohol and caffeine intake, and Parkinson's disease. *Journal of Neurology, Neurosurgery, and Psychiatry* 77:317–21.

Evans, Mike. 1996. Gifts and Commodities on a Tongan Atoll: Understanding Intention and Action in a Mirab Economy. Ph.D. diss., McMaster University.

FAO (Food and Agriculture Organization of the United Nations). 2007. Food fortification. http://www.fao.org.

Farber, Thomas. 1994. *On Water*. Ecco Press, Hopewell, N.J.

Fastcompany. 2007. We all go to the same place: Let us go there slowly. http//www.fastcompany.com.

Fatehi, Mohammed, Freshteh Farifteh, and Zahra Fatehi-Hassanabad. 2004. Antispasmodic and hypotensive effects of *Ferula asafoetida* gum extract. *Journal of Ethnopharmacology* 91 (2–3): 321–24.

Faull, Kieren. 2005. A pilot study of the comparative effectiveness of two water-based treatments for fibromyalgia syndrome: Watsu and Aix. *Journal of Bodyworks and Movement Therapies* 9 (3): 202–10.

FDA (Food and Drug Administration). 2002. Bottled water regulation and the FDA. http://www.cfsan.fda.gov.

——. 2007. Foodborne pathogenic microorganisms and natural toxins handbook: The bad bug book. http://www.cfsan.fda.gov.

Fernández-Armesto, Felipe, ed. 1995. *The European Opportunity*. Ashgate Publishing, Aldershot, U.K.

———. 2002. *Near a Thousand Tables: A History of Food*. Free Press, New York.

Fernandez-Orozco, Rebeca, Henryk Zielinski, and Mariusz K. Piskula. 2003. Contribution of low-molecular-weight antioxidants to the antioxidant capacity of raw and processed lentil seeds. *Nahrung/Food* 47 (5): 291–99.

Fifita, Patricia. 2007. Rooted and grounded: An ethnographic approach to understanding food, health, and disease in modernizing Tonga. Paper submitted in partial fulfillment of the M.A. degree, Department of Anthropology, University of Hawai'i–Mânoa.

Flagler, Joel, and Raymond P. Poincelot, eds. 1994. *People-Plant Relationships: Setting Research Priorities*. Haworth Press, Binghamton, N.Y.

Flood, Gavin D. 1996. *An Introduction to Hinduism*. Cambridge University Press, Cambridge.

Fondazione Slow Food per la Biodiversità. 2007. http://www.slowfoodfoundation.com.

Foster, Gary D., Holly R. Wyatt, James O. Hill, Brian G. McGuckin, Carrie Brill, B. Selma Mohammed, Philippe O. Szapary, Daniel J. Rader, Joel S. Edman, and Samuel Klein. 2003. A randomized trial of low-carbohydrate diet for obesity. *New England Journal of Medicine* 348:2082–90.

Fredholm, B. B. 1995. Astra Award lecture: Adenosine, adenosine receptors and the actions of caffeine. *Pharmacology and Toxicology* 76 (2): 93–101.

Fresco, Louis O. 2007. Biodiversity for food and agriculture. http://www.fao.org.

Friedman, M., and D. L. Brandon. 2001. Nutritional and health benefits of soy proteins. *Journal of Agricultural and Food Chemistry* 49 (3): 1069–86.

Fritze, Ronald H. 2002. *New Worlds: The Great Voyages of Discovery*. Sutton Publishing, Gloucestershire, U.K.

Ganss, C., M. Schlechtriemen, and J. Klimek. 1999. Dental erosions in subjects living on a raw food diet. *Caries Research* 33 (1): 74–80.

García-Solís, Pablo, and Carmen Aceves. 2005. Estudio de los factores nutricionales asociados a la prevención de cáncer mamario: Importancia de los modelos animales. *Archivos Latinoamericanos de Nutrición* 55 (3): 211–55. http://www.scielo.org.ve/scielo.php.

Garrido, Gabino, Magdalena Blanco-Molina, Rocío Sancho, Antonio Macho, René Delgado, and Eduardo Muñoz. 2005. An aqueous extract of *Mangifera indica* (Vimang-)L. inhibits T Cell proliferation and TNF-induced activation of nuclear transcription factor NF-KB. *Phytotherapy Research* 19 (3): 211–15.

Genz, Joseph H. 2008. Marshallese Navigation and Voyaging: Re-Learning and Reviving Indigenous Knowledge of the Ocean. Ph.D. diss., University of Hawai'i, Department of Anthropology.

Germanò, Maria P., Rita de Pasquale, Valeria d'Angelo, Stefania Catania, Virginia Silvari, and Chara Costa. 2002. Evaluation of extracts and isolated fractions from *Capparis spinosa* L. buds as an antioxidant source. *Journal of Agricultural and Food Chemistry* 50:1168–71.

Ghasi, S., E. Nwobodo, and J. O. Ofili. 2000. Hypocholesterolemic effects of crude extract of leaf of *Morinda oleifera* Lam. in high-fat diet fed Wismar rats. *Journal of Ethnopharmacology* 69 (1): 21–25.

Gilby, Ian C. 2006. Meat sharing among the Gombe chimpanzees: Harassment and reciprocal exchange. *Animal Behaviour* 71 (4): 953–63.

——. 2007. Chimpanzees do not trade meat for sex. Paper presented at the Annual Meeting of the American Anthropological Association, 2 December, Washington, D.C.

Giron-Calle, J., J. Vioque, Y. M. del Mar, J. Pedroche, M. Alaiz, and F. Millan. 2004. Effect of chickpea aqueous extracts, organic extracts, and protein concentrates on cell proliferation. *Journal of Medicinal Food* 7 (2): 122–29.

Gleick, Peter H. 2004. *The World's Water, 2004–2005.* Island Press, Washington, D.C.

Glombitza, K. W., G. H. Mahran, Y. W. Mirhom, K. G. Michel, and T. K. Motawi. 1994. Hypoglycemic and antihyperglycemic effects of *Zizyphus spina-christi* in rats. *Planta Medica* 60 (3): 244–47.

Goh, S. S., O. L. Woodoman, S. Pepe, A. H. Cao, C. Qin, and R. H. Ritchie. 2007. The red wine antioxidant resveratrol prevents cardiomycyte injury following ischemia-reperfusion via multiple sites and mechanisms. *Antioxidants and Redox Signaling* 9 (1): 101–13.

Gomes, A., J. R. Vedasiromoni, M. Das, R. M. Sharma, and D. K. Ganguly. 1995. Anti-hyperglycemic effect of black tea (*Camellia sinensis*) in rat. *Journal of Ethnopharmacology* 45:223–26.

Goodman, Jordan. 1995. Excitantia: How Enlightenment Europe took to soft drugs. In *Consuming Habits,* ed. J. Goodman, P. E. Lovejoy, and A. Sherratt, 126–47. Routledge, London.

Göttsch, Eggert. 1992. Purification of turbid surface water by plants in Ethiopia. *Walia* 14:23–28.

Green, Judith M., Alizon K. Draper, Elizabeth A. Dowler, Giolo Fele, Ver Hagenhoff, Maria Rusanen, and Timo Rusanen. 2005. Public understanding of food risks in four European countries: A qualitative study. *European Journal of Public Health* 15 (5): 523–27.

Grivetti, Louis, and Britta M. Ogle. 2000. Value of traditional foods in meeting macro- and micronutrient needs: The wild plant connection. *Nutrition Research Reviews* 13 (1): 31–46.

Guevara, Ameila P., Carolyn Vargas, Hiromu Sakurai, Yasuhiro Fujiwara, Keiji Hashimoto, Takashi Maoka, Mutzuo Kozuka, Yoshohiro Ito, Harukuni Tokuda, and Hoyoku Nishino. 1999. An antitumor promoter from *Moringa oleifera* Lam. *Mutation Research —Genetic Toxicology and Environmental Mutagenesis* 440 (2): 181–88.

Gurven, Michael, Kim Hill, and Felipe Jakugi. 2004. Why do foragers share and sharers forage? Exploration of social dimensions of foraging. *Research in Economic Anthropology* 23:19–43.

Guthman, Julie. 2003. Fast food/organic food: Reflexive tastes and the making of yuppie chow. *Social and Cultural Geography* 4 (1): 45–58.

Haas, Jere H., and Dennis D. Miller, eds. 2006. Symposium: Food Fortification in Developing Countries. Special issue, *Journal of Nutrition* 136(4).

Habenstein, Robert W., and William M. Lamers. 1963. *Funeral Customs the World Over.* Bulfin Pringers, Milwaukee, Wisc.

Halder, J., and A. N. Bhaduri. 1998. Protective role of black tea against oxidative damage of human red blood cells. *Biochemical and Biophysical Research Communications* 244 (3): 903–7.

Hannum, S. M., H. H. Schmitz, and C. L. Keen. 2002. Chocolate: A heart-healthy food? Show me the science. *Nutrition Today* 37:103–9.

Hartman, Thomas E., Eric Jensen, Henry D. Tazelaar, Viktor Hanak, and Jay H. Ryu. 2007. CT findings of granulomatous pneumonitis secondary to *Mycobacterium avium-intracellular* inhalation. *American Journal of Roentgenology* 188:1050–53.

Hassegawa, Regina H., Maria C. M. Ksuya, and Maria C. D. Vanetti. 2005. Growth and antibacterial activity of *Lentinula edodes* in liquid media supplemented with agricultural wastes. *Microbial Biotechnology* 8(2). http://www.ejbiotechnology.info/content/vol8/issue2.

Hattox, Ralph S. 1985. *Coffee and Coffeehouses: The Origins of a Social Beverage in the Medieval Near East.* University of Washington Press, Seattle.

Hayden, Brian. 2001. Fabulous feasts: A prolegomenon to the importance of feasting. In *Feasts: Archaeological and Ethnographic Perspectives on Food, Politics, and Power,* ed. M. Dietler and B. Hayden, 23–64. Smithsonian Institution Press, Washington, D.C.

Heard Museum. 2008. Phoenix, Arizona. http://www.heard.com.

Heath, Deborah, and Anne Meneley, eds. 2007. In focus: The techne and technoscience of food and drink. *American Anthropologist* 109 (4): 593–687.

Heber, D., I. Yip, J. M. Ashley, D. A. Elashoff, and V. L. W. Go. 1999. Cholesterol-lowering effect of a proprietary Chinese red-yeast-rice dietary supplement. *American Journal of Clinical Nutrition* 69:231–36.

Hecht, Jeff. 2007. Ancient beer pots point to origins of chocolate. *New Scientist.* November 12. http://www.newscientist.com.

Hegarty, Verona M., Helen M. May, and Kay-Tee Khaw. 2000. Tea drinking and bone mineral density in older women. *American Journal of Clinical Nutrition* 71 (4): 1003–7.

Hermann, L., L. E. Spieker, F. Ruschitzka, I. Sudano, M. Hermann, C. Binggeli, T. F. Lüscher, W. Risen, G. Noll, and R. Cotri. 2006. Dark chocolate improves endothelial and platelet function. *Heart* 92:119–20.

Hinneburg, Iris, and Reinhard H. H. Neubert. 2005. Influence of extraction parameters on the phytochemical characteristics from buckwheat (*Fagopyrum esculentum*) herb. *Journal of Agricultural and Food Chemistry* 53 (1): 3–7.

Ho, P. T. 1995. The introduction of American food plants into China. *American Anthropologist* 55:191–201.

Hockings, Kimberly J., Tatyana Humle, James R. Anderson, Dora Biro, Claudia Sousa, Gaku Ohashi, and Tetsuro Matsuzawa. 2007. Chimpanzees share forbidden fruit. *PLoS ONE* 2(9). http://www.plosone.org/article.

Hoet, Sara, Frederik Opperdoes, Reto Brun, Victor Adjikje, and Joëlle Quetin-Leclercq. 2004. In vitro antitrypanosomal activity of ethnopharmacologically selected Beninese plants. *Journal of Ethnopharmacology* 91 (1): 37–42.

Hoet, S., C. Stévigny, and J. Quetin-Leclercq. 2006. Antitryposomal compounds from *Strychnos spinosa. Planta medica* 72 (5): 480–82.

Hooper, Alex. 1989. Mutualism between man and honeyguide. In *The Walking Larder*, ed. Juliet Clutton-Brock, 347–49. Unwin Hyman, London.

Husein, M. Q., and R. T. Kridli. 2002. Reproductive responses following royal jelly treatment administered orally or intramuscularly into progesterone-treated Awassi ewes. *Animal Reproduction Science* 74 (1): 45–53.

Hviding, Edvard. 1996. Nature, culture, magic, science: On meta-languages for comparison in cultural ecology. In *Nature and Society*, ed. P. Descola and G. Pálson, 165–84. Routledge, London.

Ichihara, T., H. Wanibuchi, T. Taniyama, Y. Okai, Y. Yano, S. Otani, S. Imaoka, Y. Funae, and S. Fukushima. 1999. Inhibition of liver glutathione S-transferase placental form-positive foci development in the rat hepatocarcinogenesis by *Porphyra tenera* (Asakuka-nori). *Cancer Letters* 141:211–18.

Inness, Sherrie A. 2006. *Secret Ingredients: Race, Gender, and Class at the Dinner Table*. Palgrave Macmillan, New York.

International Bottled Water Association. 2006. Statistics. http://www.bottledwater.org.

International Herald Tribune. 2007. Honolulu company selling deep seawater as exotic ingredient. *International Herald Tribune*, 21 May. http://www.iht.com.

Ishihara, Kenji, Chiaki Oyamada, Ryoji Matsushima, Masakazu Murata, and Toshihiko Muraoka. 2005. Inhibitory effect of porphyran, prepared from dried "nori," on contact hypersensitivity in mice. *Bioscience, Biotechnology, and Biochemistry* 69 (10): 1824–30.

Ishikawa, Hideki, Ikuko Akedo, Yoshinori Umesaki, Ryuichiro Tanaka, Akemi Imaoka, and Toru Otani. 2003. Randomized controlled trial of the effect of bifidobacteria-fermented milk on ulcerative colitis. *Journal of the American College of Nutrition* 22 (1): 56–63.

Islam, Gazi. 2006. Virtual speakers, virtual audiences: Agency, audience and constraint in an online chat community. *Dialectical Anthropology* 30:71–89. http://www.springerlink.com.

Ito, Junko, Rang-Rong Chang, Hui-Kang Wang, Yong Kun Park, Masaharu Ikegaki, and Nicole Kilgore. 2001. Anti-AIDS agents. *Journal of Natural Products* 64 (10): 1278–81.

Iwuoha, C. I., and O. S. Eke. 1996. Nigerian indigenous fermented foods: Their traditional processing, inherent problems, improvements and current status. *Food Research International* 29:527–40.

Jamal, Shelina M., and Mark J. Eisenberg. 2004. The nutritional value of bottled water. In *Beverages in Nutrition and Health*, ed. T. Wilson and N. J. Temple, 321–33. Humana Press, Totowa, N.J.

Jansson, Rasmus. 1999. Dowsing—Science or Humbug? http://www.lysator.liu.se.

Japanese American National Museum. 1997. From Bentô to Mixed Plate: Americans of Japanese Ancestry in Multicultural Hawai'i. Japanese American Museum, Los Angeles, Calif.

Jardine, Nicholas. 1999. Phytochemicals and phenolics. In *Chocolate and Cocoa: Health and Nutrition*, ed. I. Knight, 119–42. Blackwell Science, Oxford.

Johns, Timothy. 2000. *The Origins of Human Diet and Medicine*. University of Arizona Press, Tucson.

Kaltwasser, J. P., E. Werner, K. Schalk, C. Hansen, R. Gottschalk, and C. Seidl. 1998. Clinical trial on the effect of regular tea drinking on iron accumulation in genetic haemochromatosis. *Gut* 43:699–704.

Kamath, Arati B., Lisheng Wang, Hiranmoy Das, Lin Li, Vernon N. Reinhold, and Jack F. Bukowski. 2003. Antigens in tea-beverage prime human V gamma 2V delta 2T cells in vitro and in vivo for memory and nonmemory antibacterial cytokine responses. *Proceedings of the National Academy of Sciences USA* 100 (10): 6009–14.

Kaplan, Hillard, and Michael Gurven. 2005. The natural history of food sharing and cooperation: A review and a new multi-individual approach to the negotiation of norms. In *Moral Sentiments and Material Interests: The Foundation of Cooperation in Economic Life*, ed. H. Gintis, S. Bowles, R. Boyd, and E. Fehr, 75–113. MIT Press, Cambridge, Mass.

Kaplan, Hillard, Kim Hill, Jane Lancaster, and A. Magdalena Hurtado. 2000. A theory of human life history evolution: Diet, intelligence, and longevity. *Evolutionary Anthropology: Issues, News, and Reviews* 9 (4): 156–85.

Kaplan, Martha. 2007. Fijian Water in Fiji and New York: Local politics and a global community. *Cultural Anthropology* 22 (4): 685–706.

Kayashita, J., I. Shimaoka, and M. Nakajyoh. 1995. Hypocholesterolemic effect of buckwheat protein extract in rats fed cholesterol enriched diets. *Nutrition Research* 15 (5): 691–98.

Keen, Carl L. 2001. Chocolate: Food as medicine/medicine as food. *Journal of the American College of Nutrition* 20:436S–439S.

Keyshistory. 2006. Fontaneda's Memoir. Trans. Buckingham Smith, 1854. http://www.keys history.org/Fontenada.html.

Kim, Dong C., Woo-Ik Hwang, and Man-Jin Jin. 2003. In vitro antioxidant and anticancer activities of extracts from a fermented food. *Journal of Food Biochemistry* 27 (6): 449–59.

Kim, N. D., R. Mehta, W. Yu, I. Neeman, T. Livney, A. Amichay, D. Poirier, et al. 2002. Chemopreventive and adjuvant therapeutic potential of pomegranate (*Punica granatum*) for human breast cancer. *Breast Cancer Research and Treatment* 71:203–17.

Kim, Soojin. 2007. Personal communication about Korean foods and celebrations by Korean graduate student of anthropology at the University of Hawai'i.

Kirshenblatt-Gimblett, Barbara. 2003. Passover. In *Encyclopedia of Food and Culture*, ed. S. H. Katz, 41–46. Charles Scribner, New York.

Kishigami, Nobuhiro. 2004. Contemporary Inuit food sharing: A case study from Akulivik, Canada. Paper presented for the International Congress of Arctic Social Sciences, 22 May, Fairbanks, Alaska.

Kleemola, Päivi, Pekka Jousilahti, Pirjo Pietinen, Erkki Vartianen, and Jaakko Tuomilehto. 2000. Coffee consumption and the risk of coronary heart disease and death. *Archives of Internal Medicine* 160 (22): 3393–3400.

Knorr, Alexander. 2006. The online nomads of cyberia. Presentation in the Workshop "Understanding Media Practices," European Association of Social Anthropologists Biennial Conference, Bristol, England, 18–21 September. http://www.media-anthro pology.net/knorr_online_nomads.pdf.

Kochilas, Diane. 2001. *The Glorious Foods of Greece*. William Morrow, New York.

Koebnick, Corinna, Ada L. Garcia, Peiter C. Dagnelie, Carola Strassner, Jan Lindemans, Norbert Katz, Claus Leitzmann, and Ingrid Hoffmann. 2005. Long-term consumption of a raw food diet is associated with favorable serum LDL cholesterol and triglycerides but also with elevated plasma homocysteine and low serum HDL cholesterol in humans. *Journal of Nutrition* 135:2372–78.

Koster, Jeremy. 2007. Food transfers among indigenous Nicaraguan horticulturalists. Paper presented at the Annual Meeting of the American Anthropological Association, 2 December, Washington, D.C.

Krauss, Beatrice H. 1993. *Plants in Hawaiian Culture*. University of Hawai'i Press, Honolulu.

Kris-Etherton, P. M., and C. L. Keen. 2002. Evidence that the antioxidant flavonoids in tea and cocoa are beneficial for cardiovascular health. *Current Opinion in Lipidology* 13 (1): 41–49.

Krishnamani, R., and M. C. Mahaney. 2000. Geophagy among primates: Adaptive significance and ecological consequences. *Animal Behavior* 59 (5): 899–915.

Kuramoto, Y., K. Yamada, O. Tsuruta, and M. Sugano. 1996. Effect of natural food colorings on immunoglobulin production in vitro by rat spleen lymphocytes. *Bioscience, Biotechnology, and Biochemistry* 60:1712–13.

Kwon, Y. S., W. G. Choi, W. J. Kim, W. K. Kim, M. J. Kom, W. H. Kang, and C. M. Kim. 2002. Antimicrobial constituents of *Foeniculum vulgare*. *Archives of Pharmacal Research* 25 (20): 154–57.

Lamb, Ursula, ed. 1995. *The Globe Encircled and the World Revealed*. Ashgate Publishing, Aldershot, U.K.

LaMoreaux, Philip E., and Judy T. Tanner, eds. 2001. *Springs and Bottled Waters of the World*. Springer, Berlin.

Lattanzio, Vincenzo, Salvatore Arpaia, Angela Cardinali, Donato di Venere, and Vito Linsalata. 2000. Role of endogenous flavonoids in resistance mechanism of *Vigna* to aphids. *Journal of Agricultural and Food Chemistry* 48 (11): 5316–20.

Laudan, Rachel. 1996. *The Food of Paradise*. University of Hawai'i Press, Honolulu.

Lavid, Noa, Ammon Schwartz, Oded Yarden, and Elisha Tel-Or. 2001. The involvement of polyphenols and peroxidase activities in heavy-metal accumulation by epidermal glands of the waterlily (Nymphaeaceae). *Planta* 212:323–31.

Lee, Cecilia Hae-Jin. 2005. *Eating Korean*. John Wiley, Hoboken, N.J.

Lee, Jung. 2002. *Korean Temples and Food*. Yeinart, Seoul.

Lei, V., W. K. Amooa-Awua, and L. Brimer. 1999. Degradation of cyanogenic glycosides by *Lactobacillus plantarum* strains from spontaneous cassava fermentation and other microorganisms. *International Journal of Food Microbiology* 53:169–84.

Lewis, George H. 2000. From Minnesota fat to Seoul food: Spam in America and the Pacific Rim. *Journal of Popular Culture* 34 (2): 83–105.

Li, Changling, Yan Zhu, Yinye Wnat, Jia-Shi Zhu, Joseph Chang, and David Kritchevsky. 1998. *Monascus purpureus*–fermented rice (red yeast rice): A natural food product that lowers blood cholesterol in animal models of hypercholesterolemia. *Nutrition Research* 18:71–81.

Lichtenstein, Alice H. 2006. Dietary fat, carbohydrate, and protein: Effects on plasma lipoprotein patterns. *Journal of Lipid Research* 47:1661–67.

Lightowler, H. J., and G. J. Davies. 1998. Iodine intake and iodine deficiency in vegans as assessed by the duplicate-portion technique and urinary iodine excretion. *British Journal of Nutrition* 80 (6): 529–35.

Lileks, James. 2007. *Gastroanomalies*. Random House, New York.

Lino, Apak, and Olila Deogracious. 2006. The in vitro antibacterial activity of *Annona senegalensis*, *Securidaca longipedunculata* and *Steganotaenia araliacea*—Ugandan medicinal plants. *African Health Sciences* 6 (1): 31–35.

Linskens, H. F., and W. Jorde. 1997. Pollen as food and medicine: A review. *Economic Botany* 51 (1): 78–87.

Long-Solís, Janet, and Luis Alberto Vargas. 2005. *Food Culture in Mexico*. Greenwood Press, Westport, Conn.

Lopez-Garcia, Esther, Rob M. Van Dam, Lu Qi, and Frank B. Hu. 2006b. Coffee consumption and markers of inflammation and endothelial dysfunction in healthy and diabetic women. *American Journal of Clinical Nutrition* 84 (4): 888–93.

Lopez-Garcia, Esther, Rob M. Van Dam, Walter C. Willitt, Eric Rimm, JoAnn E. Manson, Meir J. Stampfer, Kathryn M. Rexrode, and Frank B. Hu. 2006a. Coffee consumption and coronary heart disease in men and women. *Circulation* 113:2045–53.

Louwman, Marieke W. J., Marijke van Dusseldorp, Fons J. R. van de Vijver, Chris M. G. Thomas, Jørn Schneede, Per M. Ueland, Helga Refsum, and Wija A. van Staveren. 2000. Signs of impaired cognitive function in adolescents with marginal cobalamin status. *American Journal of Clinical Nutrition* 72 (3): 762–69.

Lovera, José e Rafael. 2005. *Food Culture in South America*. Greenwood Press, Westport, Conn.

Low Carb Diet Plans. 2006. Comparison of low-carb plans. http://www.lowcarb.ca.

Lu, Wei-Bo. 2002. Therapeutic uses of tea in traditional Chinese medicine. In *Tea: Bioactivity and Therapeutic Potential*, ed. Y.-S. Zhen, 231–41. Taylor and Francis, London.

Luard, Elisabeth. 2001. *Sacred Food*. Chicago Review Press, Chicago.

Lupien, John R. 1999. Overview of the nutritional benefits of cocoa and chocolate. In *Chocolate and Cocoa: Health and Nutrition*, ed. I. Knight, 3–8. Blackwell Science, Oxford.

Lupton, Deborah. 1994. Food, memory and meaning: The symbolic and social nature of food events. *Sociological Review* 42 (4): 664–85.

Lutz, Carroll A., and Karen R. Przytulski. 2006. *Nutrition and Diet Therapy: Evidence-Based Applications*. 4th ed. F. A. Davis, Philadelphia.

Luximon-Ramma, Amitabye, Theeshan Bahorun, and Alan Crozier. 2003. Antioxidant actions and phenolic and vitamin C contents of common Mauritian exotic fruits. *Journal of the Science of Food and Agriculture* 83:496–502.

Ma, J., Y. Li, Q. Ye, J. Li, Y. Hua, D. Ju, D. Zhang, R. Cooper, and M. Chang. 2000. Constituents of red yeast rice, a traditional Chinese food and medicine. *Journal of Agricultural and Food Chemistry* 48 (11): 5220–25.

Mabberley, D. J. 1993. *The Plant Book: A Portable Dictionary of the Higher Plants*. Corrected reprint of the 1987 edition. Cambridge University Press, Cambridge.

Madar, Z., and A. H. Stark. 2002. New legume sources as therapeutic agents. *British Journal of Nutrition* 88:287–92.

Mahaney, William C., David P. Watts, and R. G. V. Hancock. 1999. Geophagia by mountain gorillas (*Gorilla gorilla*) in the Virunga Mountain, Rwanda. *Primates* 31 (1): 113–20.

Maity, S., J. R. Vedasiromoni, and D. K. Ganguly. 1995. Anti-ulcer effect of the hot water extract of black tea (*Camellia sinensis*). *Journal of Ethnopharmacology* 46:167–74.

Manchester, Carole. 1996. *Tea in the East*. Hearst Books, New York.

Marlowe, Frank W. 2004. What explains Hadza food sharing? *Research in Economic Anthropology* 23:69–88.

Martínez, María Julia, Nancy Molina, and Elisa Boucourt. 1997. Evaluación de la actividad antimicrobiana del *Psidium guajava* L. *Revista Cubana de Plantas Medicinales* 2 (1): 12–14. http://scielo.sld.cu/scielo.php.pid.

Matalas, Antonia-Leda, and Mary Yannakoulia. 2000. Greek street food vending: An old habit turned new. In *Street Foods*, ed. A. P. Simopoulos and R. V. Bhat, 1–24. Karger, Basel.

Matz, Hagit, Edith Orion, and Ronni Wolf. 2003. Balneotherapy in dermatology. *Dermatologic Therapy* 16 (2): 132–40.

Maurer, Donna. 2002. *Vegetarianism: Movement or Moment?* Temple University Press, Philadelphia.

Maurer, H. R. 2001. Bromelain: Biochemistry, pharmacology and medical use. *Cellular and Molecular Life Sciences* 58:1234–45.

Mayo Clinic. 2005. Caffeine content of common beverages. http://www.mayoclinic.com.

Mbata, T. I., Lu Debiao, and A. Saikia. 2006. Antibacterial activity of the crude extract of Chinese green tea (*Camellia sinensis*) on listeria monocytogenes. *Internet Journal of Microbiology* 2(2). http://www.ispub.com.

McGrew, William C. 2001. The other faunivore: Primate insectivory and early human diet. In *Meat-Eating and Human Evolution*, ed. C. B. Stanford and Henry T. Bunn, 160–78. Oxford University Press, Oxford.

McKay, Diane L., and Jeffrey B. Blumberg. 2002. The role of tea in human health: An update. *Journal of the American College of Nutrition* 21 (1): 1–13.

MedlinePlus. 2006. Herbs and supplements. http://www.nlm.nih.gov/medlineplus/drug info/natural.

Meigs, Anna. 1988. Food as a cultural construction. *Food and Foodways* 2:341–59.

Mennell, Stephen. 1996. *All Manners of Food: Eating and Taste in England and France from the Middle Ages to the Present*. 2nd ed. University of Illinois Press, Urbana.

Mennell, Stephen, Anne Murcott, and Anneke H. Van Otterloo. 1992. *The Sociology of Food: Eating, Diet, and Culture*. Sage Publications, London.

Mensah, Patience, Dorothy Yeboah-Manu, Kwaku Owusu-Darko, and Anthony Ablordey. 2002. Street foods in Accra, Ghana: How safe are they? *Bulletin of the World Health Organization* 80:546–54.

Menvielle-Bourg, F. 2005. Superoxide dismutase (SOD), a powerful antioxidant, is now available orally. *Phytothérapie* 3:1–4.

Merck. 2007. Merck Manuals. http://merck.com.

Merlin, M., and W. Raynor. 2004. Modern use and environmental impact of the kava plant in remote Oceania. In *Dangerous Harvest: Drug Plants and the Transformation of Indigenous Landscapes*, ed. M. K. Steinberg, J. J. Hobbs, and K. Mathewson, 274–93. Oxford University Press, Oxford.

Messina, Mark, Christopher Gardner, and Stephen Barnes. 2002. Gaining insight into the health effects of soy but a long way to go. *Journal of Nutrition* 132:547S–551S.

Miele, Mara, and Jonathan Murdoch. 2002. The practical aesthetics of traditional cuisines: Slow food in Tuscany. *Sociologia Ruralis* 42 (4): 312–28.

Milknewsroom. 2008. Got Milk? http://www.milknewsroom.com.

Miller, Lisa, Paul Rozin, and Alan P. Fiske. 1998. Food sharing and feeding another person suggest intimacy: Two studies of American college students. *European Journal of Social Psychology* 28:423–36.

Milton, Katharine. 2002. Hunter-gatherer diets: Wild foods signal relief from diseases of affluence. In *Human Diet: Its Origin and Evolution*, ed. P. D. Ungar and M. F. Teaford, 111–22. Bergin and Garvey, Westport, Conn.

Mintz, Sidney W. 1985. *Sweetness and Power: The Place of Sugar in Modern History*. Viking Penguin, New York.

Mitani, John C., and David P. Watts. 2001. Why do chimpanzees hunt and share meat? *Animal Behaviour* 61:915–24.

Miura, Y., K. Ono, R. Okauchi, and K. Yagasaki. 2004. Inhibitory effect of coffee on hepatoma proliferation and invasion in culture and on tumor growth, metastasis and abnormal lipoprotein profiles in hepatoma-bearing rats. *Journal of Nutritional Science and Vitaminology* 50 (1): 38–44.

Mokni, Meherzia, Ferid Limam, Salem Elkahoui, Mohamed Amri, and Ezzedine Aouani. 2006. Strong cardioprotective effect of resveratrol, a red wine polyphenol, on isolated rat hearts after ischemia/reperfusion injury. *Archives of Biochemistry and Biophysics* 457 (1): 1–6.

Moody, J. O., O. O. Ojo, O. O. Omotade, A. A. Adeyemo, P. E. Olumese, and O. O. Ogundipe. 2003. Anti-sickling potential of a Nigerian herbal formula (ajawaron HF) and the major plant component (*Cissus populnea* L. CPK). *Phytotherapy Research* 19 (10): 1173–76.

Moritz, R. F. A., and E. E. Southwick. 1992. *Bees as Superorganisms: An Evolutionary Reality*. Springer, Berlin.

Moshi, Maimen J., and Zakaria H. Mbwambo. 2002. Experience of Tanzanian traditional healers in the management of non-insulin dependent diabetes mellitus. *Pharmaceutical Biology* 40 (7): 552–60.

Moskin, Julia. 2006. Must be something in the water. *New York Times*, 15 February.

Motyl, Alexander J. 2001. *Imperial Ends: The Decay, Collapse, and Revival of Empires*. Columbia University Press, New York.

Moxham, Roy. 2003. *Tea: Addiction, Exploitation, and Empire*. Carroll and Graf, New York.

Mukhtar, Hasan, and Nihal Ahmad. 2000. Tea polyphenols: Prevention of cancer and optimizing health. *American Journal of Clinical Nutrition* 71 (6): 1698S–1702S.

Muñoz de Chávez, Miriam, Adolfo Chávez Villasana, and Igor E. Vuskovic. 2000. Sale of street food in Latin America. In *Street Food*, ed. A. P. Simopoulos and R. V. Bhat, 138–54. Karger, Basel.

Mustapha, A., I. A. Yakasai, and I. A. Aguye. 1996. Effect of *Tamarindus indica* L. on the bioavailability of aspirin in healthy human volunteers. *European Journal of Drug Metabolism and Pharmacokinetics* 21:223–26.

Nabhan, Gary. 2004. *Why Some Like It Hot*. Island Press, Washington, D.C.

Nagao, F., M. Nakayama, T. Muto, and K. Okumura. 2000. Effects of a fermented milk drink containing *Lactobacillus casei* strain Shirota on the immune system in healthy human subjects. *Bioscience, Biotechnology, and Biochemistry* 64 (12): 2706–8.

Nakamura, Yasushi, Takako Iwahashi, Atsuo Tanaka, Jun Koutani, Tomoaki Matsuo, Shigehisa Okamoto, Kenji Sato, and Kozo Ohtsuki. 2001. 4-(methylthio)-3-butenyl isothiocyanate, a principal antimutagen in daikon (*Rhaphanus sativus*; Japanese white radish). *Journal of Agricultural and Food Chemistry* 49 (12): 5755–60.

Namkoong, Joan. 2006. *Food Lover's Guide to Honolulu*. Bess Press, Honolulu.

National Institutes of Health. 2006. Diabetes. http://www.nlm.nih.gov/medlineplus.

National Research Council. 1996. *Lost Crops of Africa*, vol. 1, *Grains*. National Academy Press, Washington, D.C.

Nawrot, P., S. Jordan, J. Eastwood, J. Rotstein, A. Hugenholtz, and M. Feeley. 2003. Effects of caffeine on human health. *Food Additives and Contaminants* 20 (1): 1–30.

Nazarea, Virginia D. 1999. *Ethnoecology: Situated Knowledge/Located Lives*. University of Arizona Press, Tucson.

Ndabigengesere, Anselme, K. Subba Narasiah, and Brian G. Talbot. 1995. Active agents and mechanism of coagulation of turbid waters using *Moringa oleifera*. *Water Research* 29 (2): 703–10.

Nepote, V., N. R. Grosso, and C. A. Guzman. 2004. Radical scavenging activity of extracts of Argentine peanut skins (*Arachis hypogaea*) in relation to Iis *trans*-resveratrol content. *Journal of the Argentine Chemical Society* 92 (4–6): 4–49.

Nestle, Marion. 2006. *What to Eat*. North Point Press, New York.

Newall, Venetia. 1971. *An Egg at Easter: A Folklore Study*. Indiana University Press, Bloomington.

Nicole, Catherine, Nicolas Cardinault, Olivier Aprikan, Jérome Busserollees, Pascal Grolier, Edmond Rock, Christian Demigné, et al. 2003. Effect of carrot intake on cholesterol metabolism and on antioxidant status in cholesterol-fed rat. *European Journal of Nutrition* 42 (5): 254–61.

Norton, Marcy. 2006. Tasting empire: Chocolate and the European internalization of Mesoamerican aesthetics. *American Historical Review* 111:660–91.

Norton, William. 2005. *Cultural Geography*. 2nd ed. Oxford University Press, New York.

NRDC (Natural Resources Defense Council). 2006. Bottled water: Pure drink or pure hype? http://www.nrdc.org/water.

Odunfa, S. A., and O. B. Oyewole. 1998. African fermented foods. In *Microbiology of Fermented Foods*, ed. B. J. B. Wood, 713–52. 2nd ed. Blackie Academic and Professional, London.

Ogungbamila, F. O., G. O. Onawunmi, J. C. Ibewuike, and K. A. Funmilayo. 1997. Antibacterial constituents of *Ficus barteri* fruits. *Pharmaceutical Biology* 35:185–89.

Ohira, S., T. Hasegawa, K. Hayashi, T. Hoshino, D. Takaoka, and H. Nozaki. 1998. Sesquiterpenoids from *Cyperus rotundus*. *Phytochemistry* 47:1577–81.

Ojekale, A. B., O. A. Ojiako, G. M. Saibu, A. Lala, and O. A. Olodude. 2007. Long term effects of aqueous stem bark extract of *Cissus populnea* (Guill. and Per.) on some biochemical parameters in normal rabbits. *African Journal of Biotechnology* 6 (3): 247–51.

Olaljide, Olumayokun A., Babatunde R. Ogunleye, and Temitope O. Erinle. 2004. Anti-inflammatory properties of *Amaranthus spinosus* leaf extract. *Pharmaceutical Biology* 42 (7): 521–25.

Omafuvbe, B. O., O. O. Shonukan, and S. H. Abiose. 2000. Microbiological and biochemical changes in the traditional fermentation of soybean for "soy-daddawa"— Nigerian food condiment. *Food Microbiology* 17:469–74.

Oršolić, N., L. Šver, S. Verstovšek, S. Terziæ, and I. Basiæ. 2003. Inhibition of mammary carcinoma cell proliferation in vitro by bee venom. *Toxicon* 41 (7): 861–70.

Oshodi, A. A., H. N. Ogungbenle, and M. O. Oladimeji. 1999. Chemical composition, nutritionally valuable minerals and functional properties of benniseed (*Sesamum radiatum*), pearl millet (*Pennisetum typhoides*) and quinoa (*Chenopodium quinoa*) flours. *International Journal of Food Sciences and Nutrition* 50:325–31.

Ouoba, L. I. I., B. Diawara, L. Jespersen, and M. Jakobsen. 2007. Antimicrobial activity of *Bacillus subtilis* and *Bacillus pumilus* during the fermentation of African locust bean (*Parkia biglobosa*) for Soumbala production. *Journal of Applied Microbiology* 102 (4): 963–70.

Owen, Mary. 2008. Suit blasts city's tax on bottled water. *Chicago Tribune*, 5 January, p. 13. http://chicagotribune.com.

Parkins, Wendy, and Geoffrey Craig. 2006. *Slow Living*. Oxford University Press, New York.

Parvez, K. A., K. A. Malik, S. Ah Kang, and H.-Y. Kim. 2006. Probiotics and their fermented food products are beneficial for health. *Journal of Applied Microbiology* 11 (6): 1171–85.

Patton, John. 2007. Meat and manioc: Men's and women's food-sharing networks in the Ecuadorian Amazon. Paper presented at the Annual Meeting of the American Anthropological Association, 2 December, Washington, D.C.

Pence, Gregory E., ed. 2002. *The Ethics of Food: A Reader for the Twenty-first Century*. Rowman and Littlefield, Lanham, Md.

Pereira, Juliana V., Débora C. B. Bergamo, José O. Pereira, Suzelei de Castro França, Rosemeire C. L. R. Pietro, and Yara T. C. Silva-Sousa. 2005. Antimicrobial activity of *Arctium lappa* constituents against microorganisms commonly found in endodontic infections. *Brazilian Dental Journal* 16 (3): 192–96.

Perlo, Katherine. 2003. "Would you let your child die rather than experiment on nonhuman animals?" A comparative questions approach. *Society and Animals* 11 (1): 51–67.

Peterson, Nicolas. 1993. Demand sharing: Reciprocity and the pressure for generosity among foragers. *American Anthropologist* 95 (4): 860–74.

Petrini, Carlo. 2003. *Slow Food: The Case for Taste.* Trans. William McCuaig. Columbia University Press, New York.

Pettit, George R., Dennis L. Doubek, and Delbert L. Herald. 1991. Isolation and structure of cytostatic steroidal saponins from the African medicinal plant *Balanites aegyptica.* *Journal of Natural Products* 54 (6): 1491–1502.

Phillips, J. R. S. 1998. *The Medieval Expansion of Europe.* 2nd ed. Clarendon Press, Oxford.

Pieroni, Andrea, Cassandra L. Quave, Maria L. Villanelli, Paola Mangino, Guilia Sabbatini, Luigina Santini, Tamara Boccetti, et al. 2004. Ethnopharmacognostic survey on the natural ingredients used in folk cosmetics, cosmeceuticals and remedies for healing skin diseases in the inland Marches, central-eastern Italy. *Journal of Ethnopharmacology* 91:331–44.

Pip, Eva. 2000. Survey of bottled drinking water available in Manitoba, Canada. *Environmental Health Perspectives* 108 (9): 863–66.

Plants for a Future. 2004. Hosta species. http://www.pfaf.org/database.

Pollan, Michael. 2006. *The Omnivore's Dilemma: A Natural History of Four Meals.* Penguin Press, New York.

Pollock, Nancy. 1992. *These Roots Remain: Food Habits in Islands of the Central and Eastern Pacific since Western Contact.* Institute for Polynesian Studies, Laie, Hawai'i.

Prinz, Armin, ed. 2006. *Hunting Food and Drinking Wine.* Lit, Vienna.

Probyn, Elspeth. 2000. *Carnal Appetites: Food, Sex, Identities.* Routledge, London.

Public Citizen. 2007. Ocean desalination: A technology with many pitfalls. http://www.citizen.org/california/wate.

Qian, H., and V. Nihorimbere. 2004. Antioxidant power of phytochemicals from *Psidium guajava* leaf. *Journal of Zhejiang University: Science* 5 (6): 676–83.

Radford, Andrew N., and Amanda R. Ridley. 2006. Recruitment calling: A novel form of extended parental care in an altricial species. *Current Biology* 16:1–5.

Raisor, Michelle J. 2004. Determining the Antiquity of Dog Origins: Canine Domestication as a Model for the Consilience between Molecular Genetics and Archaeology. Ph.D. diss., Texas A&M University.

Rajaram, Sujatha, and Joan Sabaté. 2000. Health benefits of a vegetarian diet. *Nutrition* 16 (7–8): 531–33.

Ramanavièiene, Almira, Viktros Mostovojus, Irina Bachmatova, and Arûnas Ramavièius. 2003. Anti-bacterial effect of caffeine on *Escherichia coli* and *Pseudomonas fluorescens.* *Acta Medica Lituanica* 10:185–88.

Rayment, P., S. B. Ross-Murphy, and J. S. G. Reid. 1996. A new polysaccharide from a traditional Nigerian plant food: *Detarium senegalense* Gmelin. *Carbohydrate Research* 284:229–39.

RDI (Reference Daily Intake). 2008. Recommended intakes for individuals. http://fnic.nal.usda.gov.

Reed, Kaye, and Laura R. Bidner. 2004. Primate communities: Past, present, and possible future. *Yearbook of Physical Anthropology* 47:2–39.

Relf, Diane, ed. 1992. *The Role of Horticulture in Human Well-Being and Social Development*. Timber Press, Portland, Ore.

Richie, Donald. 1985. *A Taste of Japan*. Harper and Row, New York.

Rios, L. Y., M. P. Gonthier, C. Remsey, I. Mila, C. Lapierre, S. A. Lazarus, G. Williamson, and A. Scalbert. 2003. Chocolate intake increases urinary excretion of polyphenol-derived phenolic acids in healthy human subjects. *American Journal of Clinical Nutrition* 77 (4): 912–18.

Ritchie, Ian. 1990. Hausa sensory symbolism. *Anthropologica* 32:113–19.

Roberts, Cynthia A. 2003. Safety of water. In *The Encyclopedia of Food and Culture*, ed. S. H. Katz, 516–21. Charles Scribner, New York.

Rogak, Lisa. 2004. *Death Warmed Over: Funeral Food, Rituals, and Customs from around the World*. Ten Speed Press, Berkeley, Calif.

Rogers, Peter J., and Hendrik J. Smit. 2000. Food craving and food "addiction": A critical review of the evidence from a biopsychosocial perspective. *Pharmacology, Biochemistry, and Behavior* 66 (1): 3–14.

Rojas, Jhon J., Veronica J. Ochoa, Saul A. Ocampo, and John F. Muñoz. 2006. Screening for antimicrobial activity of ten medicinal plants used in Colombian folkloric medicine: A possible alternative in the treatment of non-nosocomial infections. *BMC Complementary and Alternative Medicine* 6:2. http:www.pubmedcentral.nih.gov.

Rose, Lisa M. 2001. Meat and the early human diet: Insights from neotropical primate studies. In *Meat-Eating and Human Evolution*, ed. C. B. Stanford and Henry T. Bunn, 141–59. Oxford University Press, Oxford.

——. 2004. Vertebrate predation and food sharing in *Cebus* and *Pan*. *International Journal of Primatology* 18 (5): 727–65.

Rosenblat, M., Nina Volkova, Raymond Coleman, and Michael Aviram. 2006. Pomegranate byproduct administration to apolipoprotein E–deficient mice attenuates atherosclerosis development as a result of decreased macrophage oxidative stress and reduced cellular uptake of oxidized low-density lipoprotein. *Journal of Agricultural and Food Chemistry* 54 (5): 1928–35.

Ross, Paul J., Nina L. Etkin, and Ibrahim Muazzamu. 1996. A changing Hausa diet. *Medical Anthropology* 17:143–63.

Routh, Hirak B., Kazal R. Bhowmik, Lawrence C. Parish, and Joseph A. Witkowski. 1996. Balneology, mineral water, and spas in historical perspective. *Clinics in Dermatology* 14:551–54.

Rubin, Lawrence C., ed. 2007. *Food for Thought: Essays on Eating and Culture*. McFarland, Jefferson, N.C.

Rust, Petra, and Ibrahim Elmadfa. 2005. Attitudes of Austrian adults to the consumption of fruits and vegetables. *Forum of Nutrition* 57:91–99.

Ruusila, Vesa, and Mauri Pesonen. 2004. Interspecific cooperation in human (*Homo sapiens*) hunting: The benefits of a barking dog (*Canis familiaris*). *Annales Zoologici Fennici* 41 (4): 545–49.

Sabu, M. C., K. Smitha, and Ramadasan Kuttan. 2002. Anti-diabetic activity of green tea polyphenols and their role in reducing oxidative stress in experimental diabetes. *Journal of Ethnopharmacology* 83:109–16.

Saethre, Eirik. 2005. Nutrition, economics, and food distribution in an Australian Aboriginal community. *Anthropological Forum* 15 (2): 151–69.

Sahpaz, Sevser, C. Bories, P. M. Loiseau, D. Cortès, R. Hocquemiller, A. Laurens, and A. Cavé. 1994. Cytotoxic and antiparasitic activity from *Annona senegalensis*. *Planta Medica* 60:538–40.

Saleem, M., A. Alam, and S. Sultana. 2001. Asafoetida inhibits early events of carcinogenesis: A chemopreventive study. *Life Sciences* 68 (16): 1913–21.

Santetropicale. 2003. Étude d'effet d'un principe anti-inflammatoire isolé de *Borassus aethiopum*. *Le Pharmacien d'Afrique* 166 (June–July). http://www.santetropicale.com.

Savitz, David A., Ronna L. Chan, Amy Herring, Penelope P. Howards, and Katherine E. Hartmann. 2008. Caffeine and miscarriage risk. *Epidemiology* 19 (1): 55–62.

Schieffelin, Edward L. 1976. *The Sorrow of the Lonely and the Burning of the Dancers*. St. Martin's Press, New York.

Schooling, C. Mary, Sai Yin Ho, Gabriel M. Leung, G. Neil Thomas, Sarah M. McGhee, Kwok Hang Mak, and Tai Hing Lam. 2006. Diet synergies and mortality—a population-based case-control study of 32,462 Hong Kong Chinese older adults. *International Journal of Epidemiology* 35 (2): 418–26.

Seaman, Gary. 1992. Winds, waters, seeds, and souls: Folk concepts of physiology and etiology in Chinese geomancy. In *Paths to Asian Medical Knowledge*, ed. C. Leslie and A. Young, 74–97. University of California Press, Berkeley.

Seeley, Thomas D. 1995. *The Wisdom of the Hive: The Social Physiology of Honey Bee Colonies*. Harvard University Press, Cambridge, Mass.

Seeram, Navindra P., David Heber, and Risa N. Schulman. 2006. *Pomegranates: Ancient Roots to Modern Medicine*. CRC Press, Boca Raton, Fla.

Seppo, Leena, Tiina Jauhiainen, Tuija Poussa, and Riitta Korpela. 2003. A fermented milk high in bioactive peptides has a blood pressure-lowering effect in hypertensive subjects. *American Journal of Clinical Nutrition* 77 (2): 326–30.

Serafini, M., R. Bugianesi, G. Maiani, S. Valtuena, S. De Santis, and A. Crozier. 2003. Plasma antioxidants from chocolate. *Nature* 424:1013.

Sforcin, J. M. 2007. Propolis and the immune system: A review. *Journal of Ethnopharmacology* 113:1–14.

Sherman, Paul W., and Samuel M. Flaxman. 2001. Protecting ourselves from food. *American Scientist* 89:142–51.

Sherry, Frank. 1994. *Pacific Passions: The European Struggle for Power in the Great Ocean in the Age of Exploration*. William Morrow, New York.

Shimabukuro, Betty. 2002. The musubi mystique. *Honolulu Star Bulletin*. http://archives.starbulletin.com.

Shimizu, Kuniyoshi, Ryuichiro Kondo, Kokki Sakai, Supanida Buabarn, and Uraiwan Dilokkunanant. 2000. 5a-Reductase inhibitory component for leaves of *Artocarpus altilis*. *Journal of Wood Science* 46:385–89.

Shimizu, Takeo, Hiroshi Kinoshita, Shinji Ishihara, Kanae Sakai, Shiro Nagai, and Takuya Nihira. 2005. Polyketide syntheses gene responsible for citrin biosynthesis in *Monascus purpureus*. *Applied and Environmental Microbiology* 71 (7): 3453–57.

Shin, Shik, Hideki Masuda, and Kinae Naohide. 2004. Bactericidal activity of wasabi (*Wasabia japonica*) against *Helicobacter pylori*. *International Journal of Food Microbiology* 94 (3): 255–61.

Shoemaker, Candice A., ed. 2002. *Interaction by Design: Bringing People and Plants Together for Health and Well-Being*. Iowa State University Press, Ames.

Shouji, N., K. Takada, K. Fukushima, and M. Hirasawa. 2000. Anticaries effect of a component from shiitake (an edible mushroom). *Caries Research* 34:94–98.

Shovic, Anne Caprio. 1994. *Hawaiian Food Choices for Healthy Living*. University of Hawai'i Press, Honolulu.

Sibley, E. 2004. Genetic variation and lactose intolerance: Detection methods and clinical implications. *American Journal of Pharmacogenomics* 4 (4): 239–45.

Siddiqui, I. A., F. Afaq, V. M. Adhami, and H. Mukhtar. 2004. Antioxidants of the beverage tea in promotion of human health. *Antioxidants and Redox Signaling* 6 (3): 571–82.

Silk, Joan B. 2005. The evolution of cooperation in primate groups. In *Moral Sentiments and Material Interests: The Foundation of Cooperation in Economic Life*, ed. H. Gintis, S. Bowles, R. Boyd, and E. Fehr, 43–73. MIT Press, Cambridge, Mass.

Silva, Manori J., Dana B. Barr, John A. Reidy, Nicole A. Malek, Carolyn C. Hodge, Samuel P. Caudill, John W. Brock, Larry L. Needham, and Antonia M. Calafat. 2004. Urinary levels of seven phthalate metabolites in the U.S. population from the National Health and Nutrition Examination Survey (NHANES), 1999–2000. *Environmental Health Perspectives* 112 (3): 331–38.

Simoons, Frederick J. 1991. *Food in China: A Cultural and Historical Inquiry*. CRC Press, Boca Raton, Fla.

Simopoulos, Artemis P., and Ramesh V. Bhat, eds. 2000. *Street Foods*. Karger, Basel.

Simpson, Beryl B., and Molly C. Ogorzaly. 2001. *Economic Botany: Plants in Our World*. 3rd ed. McGraw-Hill, New York.

Singh, Y. N. 2004. Pharmacology and toxicology of kava and kavalactones. In *Kava: From Ethnology to Pharmacology*, ed. Y. N. Singh, 104–39. CRC Press, Boca Raton, Fla.

Slocum, Perry D., and Peter Robinson. 1996. *Water Gardening: Water Lilies and Lotuses*. Timber Press, Portland, Ore.

Smuts, Barbara. 2004. Social learning: Food. In *Encyclopedia of Animal Behavior*, ed. M. Beckoff, 593–99. Greenwood Press, Westport, Conn.

Spoon, Jeremy D. 2008. Tourism in a Sacred Landscape: Political Economy and Sherpa Ecological Knowledge in Beyul Khumbus/Sabarmatha National Park. Ph.D. diss., University of Hawai'i, Department of Anthropology.

Stanford, Craig B. 2001. A comparison of social meat-foraging by chimpanzees and human foragers. In *Meat-Eating and Human Evolution*, ed. C. B. Stanford and H. T. Bunn, 122–40. Oxford University Press, Oxford.

Steffen, Lyn M., and Jennifer A. Nettleton. 2006. Carbohydrates: How low can you go? *Lancet* 367:880–81.

Steinberg, Francene, Monica M. Bearden, and Carl L. Keen. 2003. Cocoa and chocolate flavonoids: Implications for cardiovascular health. *Journal of the American Dietetic Association* 102 (2): 215–23.

Stevens, Jeffrey R., and Ian C. Gilby. 2004. A conceptual framework for nonkin food sharing: Timing and currency of benefits. *Animal Behaviour* 67:603–14.

Strier, Karen B. 2006. *Primate Behavioral Ecology*. 3rd ed. Allyn and Bacon, Boston, Mass.

Sudheesh, S., G. Presannakumar, S. Vijayakumar, and N. R. Vijayalakshmi. 1997. Hypolipidemic effect of flavonoids from *Solanum melongena*. *Plant Foods for Human Nutrition* 51 (4): 321–30.

Sudheesh, S., C. Sandhya, Asha S. Koshy, and N. R. Vijayalakshmi. 1999. Antioxidant activity of flavonoids from *Solanum melongena*. *Phytotherapy Research* 13 (5): 393–96.

Sundram, Kalyana, Ravidgadevi Sambanthamurthi, and Yew-Ai Tan. 2003. Palm fruit chemistry and nutrition. *Asia Pacific Journal of Clinical Nutrition* 12 (3): 355–62.

Swagerty, Daniel L., Anne D. Walling, and Robert M. Klein. 2002. Lactose intolerance. *American Family Physician* 65:1845–50, 1855–56.

Takahashi, Elizo, Timothy H. Marczylo, Toshiro Watanabe, Shiro Nagai, Hikoya Hayatsu, and Tomoe Negishi. 2001. Preventive effects of anthraquinone food pigments on the DNA damage induced by carcinogens in *Drosophila*. *Mutation Research* 480–81:139–45.

Takaya, Yoshiaki, Yoshihito Kondo, Tadashi Furukawa, and Masatake Niwa. 2003. Antioxidant constituents of radish sprout (Kaiware-daikon), *Raphanus sativus* L. *Journal of Agricultural and Food Chemistry* 51 (27): 8061–66.

Takenaka, Shigeo, Sumi Sugiyama, Shuhei Ebara, Emi Miyamoto, Katsuo Abe, Yoshiyuki Tamura, Fumio Watanabe, Shingo Tsuyama, and Yoshihisa Nakano. 2001. Feeding dried purple laver (nori) to vitamin B12–deficient rats significantly improves vitamin B12 status. *British Journal of Nutrition* 85:699–703.

Taylor, Denise S., Valerie K. Fishell, Jessica L. Deistine, Rebecca L. Hargrove, Natalie R. Patterson, Kristin W. Moriarty, Beverly A. Battista, Hope E. Ratcliffe, Amy E. Binkoski, and Penny M. Kris-Etherton. 2000. Street foods in America—a true melting pot. In *Street Foods*, ed. A. P. Simopoulos and R. V. Bhat, 25–44. Karger, Basel.

Teiwes, Helga. 1991. *Kachina Dolls: The Art of Hopi Carvers*. University of Arizona Press, Tucson.

Thebtaranonth, C., Y. Thebtaranonth, S. Wanauppathamkul, and Y. Yuthavong. 1995. Antimalarial sesquiterpenes from tubers of *Cyperus rotundus*: Structure of 10,12-peroxycalamenene, a sesquiterpene endoperoxide. *Phytochemistry* 40:125–28.

Thompson, Lilian U., and Wendy E. Ward, eds. 2005. *Food-Drug Synergy and Safety*. CRC Press, Boca Raton, Fla.

Tinker, Irene. 1997. *Street Foods: Urban Food and Employment in Developing Countries*. Oxford University Press, New York.

Toda, Masahiro, Kanehisa Morimoto, Shingo Nagasawa, and Kazuyuki Kitamura. 2006. Change in salivary physiological stress markers by spa bathing. *Biomedical Research* 27:11–14.

Toussaint-Samat, Maguelonne. 1992. *History of Food*. Trans. Anthea Bell. Blackwell, Oxford.

Trang, Corinne. 2003. Coffee. In *The Encyclopedia of Food and Culture*, ed. S. H. Katz, 429–34. Charles Scribner, New York.

Tremearne, A. J. N. 1970. *Hausa Superstitions and Customs*. New impression. Frank Cass, London.

Umoh, V. J., and M. B. Odoba. 1999. Safety and quality evaluation of street foods sold in Zaria, Nigeria. *Food Control* 10:9–14.

Ungar, Peter S., and Mark F. Teaford, eds. 2002. *Human Diet: Its Origin and Evolution*. Bergin and Garvey, Westport, Conn.

United States Department of Agriculture. 2006. Food surveys. http://www.ars.usda.gov/main/site.

Urbano, Montserrat Gudiel, and Isabel Goñi. 2002. Bioavailability of nutrients in rats fed on edible seaweeds, nori (*Porphyra tenera*), and wakame (*Undaria pinnatifida*) as a source of dietary fibre. *Food Chemistry* 76:281–86.

van der Weyden, Elizabeth. 2003. The use of honey for the treatment of two patients with pressure ulcers. *British Journal of Community Nursing* 8 (12): S14–S20.

van Gennep, Arnold. 1960. *The Rites of Passage*. Trans. Monika B. Vizedom and Gabrielle L. Caffee. University of Chicago Press, Chicago.

Vayalil, Praveen K. 2002. Antioxidant and antimutagenic properties of aqueous extract of date fruit (*Phoenix dactylifera* L., Arecaceae). *Journal of Agricultural and Food Chemistry* 50 (3): 610–17.

Venskutonis, P. R., D. Gruzdiené, D. Tirzite, and G. Tirzitis. 2005. Assessment of antioxidant activity of plant extracts by different methods. *Acta Horticulturae* 677:99–107.

Viola, Herman J., and Carolyn Margolis, eds. 1991. *Seeds of Change*. Smithsonian Institution Press, Washington, D.C.

VRG (Vegetarian Resource Group). 2004. Vegetarian diets. *Newsletter* 8(3). http://www.vrg.org.

Wang, Yu, Tongle Deng, Lin Lin, Yuanjiang Pan, and Xiaoxiang Zheng. 2006. Bioassay-guided isolation of antiatherosclerotic phytochemicals from *Artocarpus altilis*. *Phytotherapy Research* 20 (12): 1052–55.

Wateryear. 2005. Facts and figures: Bottled water. (Revised 4 July 2005.) http://www.wateryear2003.org.

Watts, David P., and John C. Mitani. 2004. Hunting behavior of chimpanzees at Ngogo, Kibale National Park, Uganda. *International Journal of Primatology* 23 (1): 1–28.

Watts, Pauline Moffitt. 1995. Prophecy and discovery: On the spiritual origins of Christopher Columbus's enterprise of the Indies. In *New Worlds: The Great Voyages of Discovery*, ed. F. Fernández-Armesto, 195–224. Sutton Publishing, Gloucestershire, U.K.

Weatherstone, J. 1992. Historical introduction. In *Tea: Cultivation to Consumption*, ed. K. C. Willson and M. N. Clifford, 1–23. Chapman and Hall, London.

Weiger, Wendy A., Michael Smith, Heather Boon, Mary Ann Richardson, Ted J. Kaptchuk, and David Eisenberg. 2002. Advising patients who seek complementary and alternative medical therapies for cancer. *Annals of Internal Medicine* 137 (11): 889–903.

Weinberg, Bennett A., and Bonnie K. Bealer. 2001. *The World of Caffeine: The Science and Culture of the World's Most Popular Drug*. Routledge, New York.

White, Lynton D. 1990. *Nâ meakanu o waʻa o Hawaiʻi kahiko: The Canoe Plants of Ancient Hawaiʻi.* www.canoeplants.com, 10 September 2007.

Whitely, Peter, and Vernon Masayesva. 1999. *Paavahu and Paanaqsoʻa*: The wellsprings of life and the slurry of death. In *Cultural and Spiritual Values of Biodiversity*, ed. D. A. Posey, 403–6. United Nations Environment Programme, Nairobi.

Wiley, Andrea S. 2004. "Drink milk for fitness": The cultural politics of human biological variation and milk consumption in the United States. *American Anthropologist* 106 (3): 506–17.

——.- 2005. Does milk make children grow? Relationships between milk consumption and height in NHANES, 1999–2002. *American Journal of Human Biology* 17:425–41.

——. 2007. Transforming milk in a global economy. *American Anthropologist* 109 (4): 666–77.

Wilk, Richard, ed. 2006a. *Fast Food/Slow Food: The Cultural Economy of the Global Food System.* AltaMira Press, Lanham, Md.

——. 2006b. Bottled water: The pure commodity in an age of branding. *Journal of Consumer Culture* 6 (3): 303–25.

Wilson, Edward O. 1975. *Sociobiology: The New Synthesis.* Harvard University Press, Cambridge, Mass.

Wilson, Samuel M., and Leighton C. Peterson. 2002. The anthropology of online communities. *Annual Review of Anthropology* 31:449–67.

Wolf, Bonny. 2007. Bottled water: Is the tide turning for a top seller? National Public Radio Weekend Sunday Edition, 6 May. http://www.npr.org.

Wood, Brian. 2007. Household provisioning and food transfers among Hadza hunter-gatherers. Paper presented at the Annual Meeting of the American Anthropological Association, 2 December, Washington, D.C.

World Carrot Museum. 2008. History of the carrot. http://www.carrotmuseum.com.

World Health Organization. 2006. Diabetes. http://www.who.int/topics/diabetesmellitus.

Yamasaki, Yumiko, Hitoshi Kunoh, Hiroyuki Yamamoto, and Kazuya Akimitsu. 2007. Biological roles of monoterpene volatiles derived from rough lemon (*Citrus jambhiri* Lush) in citrus defense. *Journal of General Plant Pathology* 73 (3): 168–79.

Yanagimoto, K., H. Ochi, K. G. Lee, and T. Shibamoto. 2004. Antioxidative activities of fractions obtained from brewed coffee. *Journal of Agricultural and Food Chemistry* 52 (3): 592–96.

Ye, X. Y., H. X. Wang, and T. B. Ng. 2000. Structurally dissimilar proteins with antiviral and antifungal potency from cowpea (*Vigna unguiculata*) seeds. *Life Sciences* 67:3199–3207.

Yen, Wen-Je, Lee-Wen Chang, and Pin-Der Duh. 2005. Antioxidant activity of peanut seed testa and its antioxidative component, ethyl protocatechuate. *Food Science and Technology* 38:193–200.

Yoder, Don. 2003. Easter. In *Encyclopedia of Food and Culture*, ed. S. H. Katz, 545–47. Scribner, New York.

Young, Allen M. 1994. *The Chocolate Tree.* Smithsonian Institution Press, Washington, D.C.

Young, James H. 1978. The agile role of food: Some historical reflections. In *Nutrition and Drug Interrelations*, ed. J. N. Hancock and J. Coon, 1–18. Academic Press, New York.

Young, Linda S., and Debera J. Thomas. 2004. Celiac sprue treatment in primary care. *Nurse Practitioner* 29:42–45.

Zhao, Tingting, Quanbin Zhang, Huimin Qi, Hong Zhang, Xizhen Niu, Zuhong Xu, and Zhien Li. 2006. Degradation of porphyran from *Porphyra haitanensis* and the antioxidant activities of the degraded porphyrans with different molecular weight. *International Journal of Biological Macromolecules* 38:45–50.

Zhen, Yong-Su, ed. 2002. *Tea: Bioactivity and Therapeutic Potential*. Taylor and Francis, London.

Ziker, John. 2007. Food distribution among hunter-gatherers in northern Siberia: Tests of evolutionary hypotheses. Paper presented at the Annual Meeting of the American Anthropological Association, 2 December, Washington, D.C.

Scientific Index

Note: The letter *t* following a page number
   denotes a table.

Acacia spp., 210n4; *nilotica,* 166

Acinonyx jubatus, 8

Adansonia digitata, 115

Aframomum melegueta, 74

Alces alces, 10

Aleurites moluccana, 105

Allium spp., 101; *ampeloprasum,* 133; *cepa,*
   68; *fistulosum,* 110; *sativum,* 38;
   schoenoprasum, 133

Alocasia macrorrhizos, 96t

Alpinia officinarum, 211n5

Amaranthus spp., 41; *spinosus,* 119t

Anacardium occidentale, 133

Ananas comosus, 13

Anethum graveolens, 136

Annona senegalensis, 150

Apis mellifera, 6–7

Arachis hypogaea, 92

Arctium lappa, 133

Ardea spp., 9

Armoracia rusticana, 68

Artocarpus spp.: *atilis,* 96t, 138; *heterophyllus,* 101

Avena sativa, 40

Averrhoa carambola, 101

Azadirachta indica, 162

Bacillus spp., 150; *cereus,* 124

Balanites aegyptica, 117, 119t

Balsamita major, 144

Betula spp., 210n4

Bixa orellana, 80, 109

Borassus aethiopum, 119t

Boswellia spp.,

Brassica spp.: *juncea,* 110; *nigra,* 68;
   oleracea, 99; rapa, 97, 110

Broussonetia papyrifera, 138

Caesalpinia spp., 59

Camellia spp., 84; *sinensis,* 57

Camelus dromedarius, 53

Canis spp., 10; *familiaris,* 10; *lupus,* 10

Capparis spinosa, 137

Capsicum annuum, 57, 110

Carica papaya, 13

Carnegiea gigantea, 172

Carum carvi, 143

Cebus spp., 14

Ceiba spp., 80

Chenopodium spp.: *ambrosioides,* 94;
   quinoa, 41

Chrysanthemum coronarium, 136

Cicer arietinum, 41

Cichorium intybus, 131

Cinnamomum zeylanicum, 66

Cissus populnea, 115

Citirus medica, 137

Citrus spp., 24; *limon,* 102; *maxima,* 102;
   reticulata, 102, 135; *sinensis,* 69

Cocos nucifera, 96t

Coffea arabica, 75

Cola spp., 54, 117; *acuminata,* 146

Colocasia esculenta, 96t, 107

Cordyline terminalis, 99
Coriandrum sativum, 66, 136
Cornebacterium spp., 152
Corvus spp., 8
Corydalis ambigua, 161
Crataegus spp., 210n4
Crocus sativus, 66
Cucumis spp.: *melo*, 149; *sativus*, 32
Cucurbita spp., 72, 101, 137
Curcuma longa, 67, 96t
Cymbopetalum penduliflorum, 80

Dactylopius coccus, 31, 109
Daucus carota, 24, 28
Detarium senegalense, 149
Digitaria spp.: *exilis*, 28; *iburua*, 28
Dioscorea spp., 17, 96t

Elaeis guineensis, 116
Elettaria cardamomum, 132
Eleusine coracana, 28, 119t
Eragrostis spp., 28
Escherichia coli, 123
Eucalyptus saligna, 162
Eugenia uniflora, 101

Fagopyrum esculentum, 41
Falco spp., 8
Felis catus, 19
Ferula asafoetida, 133
Ficus spp., 119t; *carica*, 142
Foeniculum vulgare, 107
Fraxinus spp., 210n4

Gallus gallus, 8
Geotrichum candidum, 152
Glycine max, 17
Glycyrrhiza glabra, 211n5
Gossypium spp., 54
Gymnothorax javanicus, 9

Haemodorum coccineum, 161
Helianthus annuus, 41

Heliconius doris, 9
Hibiscus sabdariffa, 149
Hordeum spp., 17
Hosta plantaginea, 133
Hyacinthus spp., 135
Hyphaene thebaica, 195

Illicium verum, 107
Indicator spp., 11
Ipomoea batatas, 17, 96t

Lacifer lacca, 31
Lactobacillus spp., 152
Lactococcus spp., 152
Lagenaria siceraria, 104
Larus spp., 7
Lawsonia inermis, 146
Leishmania spp., 150, 195
Lens culinaris, 91
Lentinula edodes, 104
Listeria spp., 123
Litchi chinensis, 101
Lutra spp., 12
Lycopersicon esculentum, 32

Macadamia integrifolia, 101
Manihot esculenta, 111
Melichneutes spp., 11
Mellivora capensis, 11
Mentha spp., 68
Micrococcus cerolyticus, 11
Monascus purpureus, 108–109
Moringa oleifera, 195
Musa spp., 13, 96t
Mycobacterium spp., 184
Myristica fragrans, 66

Nelumbo spp., 135
Nicotiana tabacum, 54
Nymphaea spp., 177

Ocimum basilicum, 67
Opuntia spp., 94, 109

Orchis mascula, 92
Orcinus orca, 8
Oryza spp.: *glaberrima*, 28; *sativa*, 17

Pan troglodytes, 13
Pandanus spp.: *conoideus*, 20; *tectorius*, 138
Panthera leo, 7
Papaver somniferum, 69
Papio spp., 11
Parabuteo unicinctus, 7
Parkia filicoidea, 149
Passer domesticus, 8
Passiflora spp., 101
Pennisetum spp., 17, 111
Persea americana, 94
Petroselinum crispum, 67
Phalacrocorax spp., 11–12
Phaseolus spp., 211n4
Phoca vitulina, 8
Phoenix spp.: *dactylifera*, 117; *reclinata*, 150
Pimenta dioica, 67
Pimpinella anisum, 143
Pinus spp., 132
Piper spp.: *amalago*, 80; *guineense*, 116; *longum*, 70; *methysticum*, 96t, 138; *nigrum*, 66, 70
Pisum sativum, 143
Plantago spp., 137
Plectropomus pessuliferus, 9
Populus spp., 174
Porphyra spp., 69; *tenera*, 69
Pouteria sapota, 80
Procolobus spp., 13
Procyon lotor, 10
Prodotiscus spp., 11
Prosopis africana, 149
Prunus spp.: *dulcis*, 41; *mume*, 103; *spinosa*, 210n4
Pseudomonas spp., 184
Psidium guajava, 101
Psorospermum guineense, 149
Punica granatum, 101
Pyrus spp., 137

Quelea quelea, 9
Quercus spp., 161

Raphanus sativus, 99
Rhus coriaria, 135
Rosa spp., 141
Rosmarinus officinalis, 56
Rubus idaeus, 137

Saccharum officinarum, 17, 96t
Salix spp., 178
Salmonella spp., 123–124
Sambucus nigra, 210n4
Sciurus carolinensis, 7
Sclerocarya birrea, 119t
Secale cereale, 40
Sechium edule, 137
Sesamum spp.: *indicum*, 67; *radiatum*, 115
Shigella, 124
Solanum spp., 160; *melongena*, 107, 111; *tuberosum*, 17
Sorghum, 17
Staphylococcus spp., 124, 184
Strychnos spinosa, 119t, 195
Syzygium spp.: *aromaticum*, 66; *malaccense*, 96t

Tacca leontopetaloides, 96t
Tagetes spp., 131; *lucida*, 80
Tamarindus indica, 101, 102, 117, 134, 162
Theobroma cacao, 57, 79
Thonningia sanguinea, 115
Thymus vulgaris, 68
Trapa spp., 135
Trigonella foenum-graecum, 136
Triticum spp., 17; *aestivum*, 131
Trypanosoma spp., 150, 195
Turdoides bicolor, 8

Vaccinium spp., 130
Vanilla planifolia, 68

Vigna spp., 120; *angularis*, 107; *radiata*, 133; *subterranea*, 117; *unguiculata*, 111
Vitis vinifera, 55

Wasabia japonica, 106

Xylopia aethiopica, 115

Zanthoxylum zanthoxyloides, 69
Zea mays, 17
Zingiber officinale, 67
Zizania aquatica, 140
Ziziphus spp.: *jujuba*, 135; *spina-christi*, 119t
Zonotrichia querula, 9

General Index

acorn, 161
ADA (American Dairy Association), 43–46, 210n8
Adequate Intake (AI), 198, 212n4
aesthetics, 66, 71, 81, 103–5, 108, 119, 198
Age of Expansion, 61–64, 87
Age of Exploration, 50–52
agriculture, 20–21, 27, 43
alcoholic beverages, 26, 55, 82, 127, 129–31, 134, 141, 184
allergy, 45, 106, 170
allspice, 67
amaranth, 41; spiny, 119t, 121
analgesic, 121, 139, 149, 183
animism, 176
anise, 143; star, 107
annatto (achiote), 80, 109
anti-inflammatory agents, 121, 144, 150, 170, 196; caffeinated foods, 77–78, 84, 87, 147; edema, 102, 167; spices, 69, 75, 106, 108, 148
antimicrobials, 31, 33, 77, 87, 150, 168, 170, 184; fruit, 102, 115; spices, 38, 68–69, 106, 108, 121, 144, 148
antioxidants, 31, 101, 106, 121, 168, 170; caffeinated foods, 78, 84, 147; fruit, 102, 121,

129; legumes, 120, 144, 150; spices, 68–69, 75, 108, 121, 144, 148
anxiety, 102, 139
apples, 135, 198; mountain, 96t, 101; wild custard (*gwandar jeji*), 150, 166, 194–95
apricots, 103–4, 211n2
arrowroot, Polynesian, 96t
arthritis, 41, 75, 183, 185, 199
asafetida, 133–34, 144
association, 1, 23, 34, 38; beverages of, 76–77, 82, 86–87; foods of, 50, 65, 130, 207–8; water and, 171, 178, 182–83, 194, 196
asymmetry, socio-economic, 54, 65–66, 88, 113, 126, 130, 206–7; beverages and, 76, 80–81, 85–87, 184, 187–88, 190, 200; of spas, 181–85
Atkins Nutritional Approach, 34, 35t
avocado, 94, 101, 104

bamboo, 96t, 135, 143, 172
bananas, 13, 94, 96t, 99, 101
baobab (*kuka*), 115, 121
barley, 17, 40, 92, 131
basil, 67, 140
beans: adzuki, 107; mung, 133, 144; red, 135, 137; yellow, 211n4

berries, 130, 137

biocultural perspective, 1, 3, 47, 206

birds: hunting with, 11–12, 209n2; social foraging of, 7–9; symbolic, 127, 132

blood health: anemia, 40, 45, 87, 120, 161, 167; anti-sickling, 121, 150, 168; antithrombic, 38, 84, 102, 108–9, 144; circulation, 68, 70, 75, 108, 120; fibrinolysis, 102; gout, 77, 182, 185; hemochromotosis, 87; ketosis, 36, 209n5; thalassemia, 87

bloodroot, 161

bottled water, 3; brands, 187, 187–90, 192–93, 199; contaminants, 199–200, 202; desalinated, 201–3; enhanced, 191, 200; environmentalism and, 189, 200, 203–4; global market for, 191–92; health and, 189–90, 192–93, 198–200, 202–3; as medicine, 180, 185, 187; for pets, 201; sources of, 185–87, 190–91, 193; tap vs., 190–91, 198–200, 203–4

brazilwood, 59

bread, 131–32, 142–43

breadfruit, 96t, 138, 144

breast milk, 22, 44, 161

burdock, 133, 144

cabbage, 99, 133, 142–43; bok choy, 97, 110; Chinese mustard, 110

cacao, 57, 75–76, 78t, 79–84

cacti: nopal, 94; prickly pear, 109, 137; saguaro, 172

caffeine, 75, 77–79, 83, 147

calendrical rituals, 133–39, 142

cancer, 31, 33, 36, 108; anticarcinogenic, 70, 87, 129, 152, 168, 199; antimutagenic, 101, 106, 109, 120–21; antitumor, 69, 79, 84, 87, 144, 170, 196; breast, 45, 102, 106; chemotherapy, 170; colorectal, 40, 45, 84

canoe plants, 95, 96t

capers, 137, 144

caraway, 143

cardamom, 132, 143

cardiovascular health, 31, 33, 36–37, 39, 78, 83–84, 99, 129–30; antiatherogenic, 121, 168; artherosclerosis, 102, 144; blood pressure, 87, 152, 168; endothelial function, 78, 84; heartrate, 68; hypertension, 33, 39, 199; hypolipidemic, 121, 170; hypotensive, 75, 102, 120, 144, 170, 196; lipid mobilization, 75; pulmonary, 182; stroke, 87

carrots, 24, 28–29, 31

cassava (*rogo*), 111, 115; fermented (*gari/ kwaki*), 152–53

cats, 19, 210n7

Celiac Disease (CD), 39–41, 48

cherry, Surinam, 101–2

chickpea, 41, 144

chicory, 131

chile peppers, 57, 68–75, 79–81, 101, 148; *barkono*, 111, 147–48, 163

Chinese cosmology, 107–8, 173, 176–77, 211n5

Chinese foods, 107–9, 141, 211n3–211n4

chive, 133, 136

CHO (carbohydrate). *See* diet: low-CHO

cholesterol, 83, 87, 106, 108, 151–52, 168; diet and, 33–34; spices and, 38, 144, 195–96

Christ's thorn (*kurna*), 119t, 121

cinnamon, 66–68, 71, 81, 107–8, 143

citrus, 81, 84, 103; grapefruit, 24; lemon, 101, 132, 134, 137, 143; lime, 94; mandarin orange, 135; orange, 69, 101–2, 132, 136–37, 143; pomelo, 102; tangerine, 102

clay, 159–61

cloves, 66–67, 71, 74, 107–8, 115

cochineal, 31, 109

coffee, 75–79, 92

colors, symbolic, 28, 108–9, 128, 132, 135, 146–47

Columbus, Christopher, 51, 56–58, 61, 70, 72, 81

Committee for Responsible Medicine, 45–46

commodities, global: bottled water, 191–

192; coffee, 75–76; cotton, 54, 57; gold, 53–54, 56–57; grain, 27–28; health products, 38; ivory, 54; silk, 57, 67; silver, 57, 63; slaves, 54–56, 63; spices, 52, 57–58, 63, 65–67, 70–73; sugar, 54–55, 63; tea, 85–86

Complementary and Alternative Medicine (CAM), 36–38

consubstantiation, 19

contagion, 19–20

cooking, 16, 33, 131–32; metaphors, 156, 158, 161–62, 167

cooperation, 4–5, 14, 18; interspecific, 9–11

cordials, 75–76, 79–80, 82, 210n2

coriander, 66, 68, 134; cilantro, 136–37; cumin, 66, 68, 133, 137

corn. *See* maize

corydalis, 161

cosmogonies, 72, 207; dragonfly in, 174, 212n3; eggs in, 128; water in, 172–75

costmary, 144

cottonwood, 174

cowpea (*wake*), 111, 115–16, 120, 163

cucumbers, 32, 95, 101, 104

cuisine, 80, 94, 99; spices and, 65–66, 71–74

cytostatic effect, 121, 168

daddawa (soup base), 149–51, 162–63, 166, 212n3

Darwin, Charles, 4

date (*dabino*), 117, 121; desert (*aduwa*), 117, 119t, 121, 168

democratic ethos, 46, 77, 86, 130, 137, 182, 207–8

demographics of consumption: festival food, 137; kola, 146; medicine, 82–83; street food, 89–94, 97–98, 104–5, 113, 121–22; water, 185, 187–88, 191–92, 207; wild food, 119

dental health, 33, 170, 196, 199–200

dermatologic health, 136, 148, 151, 183–85, 202; wound, 120, 148, 196

diabetes mellitus (DM), 33–34, 38–39, 41, 48, 151; glucose modulation, 87, 102, 106, 108, 121, 144, 199–200

diet, 16, 22–24, 49, 65, 69, 89; low-CHO, 34–36; Slow Food, 26; vegetarian, 32–33

dietary diversity, 15, 25, 31–33, 123; eroded, 21, 27, 65

dietary management, 38, 48–49: of DM, 39; of GE, 41; of lactose intolerance, 42, 44

Dietary Reference Intake (DRI), 99, 199, 212n4

dill, 136

divination, 127–28; dowsing, 171–72

dogs, 10–11; bottled water for, 201

domestication, 10, 20–21, 72, 79

Dugatkin, Lee, 5

Dutch East India Company, 62, 86

earflower, 80

eggplant, 107; garden egg (*yalo*), 111, 116–17, 121

eggs, in ritual, 127–28, 131–32, 136–37, 140–41

epazote, 94

Equity Policy Center (EPOC), 126

ethnopharmacology, 3

eucalyptus, 162

European expansion. *See* commodities: global; mercantile imperialism

evolution, 2–5, 14–17, 41–42, 69, 175

exchange, 54–55. *See also* reciprocity

explorers, 51–52, 57–60, 62, 81. *See also* navigation

fast food, 25, 47, 89–90, 110, 122

fat, 33, 35t, 36, 42; steatorrhea, 40

fatigue, 36, 75, 77, 120, 161

feasting, 130–31

fennel, 107

fenugreek, 136, 144

fermentation, 33, 79, 85, 131, 167–69, 184; cassava, 152–53; *kimchi*, 99, 101; locust bean, 149–50; milk, 42, 115, 151–52 festivals, 128, 130–38, 143

fever, 108, 148–49, 196

fiber, 33, 36, 121, 147

figs (*baure*), 119t, 121, 142

films featuring food, 207–8

fish: cooperative hunting, 9–10; in ritual, 130, 132, 135–37, 140

flowers, 92, 94, 132, 148, 179; chrysanthemum, 136; hosta, 133, 144; hyacinth, 135, 144; Japanese apricot, 211n2; lotus, 135–36, 144, 173, 177; marigold, 131; purple orchid, 92; rose, 141

Food and Agriculture Organization (FAO), 125–26

Food and Drug Administration (FDA), 38, 124, 190–91, 193, 199, 203

Food and Nutrition Board, 212n4

food pyramid, 43, 47

food safety, 68–69, 123–26, 161. *See also* regulation

food sharing, 5–6, 13–14, 20–21, 48, 207; alloparenting, 22; animals, 6–12; foragers, 16–19

food-signaling, 6, 8–9

foraging, 15–20; social, 7–10

fortification, 125–26

fountain of life/youth, 181, 185–86

Fulani pastoralists, 114–15

funeral customs, 139–43

fusion foods, 25–26, 82, 94

galangal, 211n5

gardens, 177–79

garlic, 38, 68, 101, 133, 162

gastrointestinal health, 36, 69, 83–84, 87, 124, 184, 187, 196, 199; carminative, 41, 75, 102, 108, 121, 148; diarrhea, 40–41, 121, 160, 168; digestion; 68, 77, 149, 151, 202; hunger suppressant, 75; irritable bowel, 40; laxative, 102; nausea, 159–60; purgative, 185

gastronomy, 1, 31, 209n1

GE (gluten enteropathy), 39–41

gender, 173, 183, 206–7; consumption and, 80–81, 86, 92–93, 126; division of labor, 16, 131–32. *See also* Hausa

geophagia (*cin kasa*), 159–61

ginger, 67–68, 71, 74, 148, 163

Gittleman, Anne: Fat Flush Plan, 35t, 36

globalization, 21, 47, 64, 91, 137, 139, 147. *See also* commodities, global

"Got Milk" campaign, 43

grains, 136, 156, 164–65; African, 27–28

grapes, 55, 129–30, 135

grape ivy (*malaiduwa*), 115, 150, 168

groundnut (*gyada*), 92, 143, 211n7; Bambarra (*gurjiya*), 117; Hausa use of, 111, 114–17, 120, 150, 156; paste (*karago*), 117

guava, 101–3, 117, 121

Hamilton, William, 4–5

Hausa: exchange, 146–47, 154–56, 162–63; folklore, 127, 146–47; gender, 113–14, 121–22, 132, 153, 155–57, 166, 194; medicine, 147–49, 155, 166, 196; social spaces, 111, 113; spices, 115–16, 147–51; street food, 114–22; subsistence, 21, 111, 117, 119, 151; water sources, 193–94. *See also* lifecycle

Hawai'i, 95–98, 102, 107, 138–39, 202. *See also* "Local Food"

hawthorn, 210n4

health effects of: bee products, 169–70; caffeinated beverages, 77–79, 82–84, 87; diet, 26, 29, 31, 33, 36; European expansion, 64–65, 88; fermentation, 167–68; geophagia, 159–61; Hausa foods, 120–22, 147–50, 195–96; kava, 139; milk, 45, 47, 152; ritual foods, 144–45; spices, 67–71, 74–75, 108, 144; street foods, 99–103, 105–6, 123–25; water, 171, 182–85, 197–98, 202–3; wine, 129–30

heirloom plants and animals, 27–28

henna, 146

honeybees and products, 6–7, 11, 145, 168–70, 206

honeyguides, 11

hormones, 45, 68, 170; estrogen, 109;
    insulin, 34, 36, 38–39, 108

horseradish, 68, 74, 131; drumstick tree,
    195–96; *wasabi*, 106

hunting, 13–14, 16–17; birds, 11–12; dogs,
    10–11; otter, 12

Huxley, Thomas, 4

hydration, 171, 196, 198

hydrotherapy, 180–85

identity: bathing, 182, 187; beverages, 138,
    204; diets, 32–34, 38; disease, 48; food,
    23, 65, 89, 93–95, 123; local Hawai'i, 97–
    98

immune function, 22, 40–41, 78, 109, 183;
    foods and, 70, 102, 106, 120–21, 152, 168,
    170

inclusive fitness, 4–5

infectious disease, 33, 181; anthelmintic,
    150, 195; antibacterial, 75, 102, 108–9,
    144, 150, 195–96; antibiotic, 37, 45; anti-
    fungal, 69, 75, 101–2, 120, 139; antipara-
    sitic, 150, 160, 195; antiprotozoan, 150–
    51, 168; antischistosomes, 102; anti-
    trypasomal, 121, 196; antiviral, 120, 144,
    196; cholera, 54, 184, 188; dengue, 133;
    distemper, 84; dysentery, 184; influenza,
    65; leishmania, 170; malaria, 121, 133;
    measles, 65; plague, 65; smallpox, 65;
    tuberculosis, 83; typhoid, 83, 184, 188;
    yellow fever, 187

insects, 95; dragonfly, 174, 212n3; heliconid
    butterfly, 9; lac, 31; scale, 31, 109. *See
    also* Honeybees

International Bottled Water Association,
    198

jackfruit, 101

kava, 96t, 138–39

kayan kwadayi (desired goods), 113, 122,
    145–46, 155–56, 162–63, 166–68

kijinjiri, 150

kola nuts (*goro*), 54, 117, 146–47, 154–56,
    163, 166

Korean foods, 99, 136–37

kulla, 115, 148

kulle (purdah), 113–14, 194, 211n6

lactose intolerance, 38, 41–48, 209n6,
    210n7

leek, 133

leisure, 76, 113, 181–82

lentils, 91, 133, 144

León, Juan Ponce de, 60, 186

lethargy, 84, 149

life-cycle, 80, 128, 138, 146; birth, 158;
    circumcision, 163, 166–67; death, 139;
    marriage, 156–57; naming, 153–55;
    post-partum, 161–63; pregnancy,
    157–59

lipstick tree, 80, 109

liver health, 68, 87; hepatitis, 124, 161;
    hepatotoxicity, 139

"Local Food" (Hawai'i), 97–98, 110; fruit,
    101–2; *manapua*, 106–9; *musubi*, 103–6;
    Plate Lunch, 98–101; *saimin*, 109–10

locust bean tree, 149. *See also daddawa*

loli, 149, 151

longevity, 33, 110, 141, 186

lychee, 101, 103

Magellan, Ferdinand, 51, 60–61

maize, 17, 27, 54–55; in ritual food, 130,
    134, 137, 140–43

malnutrition, 40, 65, 161; scurvy, 77

mangos, 95, 101, 103, 117, 119, 121

marketing, 24; milk, 43–48; water, 193,
    201–4

marula (*danya*), 119t, 121, 168

meat, 69, 127, 129, 209n3; richness of,
    145

meat dishes: *cha shao*, 107–8; ritual, 131–
    38, 140–44; street, 92, 94, 97–99, 105,
    110; *tsire*, 114, 132, 156, 163

melons, 149; watermelons, 95

"melting pot," 93–94

mercantile imperialism, 50–55, 87–88; Dutch, 59, 62–64, 67, 85; English, 57, 59, 61, 64, 85; French, 59, 61, 64; Italian, 55, 63, 66, 72; Portuguese, 27, 55–56, 58–61, 63–64, 66, 72–73; Spanish, 57, 59–61, 63–64, 72–73, 81, 109. *See also* commodities, global

mesquite, African, 149

metaphors: eating/reproduction, 149–50, 155, 167; egg, 127–28; cooking, 156, 158, 161–62, 167; pollution, 162–63, 166–67; public/private, 132; water, 172–75, 181. *See also* color; number

milk, 43–48, 210n8. *See also* lactose intolerance; *nono*

millet, 17, 136, 142; finger, 28, 119t

mimosa, thorn, 166

mint, 68

modernity, 25, 28, 47, 111, 197

monkey orange (*kokiya*), 119t, 121, 195–96

mulberry, paper, 138

mushroom, 94, 143; shiitake, 104, 106

mustard, 68, 74

mutualism, 5, 8, 11

National Institutes of Health (NIH), 41

Native American customs, 19, 140, 161, 172–74, 212n3

navigation, 55–58, 60–63, 66, 87–88, 173. *See also* explorers

neem, 162

neurological health, 36, 68, 77, 83, 139, 199–200; lumbago, 75; neuralgia, 75; Parkinson's, 79

Nigeria. *See* Hausa

nono (fermented milk), 114–15, 121, 146, 151–52

nori seaweed, 69–70, 103–6

numbers, symbolic, 134–36, 140, 158, 163, 173; five, 107–8, 136, 211n2

nutmeg and mace, 66–67, 71, 143

nutrients, 24–25, 29, 33, 167; in bee products, 169–70; in fermented food, 150, 152–53, 167–68; fortification of, 125–26; in milk, 46–47; in street food, 99–101, 123, 125. *See also* malnutrition; vitamins and minerals

nuts, 136, 211n7; almond, 41, 44, 132; cashew, 133; chestnut, 136; *kukui*, 105; macadamia, 101; pine, 132, 136; walnut, 92, 132, 134; water chestnut, 135, 143

oats, 40, 131

obesity, 33, 39, 45, 99

offerings, 131, 133, 140–41, 179

onions, 68, 84, 133

ophthalmic health, 39, 77, 84, 139

organic food, 24, 29, 30t

origin stories. *See* cosmogonies

osteoporosis, 33, 36, 41, 45, 87, 199

palatability, 33, 66, 69, 79, 161, 167

palms, 168; coconut, 96t, 101, 134; doum, 195; palmyra fan (*giginya*), 119t, 121; red, 116, 121

pandanus: fruit, 138, 144; red, 20

papayas, 13, 101–3, 117; wild (*gwandar jeji*), 150, 166, 194

paprika, 110

parsley, 67, 131, 136

passion fruit, 101–2

peaches, Sun Crest, 25

peppers: Benin, 116, 148; black, 66–72, 74, 133; flower, 69, 74, 107–8, 115, 148; guinea, 115, 148; health and, 74–75; long, 70–71, 74; melegueta, 74, 115, 148; rough leaf, 80

Petrini, Carlo, 26

pharmacologic potential. *See* health

pica, 159–60

pineapple, 13, 95, 101–2

plantains, 137; lily, 133

Plate Lunch, 98–101

POGs, 102

political economy, 47–48, 88, 121–22, 206–7
Polynesia, 138–39
pomegranates, 101–2
poppies, 69–70; opium, 86
potatoes, 17, 54, 160; sweet, 17, 96t
presentation, 94, 99, 103–5, 131, 145
preservation, 33, 68, 71, 101, 117, 121, 128.
    See also food safety
primates, non–human, 11–14, 22
prohibitions, food, 19–20, 32, 72, 129, 131,
    133. See also diet
provisioning, 6, 8, 14, 16, 207. See also food
    sharing
public food. See street food
pungency, 68, 74, 106, 133

quinoa, 41

radishes, giant white (daikon), 99, 101, 103–
    4, 133
rain, 172–74
reciprocity, 80, 141, 146, 156, 162–163
recruitment calling, 8–9
redistribution, 130, 142, 151, 167–68, 207
regulation: of food, 92–93, 122–26; of sup-
    plements, 38; of water, 187, 190, 193, 199.
    See also food safety; preservation
religion: food prohibitions and, 32, 129, 131;
    spread of, 51, 54, 56–59; water and, 180–
    81, 196–97. See also cosmogonies; fes-
    tivals; life-cycle
reproduction, plant, 3–4
reproductive health: birth defects, 41;
    childbirth, 120, 161; failure to thrive, 120,
    161; fertility, 170, 182; hysteria, 182;
    postpartum, 132, 161–63; pregnancy, 79,
    158–59. See also life-cycle
respiratory health, 45, 75, 87, 120, 139
rice, 17, 24, 27, 44, 151, 211n4; red yeast
    (hong qu mi), 108–9; West African red,
    28; wild, 140
rosemary, 56, 141
rye, 40

saffron, 66, 144
salt, 53, 111, 131; desalination, 201–3; in
    foods, 85, 99, 101, 107, 211n4; sodium car-
    bonate (gishiri/kanwa), 115–16, 163
sapote, 80
scallion, 110
senescence, 129
sesame, 67, 69; benniseed, 115, 120
Silent Spring (Carson), 188–89
sleep, 83, 139
sloe, 210n4
Slow Food (SF), 25–27, 29, 31, 209n4
snowpea, 143
sociability, 1, 16, 145, 209n1; alliance, 18–19,
    130; of bathing, 181–82, 187; of beverages,
    76–77, 80–81, 85–87, 138, 171, 189, 196;
    kola and, 146, 154–55; online, 23–24, 77;
    popularity, 120
social spaces, 1, 16; agorae, 91–92; choco-
    latehouses, 81–82; coffeehouses, 76–77;
    convivia, 26–27; gida, 113, 166; hanya,
    111; kasuwa, 113; teahouses, 86, 211n3; TV
    and cinema, 207–8; water–related, 181–
    84, 187, 189–90, 194, 207
sociobiology, 5
sorcery repellant, 66, 120, 147–48, 158, 162
sorghum (dawa), 17, 111, 115; guineacorn, 15
sorrel, red, 149
soybeans, 17, 33–34, 44, 99, 133
Spam, 104–5, 110
spas and springs, 179–80, 182–85, 207
spice, 50, 67–70, 75, 143–44; trade, 52, 57–
    58, 63, 65–67, 70, 72–73
spice complex: Chinese five–spice, 107–8,
    211n5; Japanese seven–spice, 69; yaji,
    115–16, 121, 148–49, 162–63, 166
Spice Islands (Maluku), 59–62, 66–67
squash, 72; bottle gourd, 104; calabash, 145,
    172; chayote, 137; pumpkin, 101; yellow,
    137; zucchini, 137
star fruit, 101–2
stimulants, 77, 83
street food, 2, 89–91; Greek, 91–92; Hausa,

110–23; Hawai'i, 97–110; Mexico, 94–95; New York, 93–94
stress, 78, 183–84, 202
sugar: cane, 17, 54–55, 63, 96t, 143; additive, 81–82, 101, 145, 207; health and, 22, 39, 41, 200
sumac, 135
sunflowers, 41, 92, 136
supplements, 38, 139, 202
synergies, 69
synergies, 69

tallow, 149, 151
tamarind, 101–2, 127, 162
taro, 96t, 107; giant, 96t
tarragon, Mexican, 80
taste, 66, 68, 103, 134, 108, 147–49, 198–200
tea, 57, 84–87, 136, 210n2
therapeutic landscape, 175–80
thyme, 68
ti, 99
tiger nut (aya), 116–17, 121, 211n7
tobacco, 54, 142
tomato, 32, 72, 92, 111
totemism, 176
toxin reduction, 33, 160–61
trade routes, ancient, 52–54, 72. See also navigation
trophalaxis, 6
turmeric, 67–68, 96t

ulcer, 75, 87, 170
ume, 103–4, 211n2
ungozoma (midwife), 155, 158, 162
United States: diet, 43–46, 137, 208; gardens, 178–79; hydrotherapy, 182–83; "melting pot," 93–94; water management, 186–93, 199–200, 203–4

U.S. Department of Agriculture (USDA), 29, 30t, 43, 47, 122
U.S. Environmental Protection Agency, 189, 190
urban: diet, 44, 47; rural vs., 110–13, 119, 125. See also street food
urinary health: diuretic, 75, 83, 139, 147; kidney, 36, 39, 129, 187

vanilla, 68, 80–81, 143
vitamins and minerals, 24, 33, 36; calcium, 42, 46–47, 199; destabilizers, 30t; flouride, 200; in foods, 33, 70, 101, 103, 106, 121, 144, 147

Wallace, Alfred Russel, 4
wanzami (barber-surgeon), 155, 163, 166
warming, 68, 158, 161, 163, 165–67
water: animals, 173–76; bathing, 162, 180–82, 196–97, 207; health and, 179–84, 188, 190, 196–98; mineral, 180, 183, 185, 191–92, 199; municipal, 186–90, 200, 203; plants, 177–78; purifying, 188, 190–91, 194–95, 204; ritual, 133, 140, 142–43, 162, 171–75, 180–81; vessels, 158, 172, 179, 187, 189, 194–97, 201. See also bottled water
water lilies, 177
Watsu, 183
weapons, medicine against, 120, 150
weight loss, 40, 45–46, 83, 161; diets, 34–36, 202
wet nurse, 22, 206
wheat, 17, 27; buckwheat, 41, 144; gluten, 40–41; spelt, 131
wild and semiwild species, 20–21, 31, 119, 121

yams, 17, 96t, 138
yeast, 135, 152

About the Author

Nina Etkin (deceased) was a professor of anthropology and was the graduate chair at the University of Hawai'i, where she coordinated the medical anthropology concentration. She was also appointed to the Department of Ecology and Health of the University of Hawai'i Medical School. She earned a BA in zoology from Indiana University and an MA and PhD in anthropology from Washington University–St. Louis.

Etkin was best known for her pioneering work on the pharmacologic implications of plant use, especially the interrelations among foods and medicines. Her research addressed both cultural and pharmacologic aspects of botanicals and human cultures, including polypharmacy and the role of complementary and alternative medicines in integrative medicine in the United States. She had field experience in northern Nigeria; in Maluku, eastern Indonesia; and in Hawai'i. Etkin combined in-depth ethnography with laboratory studies through an interdisciplinary perspective that linked physiology, culture, and society to understand the dialectics of nature and culture in diverse ecologic and ethnographic settings.

Etkin was one of the two recipients of the 2009 Distinguished Economic Botanist Award from the Society for Economic Botany, and she was awarded the prestigious Hawai'i Regents' Medal for Excellence in Research. Her extensive list of publications includes *Edible Medicines: An Ethnopharmacology of Food* and *Eating on the Wild Side: The Pharmacologic, Ecologic, and Social Implications of Using Noncultigens*, both published by the University of Arizona Press.